THE STUDY OF PLAY:
Problems and Prospects

THE STUDY OF PLAY:
Problems and Prospects

Proceedings
of the
First Annual Meeting
of the
Association for the Anthropological Study of Play

edited by

David F. Lancy
B. Allan Tindall

Leisure Press
P.O. Box 3
West Point, N.Y. 10996

A publication of Leisure Press
P.O. Box 3, West Point, N.Y. 10996
Copyright© 1977 by **THE ASSOCIATION**
FOR THE ANTHROPOLOGICAL STUDY OF PLAY
All rights reserved. Printed in the U.S.A

ISBN 0-918438-06-3

Cover drawing by James Aponovich used with
the permission of New England College

Back cover drawing by David Frederick,
Miami University Audio-Visual Dept.

Publisher's note: This is the 2nd printing of this text. The title of the book for the 1st printing was: *The Anthropological Study of Play: Problems and Prospects.* In response to a request from Professor Lancy, the title was changed for this printing.

CONTENTS

CHAPTER IV: EXPRESSIVE ASPECTS OF PLAY

CHAPTER V: OBSERVATIONAL STUDY OF PLAY IN PRIMATES AND YOUNG CHILDREN

CHAPTER VI: SOCIO-PSYCHOLOGICAL ASPECTS OF PLAY AND HUMOR

APPENDIX A

preface

WINDS OF CHANGE

Michael A. Salter
University of Windsor

In pondering the format of this preface, I began to realize that the words I ultimately penned would be coloured by my emotions. Feelings of satisfaction and relief were being charged by an undercurrent of excitement. If, therefore, it appears at times that my enthusiasm overrides my objectivity, so be it; for it is not every day that a vision becomes a reality.

The vision — to draw together, from different disciplines, scholars capable of promoting the type of research and interaction necessary to better understand the nature, function and place of that phenomenon we label "play," within the varied societies of our Global Village.

The reality — The Association for the Anthropological Study of Play — TAASP.

Permit me to recap, as succinctly as possible, the genesis of this organization. It was becoming obvious, as we moved into the 1970's, that an increasing number of intellectuals were beginning to analyze play from an anthropological perspective. In essence, they had taken up the gauntlet cast down a decade earlier by such scholars as John Roberts and Brian Sutton-Smith. Among the first to recognize and attempt to foster this burgeoning interest were Alyce Cheska, Howard Nixon and Edward Norbeck. Operating independently they organized "mini-conferences" in Minneapolis (April, 1972), Burlington, Vermont (April, 1973) and New Orleans (December, 1973).

The success of these meetings, together with some gentle "arm-twisting" by Alyce Cheska in May, 1973 prompted me to examine the possibility of bringing together under one umbrella the many persons sharing this concern and focus of research. There followed a period of correspondence with a variety of professional organizations and potentially interested scholars. Questionnaires, announcements, explanatory briefs and notes of information and speculation were sent winging throughout North America. This activity paved the way for a May, 1974 gathering of some two dozen interested persons in London, Ontario.

Meeting in conjunction with the North American Society of Sport History, these individuals forged the framework of the Association by electing for a one year term a twelve-man Steering Committee comprised of the following:

Chairman: Michael A. Salter, University of Windsor
Secretary-Treasurer: Alyce Cheska, University of Illinois
Members: Kendall Blanchard, Middle Tennessee State University; Francis J. Clune, Jr., SUNY at Brockport; R. Gerald Glassford, University of Alberta; Joseph Royce, University of California at Berkeley; Frank A. Salamone, SUNY at Brockport; Peggy Stanaland, Eastern Kentucky University; B. Allan Tindall, SUNY at Buffalo; Phillips Stevens, Jr., SUNY at Buffalo; D. Margaret Toohey, California State University at Long Beach; and David Q. Voight, Albright College.

The Steering Committee, charged with the responsibility of structuring and promoting the growth of this fledgling organization, established six working committees, to wit: Constitution Committee — Tindall, Stanaland, Royce; Membership Committee — Clune, Salter, Toohey; Programme Committee — Stevens, Voight, Glassford; Nominating Committee — Blanchard, Salamone; Time and Site Committee — Salter; Budget Committee — Cheska. That the Association evolved in less than twelve months, from a mere concept to a tangible entity, complete with its own letterhead, newsletter and solid core of members, is largely due to the enthusiasm, imagination and perseverance of these working groups. Their efforts culminated in the First Annual Meeting of The Association for the Anthropological Study of Play in Detroit (April, 1975); their reward is housed between the covers of this volume.

In my opening gambit I alluded to a personal state of excitement tempered somewhat by feelings of satisfaction and relief. I was referring, of course, to the satisfaction that stems from a certain measure of success* and the relief associated with the knowledge that TAASP will continue to thrive under the capable and dedicated leadership of its new executives, namely:

President - B. Allan Tindall, University of California at Berkeley;
President-Elect — Phillips Stevens, Jr., SUNY at Buffalo;
Immediate Past-President — Michael A. Salter, University of Windsor
Secretary-Treasurer — Alyce Cheska, University of Illinois
Publications Editor — David F. Lancy, University of Pittsburgh
Members-at-Large — Elinor Nickerson, San Ramon Valley High

---

*At this point I would like to express my sincere appreciation on behalf of TAASP to the following organizations for their assistance during our formative stages: The Faculty of Human Kinetics at the University of Windsor, The North American Society for Sport History, The Central States Anthropological Society, The American Ethnological Society and the many professional associations who have carried TAASP information in the pages of their journals and newsletters.

School, California; Peggy Stanaland, Eastern Kentucky University and Kendall Blanchard, Middle Tennessee State University.

Excitement? How any scholar interested in the concept of play could fail to experience some stirrings of excitement following the Detroit conference is beyond me (although I must admit to certain biases!), for finally sociologists, educators, psychologists and anthropologists had assembled in one room to listen to and discuss topics of mutual concern. Hopefully, this intermingling of disciplines and the resultant interactions will lead to the rending of traditional academic barriers and culminate in hitherto unsuspected payoffs.

However, let us not waltz off in a euphoric state, for much still has to be done if we hope to truly understand the play world of man. While the annual coming together of academics is a step in the right direction, I would, in closing, pose this question: "What do *you* intend to *do* with the information gleaned from these proceedings?" I leave the following thought for you to mull over: I believe that the members of TAASP must do more than merely act as the generators and receptacles of knowledge. I suggest that they have an obligation to disseminate the knowledge they accumulate and to act as catalysts in the implementation of that knowledge at the "grass-roots" level.

CHAPTER I

Theoretical Approaches in the Study of Play

Introduction

When one considers "the study of play" in historical perspective an interesting paradox is apparent. Legions of historians, philosophers and social scientists have looked at Man, Society, and Culture and seen no play at all. By contrast, a minority of scholars, led by Johan Huizinga, have seen nothing but play when they looked at Man, Society, and Culture.

The lack of concern for play is explained by Norbeck in terms of the seriousness engendered by the Protestant ethic. Another reason for this neglect might be in the great difficulty of defining play operationally or theoretically; or the difficulty of separating play from "not-play." The "all is play" school hasn't been very helpful in this regard, but, as the papers by Carlton, Kilmer, Mouledoux, and Norbeck attest, this is very much a timely and urgent issue.

A second issue of central importance concerns the functions or uses of play. All too often, investigators assume a particular function and proceed to describe play, rather one-sidedly, strictly in terms of the preferred function. Schwartzman and Barbera describe four assumed functions which have dominated research in Africa and South America: (1) play as socialization, (2) play as recreation, (3) play as projection, and (4) play as functionless. As they point out, these functions of play, like theories of play, are much more a product of the ethos of the (Western) observer than of careful analyses of grounded or emic data.

A science of play will require well-ordered and testable theories and statements about the functions of play must now be treated as hypotheses. This search for theory and hypotheses to be derived therefrom can be best visualized in terms of the creation of a taxonomy. Huizinga would place play at the head of any taxonomy of human endeavors and would include as subcategories ritual, law, war, politics, poetry, philosophy, etc. Norbeck (1974) reduces the scope of play considerably, but in his definition, the subcategories of play would still stretch from sports to the arts, and from humor to ecstatic psychic states. In Carlton's taxonomy, sports are kinetic art forms; in other words, sports form a subcategory of art or aesthetics. By taking this position, he accounts very well for the role of spectator, a role which is otherwise badly handled in most theories of sport. Finally, in Kilmer's taxonomy, sport is a subcategory of ritual. He sees sports as fulfilling many of the characteristics and functions ascribed to ritual. In sports, power is allowed to build-up under the tightly controlled conditions of rules in order to satisfy the power needs of individuals.

Another approach to the creation of a play theory has been to concentrate on the lower levels of the taxonomy. Doyle (Chapter V) reviews attempts to taxonomize the play activities of American children aged 2-6. Roberts and his associates have taxonomized games, into games of strategy, chance, and physical skill. Callois (as discussed by Mouledoux) devotes his attention to games and has identified four types or characteristics: competition, chance, vertigo, and mimicry. Vertigo, in particular, is a game-characteristic which Callois appears to have "discovered" and which has received little attention from others. Mouledoux has found Callois' theory extremely useful in guiding her research and that of her students. It seems to be the case that by working at lower levels in the play taxonomy operational definitions and thereby effective research strategies are much easier to come by.

A third approach to play theory is via the ethnoscientific method. Here, folk taxonomies of play are elicited from informants. The categories and relationships depicted are those used by native peoples in ordering their experience. This method is exemplified in the papers by Blanchard and von Glascoe (Chapter III). The great advantage of such an approach is that relationships between play and other features of a society are more easily assessed. The principle disadvantage is that cross-cultural comparisons are problematic.

To return briefly to the question of function, as Carlton and Doyle (Chapter V) point out, even today research on play is often dominated by an applied functionalist perspective. Efforts to manipulate play behavior in accord with the results of research may be extremely premature until further light is shed on the more general issues of the functions of play in *animals,* in organism *development,* in *social relations,* in *enculturation,* and so on. The papers is this chapter illustrate approaches to theorizing about play and its functions. In subsequent chapters, these and other theories are applied directly to play behaviors in a variety of settings and in human and non-human primates. The works in this volume, therefore, very adequately represent the range of contemporary issues in the study of play.

THE STUDY OF PLAY—JOHAN HUIZINGA AND MODERN ANTHROPOLOGY
(Johan Huizinga Address)
Edward Norbeck
Rice University

The contributions to the anthropological study of play of the Dutch culture historian Johan Huizinga are examined against the background of his personal and professional history and his views of culture and society. So examined, his writings are seen to have added value for anthropological research, particularly in broadening the field of study and in suggesting new topics and, correspondingly, new approaches.

I WISH FIRST to offer congratulations to The Association for the Anthropological Study of Play upon its successful establishment and to express thanks to the moving spirits whose efforts led to its founding. I am honored to have the privilege of delivering the first Johan Huizinga Address at this gathering, the first annual meeting of the newly formed association.

For more than one reason it is appropriate that my remarks give attention to Johan Huizinga and his role as a pioneer in the study of human play. Against the background of his life and times and his career as a Dutch historian of culture, Huizinga's writings seem to me to take on meaning that they otherwise lack and his contributions to the study of play appear to have value of which I think anthropologists have been largely unaware. Acting on this judgment, I shall discuss Huizinga's study of play in a context of his personal history and his views of the nature of culture and civilization. As a preliminary step, I shall first discuss, somewhat speculatively, certain aspects of the history of the emergence of play as a subject of scientific inquiry.

A relevant question arises in connection with the founding of The Association for the Anthropological Study of Play, an event that happened in 1974. Why has this organization, and play as a subject of study, been so late in developing? For some time, various of us have held that the undesirable effects of the complex of attitudes and values we call the Protestant ethic have included the retarding of our recognition of play as a valid subject of scientific study. I have also suggested that the late emergence of play as a topic of study is a reflection of a broad general trend of the growth of science and of related changes of attitudes about the nature of the universe, the human condition, and propriety of behavior (Norbeck 1971, 1974). I have called my speculations along this line "Man's Rediscovery of his Animal Nature," a phenomenon that I think is recent. I mean to say that the educated public of our nation and many other nations has only recently become willing to acknowledge openly that man-animal behavior, such as sexual activity, is a vital part of human existence and something that need not be disguised, concealed, or kept secret as being unseemly conduct. The

13

anthropological version of this view seems only slightly different. I think we now have the opinion that, although important in the development of human society, what we have called "the cultural molding of basic primate urges" may have gone dangerously far in channeling and suppressing universal human traits that are part of our biological inheritance, traits that cannot be strongly suppressed without harmful consequences. The world now seems safe for all of us to acknowledge that we breathe, eat, excrete, sleep, have sexual lives, and do many other similar things that are the universal behavior of all species of the mammalian class.

For many decades the grand taboo in the scientific study of human beings was the subject of sexuality. But the study of play has been even slower to develop—and play, we may note, is fundamentally man-animal behavior. Only its specific forms are learned, cultural acts. Taboos are rules explicitly prohibiting behavior that might otherwise be followed. No such explicit restriction seems to have prohibited the study of play. For the most part, we did not study play because it was somehow beneath our attention, so that no overt expression of prohibition existed. Sexuality became an appropriate subject for scientific study a number of years ago, but I wonder if play is even now wholly respectable, if it is generally regarded as a subject of study that is truly worthwhile. Unless students of play concern themselves with play therapy or other aspects of play that appear to have immediate, practical value, I think they are still generally faced with the need to justify their interests. In support of this statement, I shall note that the latest edition of *Encyclopedia Americana* contains only an article on play therapy among children. Nevertheless, in our roles as social scientists I think we are now both free to study play and increasingly willing to do so. As various of us have noted, however, our new-found interest has presented a curious dilemma: we must usually be serious in our study of play.

These remarks are not to say that the study of all forms of play were formerly disrespectable or that it had been discouraged for other reasons. The realm of aesthetics has been a notable exception, although it has never been a major topic of anthropological study and it has not generally been regarded as play. Anthropologists did not ignore entirely other forms and aspects of play. If one searches through anthropological writings before the 1960's, some interest in one or another aspect of human play is evident from the time of Tylor, whose interest lay in games in their relation to the subject of cultural diffusion. Sports, games—at one time, notably the cat's cradle—and aesthetic activities of various kinds have often been dutifully described by anthropologists.

A vast amount of useful data on these and other forms of play may in fact be found in 19th and 20th century ethnological accounts, but many of these activities are not identified as play and they are often described under the heading of religion. Physical anthropologists of the past have sometimes described the play of primates, and this interest continues today. A few vintage writings, such as the doctoral dissertation of Julian Steward and a subsequently published article summarizing it (Steward 1930), concern the topic of wit and humor, a subject about which anthropological understanding remains very small. But anthropologists of the past rarely concerned themselves with play as a generic subject. The most notable exception was A. L. Kroeber, whose textbook *Anthropology*, published in 1948, contains several pages on play as a general subject and on certain specific aspects of play, and who for years conducted graduate seminars at Berkeley that consisted of reading about and actually playing games of the Indians of the Great Plains and California. Margaret Mead has also shown an interest for many years in the general subject of play.

The upsurge in anthropological interest in human play has been very recent and sudden. To date it has resulted in a collection of writings covering a range of facets or sub-topics that includes such diverse subjects as the biological significance of human play, play and psychopathology, play elements in the liminoid stage of rites of passage, ritual humor, play as inverted behavior, and, of course, the play of children. An examination of the program of papers being delivered at this meeting gives evidence of a still broader range. No substantial general or comprehensive work has yet appeared, however, a circumstance that appears to reflect the pioneering stage of our research.

I think it is reasonable to describe the present anthropological attitude toward the subject of play as evincing both interest and encouragement: play should be studied. My view is stronger. Play is a conspicuously striking and universal kind of human behavior that is genetically based and culturally modified. If anthropology is to reach its objective of gaining an understanding of the human organism and its ways of life, I think that play must be studied. In my view, play should not be regarded as interlude in human behavior, a dispensable if refreshing indulgence, but as a vitally important activity of human life that in fact exists among the members of all human societies although its manifestations are sometimes masked by cultural conventions so that it is not readily obvious. As a field of study committed more strongly than other fields to cross-cultural or comparative observation, anthropology has perhaps an especially important role in the study of human play.

The roots of the anthropological interest in play, and of my own view of play, do not appear to be strongly or clearly evident in the history of anthropology. Rather, I suspect, they lie in other scholarly fields, biology, psychology, and, farther back in time, in philosophy, perhaps especially in some of the writings of Friedrich Schiller. One thing appears to be certain. One root lies in the writings of Johan Huizinga, who, in turn, undoubtedly drew some of his ideas from earlier scholars such as Schiller. This address honors Huizinga, a circumstance indicating that at least one group of anthropologists regards his writings as important in the anthropological study of play. This opinion seems to be well founded; Huizinga's works contain much that is interesting and of potential value in the anthropological study of play.

Biography of Johan Huizinga

Johan Huizinga, a citizen of Holland, was born in Groningen in 1872 and died in 1945. His advanced education was gained at the universities of Groningen and Leipzig, where he was trained as a linguist, specializing in Sanskrit. Later, while serving as a high school teacher in Haarlem and as a teacher of Indic studies in Amsterdam, his interests turned to history. In 1905 he became a professor at Groningen and in 1915 was appointed professor at Leiden University, where he later served as rector. Until recent years he was best known for his books on cultural history and essays on the philosophy of history, of which the most noted work was *The Waning of the Middle Ages*, first published in Dutch in 1919 and later translated into German and English. To those who are assembled here, his notable work is *Homo Ludens*, and I suspect that this book will in the future be regarded as his most distinguished writing. My remarks here will concern principally *Homo Ludens*, but I shall commend *The Waning of the Middle Ages* as also being valuable to those interested in the subject of human play and its course of history in Europe.

Huizinga's view of culture does not accord with conventional anthropological ideas, past or present. He defined culture as the state of a community "when the domination of nature in the material, moral and spiritual realms permits a state of existence which is higher and better than the given natural conditions", a state of "harmonious balance of material and social values" (Cheyette 1793:408; see also Weintraub, 1966). Huizinga's definition of culture thus involves a value judgment and it closely resembles a traditional non-anthropological meaning of the term as being refinements of life or "civilization".

Huizinga is described by a biographer (ibid) as being a cultural conservative, strongly elitist, and in later years deeply despondent over the future of European civilization. Huizinga's concern over the future of civilization is strongly evident in his cultural history, *The Waning of the Middle Ages* and in *Homo Ludens*. He describes the Middle Ages as a time of violence, a period that carried the smell of both blood and roses. People sought refuge from the perils of the times by creating a life of fantasy, by idealizing knighthood, romantic love, and religious sensibilities, essentially as forms of play, and by rich development of play in the forms of aesthetics and bodily adornment. In *Homo Ludens* he describes the Middle Ages as a time of "joyous unbuttoned play" and sees in later times both a decline in play and a decline in the quality of civilization. In his view, a harmonious balance of play and "earnest", a word that he uses as a noun, are necessary for civilization to flourish, and that balance is achieved by the use of suitable play forms as vehicles for, and mediators of, the earnest. After the Middle Ages, Huizinga states, appropriate forms of play waned and disharmony grew.

Much of Huizinga's pessimism over the future of European civilization appears to have stemmed from his observation of historic events in Europe in the 1920's and 1930's, including the rise of the Nazis, whose forms of play he regarded as being debased. A passage in *Homo Ludens* expressing disapproval of developments in Europe is easily recognizable as referring to Germany. Leiden University was closed by the Germans in 1941. As one of a group of professors of the university who were regarded as being unsympathetic with the German cause and uncooperative with German policies concerning the university, Huizinga was interned.[1] Later released from custody because of poor health, he died soon thereafter, in 1945.

Homo Ludens

Against the biographic background sketched above, the contents of *Homo Ludens* appear to me to take on greater meaning. In this book Huizinga first presents an elaborate definition of play, a subject to which I shall later return, and discusses the development of the linguistic concept of play, which he concludes is late in human history and well developed in Germanic or northern European languages but later in its development than the concept of work. I think it is still surprising for most of us to learn that various languages lack a generic term for play and lack a concept of work and play in binary opposition. The main focus of *Homo Ludens* is the question of the extent to which culture, as defined by its author, results from play. In Huizinga's own words, his goal is "to ascertain how far culture itself bears the character of play" (p. 4). This question is answered by an investigation of the extent to which culture expresses itself in the forms of play. Huizinga is careful to describe his work as concerning the play forms *of* culture rather than the play forms *in* culture, indicating that play is the vehicle for many activities known by other names. He examines ritual, law, war, politics, knowledge, poetry, imagery, philosophy, and various fields of aesthetics, and concludes (p. 173):

> It has not been difficult to show that a certain play-factor was extremely active all through the culture process and that it produced many of the fundamental forms of social life. The spirit of playful competition is, as a social impulse, older than culture itself and pervades all life like a cultural ferment . . . We have to conclude, therefore, that civilization in its earliest phases, played. It does not come *from* play like a babe detaching itself from the womb; it arises *in* and *as* play and never leaves it.

Elsewhere (p. i), he summarizes this conclusion in the statement that ". . . civilization arises and unfolds in and as play."

If this book is examined from the viewpoint of its organization and mode of execution, its contents bear a number of resemblances to anthropological ideas and procedures, some of which are curiously modern. The entire work may

---

[1]This information was given in personal conversation by the wife of a colleague of Huizinga at Leiden University, who stated that her husband was also one of a group of 17 professors disfavored by the occupying Germans.

be described as being organized around central themes that are reminiscent of the ideas of Ruth Benedict and other anthropologists concerning "configurations" or "patterns" and also resemble more recent anthropological concepts of binary opposition. Huizinga's master pattern in the growth of civilization consists of play forms. In the play forms he sees as the dominant and distinguishing motif the element of agonism or contest. This theme, in turn, relates to a larger idea of binary opposition, the balance between play and earnest. He describes play and earnest (or "seriousness") as the "two cardinal moods of life" of the Middle Ages, and holds that they must be in harmonious balance, a state which is achieved through the existence of appropriate forms of play. These involve agonism or contest, which means *regulated* contesting, bound by the rules of play. The competitive spirit, he holds, is innate among human beings, and, if expressed in play forms, it is permissively controlled in a way that fosters the development of culture.

Some of the roots of these ideas of Huizinga appear to be traceable to Friedrich Schiller, who also presents a view of human play expressed in a scheme that may be called binary opposition and who identifies play with aesthetics or beauty. In his series of essays of 1795 translated into English under the title *On the Aesthetic Education of Man*, Schiller states that ". . . man plays only when he is in the fullest sense of the word a human being, and he is fully a human being only when he plays (1967:107)." Schiller sees human life as being governed by two drives operating by reciprocity, which, in turn, constitutes a third drive. He states, "The sense-drive demands that there shall be change and that time shall have content; the form-drive demands that time shall be annulled and that there shall be change. That drive, therefore, in which both the others work in concert . . . , the play drive, . . . would be directed towards annulling time within time, reconciling becoming with absolute being and change with identity (1967: 97)." These more or less shadowy ideas of Schiller are also reminiscent of 20th century anthropology, resembling views concerning structure and function as well as of balanced opposition.

Returning now to Huizinga, it is appropriate, and perhaps necessary, to observe that some of his ideas are not generally acceptable to modern anthropologists. Our definition of culture is very different from that of Huizinga, and it is doubtful that most of us find acceptable various of his other ideas; for example, the views that the cardinal trait of play is agonism, that human beings are innately competitive—he refers to "the human need to fight" (1950:61)—and that archaic society was founded upon contest or agonism (1950:58). The issue now turns to the question of the value of Huizinga's works to the modern anthropological study of play.

If the circumstances of Huizinga's intellectual and personal background are considered, so that his writings may be appropriately understood, his writings on play constitute a heuristically rich contribution in a number of ways. Among these are his discussion of linguistic concepts of play, a subject about which our knowledge has not advanced since Huizinga's time; the organizing theme of his book, which, in anthropological eyes today, may well be regarded as an interpretation of human play in its relationship to the culture as a whole; and numerous suggestive ideas embodying the idea of binary opposition, which may have value in modern studies of symbolism and cognition and which bear a resemblance to the views of Victor Turner (e.g., Turner, 1974) concerning play, ritual and symbolism. Huizinga's broadening of the concept of play appears to me to be the contribution of greatest and most immediate importance to us.

As modern anthropologists interested in the subject of human play, we are all concerned with play as a concept. We thus face the problem of defining it—and, to my knowledge, no consensus exists in its definition. For the most part, we have proceeded in our studies without defining play, assuming that everyone knows its meaning. An examination of such definitions as do exist shows disagreement. For example, Kroeber (1948) includes all of science in play; Huizinga and others do not. I think it appropriate to include in the category of play the entire realm of aesthetics, as Huizinga does, but others do not think so.

Huizinga defines and redefines play, discussing a large variety of traits that he sees as distinguishing it. The terms of description he uses include the following, which, for convenience, I have sometimes paraphrased:

voluntary, free, freedom

may be deferred or suspended at any time

not a task, not ordinary, not real

essentially unserious in its goals although often seriously executed

outside the immediate satisfaction of wants and appetite and the individual satisfaction of biological needs

a temporary activity satisfying in itself, an intermezzo or interlude, but an integral part of life and a necessity

distinct in locality and duration

repetitive

closely linked with beauty in many ways but not identical with it

creates order and is order; has rules, rhythm, and harmony

often related to wit and humor but not synonymous with them

has elements of tension, uncertainty, chanciness

casts a spell over us, is enchanting, captivating, intensely and utterly absorbing, joyous, has illusion

older than civilization or culture, it sub-serves culture and becomes culture

outside the antitheses of wisdom and folly, truth and falsehood, good and evil, vice and virtue, has no moral function

Whether or not all of these traits and additional characteristics which Huizinga discusses will turn out eventually to be useful in formulating an appropriate working definition of play is unpredictable. Huizinga has, however, provided a richer working base for such a formulation than may be found elsewhere.

As a culture historian, Huizinga does not concern himself with the biological significance of play as a trait of the species *Homo sapiens*, a subject that is better handled by physical anthropology and the biological sciences. Directly or indirectly, however, he deals with most of the major topics of the modern study of play in cultural and social anthropology. These include the relationships between play and other elements of culture (that is, play as related to values, ideals, war, law, politics, ritual, and the like); human play and its cultural expression; the functional significance of play in a cultural sense, and the relationship between work and play. Our modern concern with the therapeutic value of play is also clearly evident in *Homo Ludens*, appearing as an important but largely implicit theme that concerns the health or welfare of European civilization.

Huizinga's treatment of aesthetics as forms of play merits special attention. I think it invites our entry into a large realm of investigation into which we have so far scarcely ventured. I shall select here only one example, his treatment of bodily adornment, that is, clothing and hairdress. This is a subject about which anthropology has been notably silent. The only well-known writing on this subject is the aging work of A. L. Kroeber and Jane Richardson (1940) on European dress styles, which principally concerns patterns discernible in trends of fashion. We learn from introductory textbooks in anthropology that all peoples have aesthetic impulses and adorn their bodies within a varied but nevertheless limited range of ways. We have rarely dealt with fashions, however, and we have not regarded hair and clothing styles as forms of play that relate to other elements of culture beyond social statuses and, perhaps, traits of personality. Huizinga does so interestingly and informatively. I suggest that, following the lines of Huizinga's thinking, the tracing in an anthropological context of modes of bodily adornment in our nation during the past several decades would also be informative.

Another feature of Huizinga's *Homo Ludens* merits special attention, his view that the quality of culture or civilization is declining. As we all know, this opinion is a popular view today that we hear expressed frequently. In this context, Huizinga writes of the decline of play after the Middle Ages and its heightened decline in modern times. Referring to modern social life and politics, he sees the existence of false play, calling it "Puerilism", "a blend of adolescence and barbarity" (p. 205). Referring to sports and athletics, he speaks of "play stiffening into seriousness but still being felt as play . . . (1950:199)." Sport, he states, has become a thing *sui generis*, neither play nor earnest (ibid). He sees other play forms as having changed similarly: for example, war is no longer a noble game; the play element in art has waned; the modes of dress have become similarly serious. Stating that civilization is rooted in "noble play", he cautions that we cannot afford to neglect the play element (1950:210), particularly in international relations.

These statements seem to me both provocative and profound, and they allow me to bring this discussion to an end with a note of cheer. They lead me to think that perhaps Huizinga's death came too soon, that his observation of the decades since his death might in some ways serve to lighten his pessimism about the future of civilization. As we have noted, much of Huizinga's discussion of play concerns the branches of aesthetics. We in this room have all observed great changes in every field of aesthetics and, I think, a strong resurgence of playfulness in them. Perhaps only because I am not young, I have privately called the last decade "The Age of Ugliness." Modern music, painting, dance, and, certainly, styles of clothing and hairdress are often described by our middle-aged and aged citizens as ugly, bizarre, strident, harsh, unpleasant, or by much less polite words. Knowing that my view reflected personal bias, I have sometimes wondered how our modern university students could possibly induce themselves to wear such unbecoming clothing. Canons of taste, fashion, and beauty have obviously changed greatly. The new forms have vibrant life, and it is certain that the uncomplimentary terms I have just recited do not represent the opinions of much of our nation, those who endorse the modern modes of aesthetics.

It also seems certain that in these matters much greater freedom than existed in former times is tolerated and, in fact, encouraged today. The element of play seems clearly evident in the general atmosphere of freedom in modern aesthetics, including bodily adornment. In this matter, some of us cling to the past and are timid players or sit on the sidelines, but we may at almost any moment readily see among our fellows many who are exuberantly enthusiastic players. The glorious clothing of many male members of our society is one example— and it is useful to note that the extension to males of the freedom to adorn oneself fancifully is a radical departure from the past. Much of modern clothing is best labeled as "costume", a term that connotes its playful element. A male wearing a plumed hat, one earring, trousers and shirt of radiantly glorious colors, and viewing the world from the eminence of shoes with platform soles and high heels is surely playing.

I have no doubt that in bodily adornment as well as in modern music, dance, painting, and sculpture the traits of order, rhythm, cadence—in short, rules—always exist. These are also traits that distinguish play. Many other traits of play as described by Huizinga may also be seen in modern aesthetics—if the scales resulting from earlier sets of values are removed from our eyes.

A noteworthy development of modern times that might well have had meaning for Huizinga is the changing national attitude toward play to which I have already referred. Play becomes less and less an unnecessary frivolity, frailty or sin, something in which we "indulge". More and more, it is regarded by the average citizen as normal, natural, and necessary human behavior. If, as Huizinga contends, the element of play is necessary not only for human existence but for the continued development of culture, perhaps we are now preparing to soar to new cultural heights. Now that we seemingly have the freedom to study play, I shall hope that one of the new heights of cultural development will be an understanding of the subject, and I wish the Association for the Anthropological

Study of Play good speed in the pursuit of its goals.

REFERENCES

Cheyette, Fredric
    1972 *Encyclopedia of World Biography*, New York: McGraw-Hill, pp. 407-408.
Huizinga, Johan
    1927 *The Waning of the Middle Ages*. London: Edward Arnold (First published 1919, in Dutch).
    1950 *Homo Ludens*. Boston: Beacon Press (First published 1944, in German).
Kroeber, A. L.
    1948 *Anthropology*. New York: Harcourt, Brace and Co.
Kroeber, A. L., and Jane Richardson
    1940 *Three Centuries of Women's Dress Fashions*. Anthropological Records 5:2. Berkeley: University of California.
Norbeck, Edward
    1971 *Man at Play*. Natural History 80,10:48-53.
Norbeck, Edward, ed.
    1974 *The Anthropological Study of Human Play*. Rice University Studies 60,3.
Schiller, Fredrich
    1967 *On the Aesthetic Education of Man*. Trans. by E. M. Wilkinson and L. O. Willoughby. Oxford: The Clarendon Press.
Steward, Julian H.
    1930 *The Ceremonial Buffoon of the American Indian*. Papers of the Michigan Academy of Letters, Arts and Science 14:187-207.
Turner, Victor W.
    1974 *Liminal to Liminoid in Play, Flow and Ritual: An Essay in Comparative Symbology*. Rice University Studies 60,3:53-92.
Weintraub, Karl J.
    1966 *Visions of Culture*. Chicago: University of Chicago Press.

CHILDREN'S PLAY IN AFRICA AND SOUTH AMERICA:
A REVIEW OF THE ETHNOGRAPHIC LITERATURE

Helen B. Schwartzman   Linda Barbera
Institute for Juvenile Research   Institute for Juvenile Research
Chicago, Illinois   Chicago, Illinois
                                              and
                                   Northwestern University
                                      Evanston, Illinois

Anthropologists, in their efforts to study the "serious" and "important" aspects of societies, have often neglected the activities of children—particularly children's play, so a review of the ethnographic literature on Africa and South America was undertaken. I expected that this review would reveal the existence of a fairly diverse array of descriptions of children's play behavior. However, our analysis of these accounts demonstrates that anthropologists present and interpret information on children's play in only four different ways. These four perspectives or "metaphors for play" are:

1)   play as imitation of and/or preparation for adult life,
2)   play as a game or sports activity,
3)   play as projection or expressive activity, and
4)   play as unimportant or as a "miscellaneous" pastime.

These descriptions frequently are interpreted as reflecting the socio-cultural patterns or emphases of the society which is the subject of the monograph.

In this paper a different interpretation of these descriptions is suggested. Here it is proposed that these four 'metaphors' for children's play can best be understood not in reference to the culture of the studied (i.e., "native") society but rather in reference to the culture of the student (i.e., the anthropologist). In short, it is argued that ethnographic reports of children's play behavior have been influenced at least as much by past and present anthropological (and generally Western) ideas about this topic as by the reality of this phenomenon as constructed by members of the society under investigation.

In order to present this approach a discussion and illustration of each metaphor and its use by anthropologists in their descriptions of children's play in African and South American ethnographies will be offered. Each of these discussions will also relate the use of a particular metaphor for play to the 'culture' of the anthropologist; and a number of suggestions for why the above four metaphors have been, and are still, persistently employed by ethnographers in their descriptions of this activity will be made.[1]

---

[1] For the African portion of this review only ethnographies reporting information on societies existing south of the Sahara Desert are considered. The specific geographic areas of Africa represented by these works are West Africa, East Africa, East Sudan/East Horn area, Central Africa and South Africa. For each area, a number of ethnographic, and where

Play as Imitation

Children's play is frequently characterized as imitative or mimetic activity in a number of African and South American ethnographies. In these descriptions it is generally said that this sort of activity is important for children to engage in because it provides them with an opportunity to learn, prepare, and practice adult social roles and activities. Kenyatta's discussion of Kenyan Gikuyu children's play is typical of this approach. He states that

> children do most things in imitation of their elders and illustrate in a striking way the theory that play is anticipatory of adult life. Their games are, in fact, nothing more or less than a rehearsal prior to the performance of the activities which are the serious business of all members of the Gikuyu tribe (1939:101).

Leis also utilizes this metaphor in his description of the play of Nigerian Ijaw children as consisting of "sporadic and simple imitation, almost like follow-the-leader" (1972:76). Bird's article in the *Handbook of South American Indians* (Steward, 1946-51) repeats this theme in reference to Alacaluf children, "As far as observed, children content themselves with imitating their elders, occasionally making miniature huts, weapons, and baskets . . ." (Vol. I:78). And according to Mishkin the play of the Central Andean Guechia children seems always to "hinge on the imitation of and preparation for adult life" (Vol. II:458).

Again and again this view of play as imitation appears in the ethnographic literature of both Africa and South America.[2] The recurrence of this metaphor

---

relevant, psychological and educational accounts are considered. Specific attention is paid to reports providing information on socialization and child-rearing practices. All of the accounts (with the exception of one) reviewed on African societies are available in English and cover the time period 1913-1974.

The ethnographic literature reviewed for South America falls into two categories. The *Handbook of South American Indians*, edited and compiled by Julian Steward (in conjunction with Robert Lowie, John Cooper and Leslie Spier), and published in six volumes from 1946-1951, is reviewed as one major reference source with accounts from over 100 contributors. The South American cultural areas discussed in the *Handbook* are marginal hunting and gathering tribes of Eastern Brazil, Gran Chaco, Pampa, Patagona, and Tierra del Fuego; Andean civilizations; tribes of the Tropical Forests and Savannas; and Circum-Caribbean cultures. In addition to an extensive review of relevant material appearing in *Handbook* articles, a number of recent (1944-1973) ethnographies written on South American cultures are examined. It is felt that this review of more contemporary ethnographies, along with the analysis of *Handbook* articles, which summarize a variety of historical and ethnographic works from 1600-1940, adequately covers the range of anthropological material available on South American societies.

[2] See, e.g., Hopen (1958:69-70) and Stenning (1965:391) on the Fulani of Nigeria; Ottenberg (1965:23) on the Ibo of Nigeria; Smith (1965:144-145) on the Hausa of Nigeria; Bohannan and Bohannan (1958:374) on the Tiv of Nigeria, Messing (1961:435-437) on the plateau Amhara of Ethiopia; Klima (1970:54) on the Barabaig of Tanzania; Edel (1951:176-177) on the Chiga of Uganda; Turnbull (1961:129) on the Mbuti Pygmies of the Congo; Schapera (1930:267) on the Hottentot, and Kuper (1965:490) on the Swazi of South Africa; and Marshall (1965:264) on the Kung Bushmen. On South American Indians, see,

in these works can be linked to the history of early anthropological, psychological and educational conceptions of "primitive" children's activities in general (see Raum, 1940 for a detailed discussion of this history as well as a critique of descriptions of play as imitation). Anthropology was, in part, formulated in response to an accumulation of explorers', travellers', missionaries', and colonial administrators' reports about the customs of "native" peoples. These reports often portrayed children's activities as desultory, passive, aimless and totally lacking in imagination. For example Baker, a missionary writing in 1913 about the children of Rhodesia, states:

> The children of this land are non-entities. Nothing at all is done for them. They feed, sit about and sleep, and in this manner they grow until it comes time for them to get about for themselves, to do something in the gardens, or to seek work from the white man. They have no nurseries, no toys, no books, no treats, no tea-parties and no instructions from their parents and friends. They are here and that is all. Their lives are one big nothing. (1913:20).[3]

Many of these accounts soon became incorporated into various anthropological and also psychological and educational reports and theories about the behavior of "primitive" children (e.g., F. C. Spencer, 1899; Monroe, 1906). In this material, imitation of and passiveness and submissiveness toward adults in "primitive" societies came to be viewed as the only way available for these children to learn and hence become socialized.[4] Play (if noticed or reported at all) came to be interpreted as merely another form of imitative behavior on the part of the child.

The specific development of both the British functional and American culture and personality schools of anthropology in the twentieth century did little to challenge, and probably much to reinforce, the validity of these early descrip-

---

e.g., Holmberg (1969:207-208) on the Siriono of Eastern Bolivia; Chagnon (1968:85) on the Yanomamo; and numerous authors contributing to the Handbook of South American Indians (Steward, 1946-51, Volumes I-VI).

[3] A more recent example of an ethnographic portrayal of children in this manner may be found in Ashton's (1952:36) description of the lack of ingenuity and imagination evidenced in South African Basuto children's play. He also states that most children's games "are aimless . . . and desultory and consist chiefly of roaming about, playing hide and seek, digging on ash heaps, making slides" (1952:35).

[4] Imitation, however, came to be interpreted not just as the dominant mode of learning for children in primitive societies but also as the dominant approach to learning for adults in these societies. Though children in Western societies were also thought to engage in many imitative learning activities in their early years, it was felt that they soon moved into more "sophisticated" formal learning contexts such as schools. "Primitives" in general came to be characterized as children; and likewise Western children often came to be characterized as "primitives".

tions of children and their play.[5] For example, Mead in her now classic ethnography *Growing Up in New Guinea* (1930) suggests that imitation is important and crucial for the production of active, imaginative play in children. In this account the Manus child is depicted as engaging in a listless, desultory, and boring play life because he/she is left out of adult life and kept separate from his/her elders and is therefore unable to imitate their activities in play (1930:100). Malinowski (1944) may also be seen to have contributed to the perpetuation of this metaphor by contending that the function of play is to prepare children for the assumption of adult economic roles. Fortes (1938:44), however, is significant to note for his critique of 'simple and mechanical' views of mimesis in reference to his interpretation of Tallensi children's play.

More recently the work of Whiting and Child (1953), culminating in the *Six Cultures* series edited by B. Whiting (1966), also implicitly suggests a view of children as passive imitators of adults.[6] In these works the role of adults as the primary socializing, "training", "rearing", or cultural "transmission" agents for children is emphasized again and again. A child's influence on adults, or the possibility that peers may also function as socializing figures, is only briefly mentioned. This "one way" or unidirectional theory of socialization assumes that children are incomplete, incompetent, asocial and acultural beings whereas adults are seen as complete, competent, social and supremely "cultural" (Mackay 1974: 181). This approach also reflects the extreme child-centered orientation of many American adults. That is, if adults are thought to be always directing their activities toward children (i.e., "rearing" them), then it becomes, at least, implicitly assumed that children will likewise direct most of their activities toward adults (i.e., imitate them). These general cultural assumptions as they appear in many childhood socialization studies like Whiting and Child (1953) need to be questioned and reevaluated (as by Raum 1940; and Shimahara 1970) and researched (as by Mackay 1974) before becoming incorporated in anthropological works.

Play as Game

Play is often described as game activity not only by ethnographers but by many individuals from different disciplines with various interests in the study of play. The words play and game have and are frequently used interchangeably even though various individuals have attempted to differentiate types of play (e.g., Piaget's 1962 discussion of sensory-motor play; symbolic play; and games-with-rules).

---

[5]It is interesting to note here that Freud, an acknowledged influence on both these schools of anthropology; maintains that:

> Mimicry is the child's best art and the driving motive of most of his games. A child's ambition aims far less at excelling among his equals than at mimicking the grown-ups (1905:227).

[6]Robert Sears, who has exerted a great influence on the Whiting and Child socialization studies, views children's play as a type of learning process which fosters identification through *role practice* (1957).

In anthropology, formalized games are often reported in ethnographic works to the exclusion of accounts of other types of children's play behavior. For example a great deal of attention has been paid to the study and description of various versions of the characteristic African game of *mancala* which is generally played by adults (e.g., Culin 1894; Anna 1930; Powell-Cotton 1931; Matson 1957; Alamayahu 1959). Much less attention has been focused on the description and analysis of children's versions of this game or other types of children's play in African societies. Leacock's (1971) discussion of Zambian children's play, however, is an important recent exception.

This focus on the formalized games of a society may be related, as Raum (1940: 7,21,22) has suggested, to the early ethnographers' interest in reporting only the spectacular, conspicuous and ritualized events of "primitive" societies. Formalized games, complete with elaborate rule structures which organize the place, time, objects (toys), and persons involved in a game, would obviously appear to the ethnographer as more conspicuous and spectacular than non-structured play activities. Also, the actual system of rules organizing the game would be likely to be known and remembered by a larger number of individuals than the more idiosyncratic and spontaneously developed sorts of rules organizing relatively non-structured play activities. J. Henry and Z. Henry in their discussion of *Doll-Play Among Pilaga Indian Children* (1944) and Raum in his descriptions of *Chaga Childhood* (1940) are among the very few ethnographers to have called attention to the anthropologist's tendency to study and report only formalized game activities.

The repeated use of the game metaphor is probably best reflected in the organization of the articles appearing in the *Handbook of South American Indians*. In this reference, special subsections entitled "Games" and "Games and Toys" were created for each article in order to insure the presentation of this sort of material (see, e.g., Metraux, Volume I: 336 on the Mbaya; Bird, Volume I: 55-79 on the Alacaluf; Park, Volume II: 865-886 on the tribes of Sierra Nevada de Santa Marta, Columbia; Herandez del Alba, Volume II: 915-960 on the Highland Tribes of Southern Columbia; and Levi-Strauss Volume III: 229-305 on the Tupi Cawahib).

The game metaphor also is characteristically employed by ethnographers who use the presence or absence of particular sorts of games or toy objects in a culture as evidence of possible culture contact between societies. For example Cooper in the *Handbook* uses this approach in discussions of Chacoan and Araucanian societies (Volume V: 506-507,510).

Play as Projection

Psychologists and psychiatrists have often viewed the play behavior of children as a type of methodological or clinical projection-eliciting technique similar to a Rorschach or TAT test. This perspective on play has proven quite useful for studying, as well as treating, the intra-psychic anxieties and interpersonal conflicts of young children (e.g., Axline 1947, 1955; A. Freud 1937; Erickson 1940). Anthropologists interested in the study of culture and personality relationships have occasionally employed this projection metaphor in their interpretations of children's play. In these instances play is typically portrayed as an activity which is expressive of a child's inner drives and anxieties which are in turn related to the influence of cultural patterns.

Centner (1962) adopts this approach in a description and analysis of the play of the Baluba and Basanga-Bayeke children of Central Africa. This work is, to our knowledge, the most extensive and detailed presentation of information on children's play available in the African literature. Centner views play as expressive of, as well as influential in the development of a child's personality. Culture is seen as both reflected in and affected by play and the individual personalities of players.

Jules and Zunia Henry's (1944) description and analysis of the doll play behavior of Argentenian Pilaga children also utilizes the projection metaphor. However, this presentation is actually a study of the sibling rivalry of Pilaga children as this is expressed in their doll play and patterned by Pilaga culture. In this work the Henry's provide the reader with a great deal of information about the form which sibling rivalry takes in Pilaga society, but very little information about the various forms of children's play in this culture.

In the *Six Culture* series (B. Whiting 1966), games are discussed, after the work of Roberts, Arth, and Bush (1959), as expressive models of a culture as well as projections of a child's personality. Specific sorts of games (e.g., games of physical skill, games of strategy, games of chance) are also related to particular sorts of child-rearing practices. This use of the play as projection metaphor is reflected in a number of more recent articles building on the original work of Roberts, et. al. (e.g., Roberts and Sutton-Smith 1961; Sutton-Smith, Roberts and Kendon 1963; Sutton-Smith and Roberts 1970).

The projection metaphor is beginning to appear more frequently in the anthropological literature. It is our suggestion that the adoption of this perspective will only yield important information about play if it produces actual studies of play or games in cultural context (e.g. Centner) and does not produce studies *which only use play* to study some other type of activity (e.g., sibling rivalry as in J. and Z. Henry).

Play as Unimportant

Anthropologists have been unconcerned with the study of children in general (see Henry 1960, Diamond 1971)and children's play in particular.This lack of concern is coupled with a general disregard for, or disinterest in, play in Western societies (see Norbeck 1971). The format of many ethnographies reflects this lack of interest in that play either is not included as a legitimate ethnographic topic or reports of this activity are combined with a number of unrelated topics in a "miscellaneous" section. In many of the *Handbook* articles play is often

28

interpreted as separate from social activities and more properly grouped with narcotics and intoxicants. If play is discussed, little detailed description follows. And though the physical construction of toys or play objects may be mentioned the social construction of play activities is not.

Ethnographers may, in fact, collect information on children's and adults' play activities but simply exclude it from their ethnography. This is true of Paul and Laura Bohannan's reports on the Tiv. The ethnographic reports (1953, 1965) do not include mention of children's play activities; however, in the publication of their field notes (1958:374-379), descriptions of children's play activities do appear. This exclusion probably also occurs in many 'problem oriented' monographs. Often in these accounts socialization practices are not discussed and children's play may likewise be judged as irrelevant to the topic. Consequently, play is either not observed by the ethnographer or, if observed, simply excluded as irrelevant to the 'problem'.

It has been suggested that in some societies children do not play because they are put to work at an early age (e.g., Sutton-Smith 1974; commenting on the Gusii material of Robert and Barbara LeVine 1966; Wagley 1964 discussing children's play in an Amazon town). This seems questionable, for it is well known that children play in many non-Western societies even though they take on work responsibilities much earlier than Western children. In the few cases where this has been contended, the ethnographers note, interestingly enough, that the children in these societies actually do play but what or how they play is either not mentioned or only briefly described. This approach, again, seems to say more about the author's view of play than about its actual significance in the society.

Play is also treated as unimportant and therefore only briefly mentioned by a few ethnographers concerned specifically with the study of socialization practices (e.g., Hake 1972; Kaye 1960; R. and B. LeVine 1966; Peshkin 1972). Even though many of these authors do not specifically subscribe to the Whiting and Child (1953) and B. Whiting (1966) approach it is our suggestion that this view of socialization has had, since its first use in the 1950's, a great effect on determining what specific child-rearing techniques are considered important to study. Many of the 'critical child rearing variables' suggested by Whiting and Child (1953) have been adopted from Robert Sear's theories about child development. Sears does not consider play to be a critical variable for the study of child rearing practices and has in fact, only infrequently researched this phenomena, (e.g., 1946). The critical variables usually discussed by Sears are "the behavioral systems of feeding, toilet training, dependency, aggression, competition and identification" (Maier 1967:197). And it is not surprising to find that these are the critical variables emphasized by the Whiting and Child school and reported on in most ethnographies written since the 1950's which focus on the topic of childhood socialization. It is our view, however, that the widespread use of this approach specifically dictates against the collection of significant information on children's play behavior and continues to foster a view of play as unimportant.

Conclusion

In this review it is suggested that ethnographers of African and South American societies describe and interpret children's play from only four different perspectives (i.e., as imitation, as a game, as a projection, or as unimportant). It is also proposed here that each of these perspectives or metaphors for play reflect the culture of the anthropologist as much as the culture of an African or South American society. In illustrating the relationships existing between the culture of the anthropologist and these four perspectives on play it is not our intention to assert that anthropologists abandon the use of any or all metaphors for play; for in our view metaphors are a basic part of all descriptive and interpretive efforts.[7] It is, however, our suggestion that anthropologists acknowledge the use, source, and influence of these metaphors for play with the expectation that this will lead to a more careful appraisal of their work.

REFERENCES

Alamayahu, S.
    1959 "The Game of Ganna" in *Ethnological Society Bulletin*, Addis Ababa, 9:9-27.
Anna, M.
    1930 "The Mueso Game Among the Basoga", in *Primitive Man*, Washington, D.C. 11:71-74.
Ashton, H.
    1952 *The Basuto*, London: Oxford University Press, 1967 Edition.
Axline, V. M.
    1947 *Play Therapy: The Inner Dynamics of Childhood*, Boston: Houghton Mifflin Co.
    1955 "Play Therapy Procedures and Results" in *Orthopsychiatry*, 25:618-626.
Baker, H. J.
    1913 *Children of Rhodesia*, London: Charles H. Kelly.
Bohannan, P.
    1965 "The Tiv of Nigeria", see Gibbs (ed.)
Bohannan, P. and L.
    1953 *The Tiv of Central Nigeria*, London: International Institute (Western Africa, Part 8, in the Ethnographic Survey of Africa.)
    1958 "A Source Notebook on the Tiv Life Cycle" in *Three Source Notebooks in Tiv Ethnography*, Human Relations Area File.
Centner, T. H.
    1962 *L'Enfant Africain et ses Jeux*, Elisabethville: CEPSI.
Chagnon, N.
    1968 *Yanomamo: The Fierce People*, New York: Holt, Rinehart and Winston.

---

[7]The role and importance of metaphor in all scientific activities has been discussed in a number of works (e.g., Hesse, 1966; and Turbayne, 1970). In anthropology the importance of metaphor has recently been discussed by Wagner, 1975. An attempt to "re- metaphorize" the study of children's make-believe play activity appears in Schwartzman (1974).

Culin, S.
    1894 "Mancala, The National Game of Africa" in *Annual Report of the United States National Museum*, Washington, D.C., pp. 597-606.
Diamond, S.
    1974 "Introduction" in *Doll Play of Pilaga Indian Children* (J. and Z. Henry), New York: Vintage Books.
Edel, M.
    1957 *The Chiga of Western Uganda*, New York: Oxford University International African Institute.
Erikson, E. H.
    1940 "Studies in The Interpretation of Play: Part I: Clinical Observations of Play Description in Young Children" in *Genetic Psychology Monographs* 22:557-671.
Fortes, M.
    1938 "Social and Psychological Aspects of Education in Taleland" in Supplement to Africa, vol. XI, no. 4.
Freud, A.
    1937 *The Ego and Mechanisms of Defense*, London: Hogarth.
Freud, S.
    1905 *Jokes and Their Relation to The Unconscious*, New York: W. W. Norton and Co. (1963 edition).
Gibbs, J. L. (ed.)
    1965 *Peoples of Africa*, New York: Holt, Rinehart and Winston.
Hake, J. M.
    1972 *Child-Rearing Practices in Northern Nigeria*, Nigeria: Ibadan University Press.
Henry, J.
    1960 "A Cross-Cultural Outline of Education" in *Current Anthropology*, 4:267-305.
Henry, J. and Z.
    1944 *Doll Play of Pilaga Indian Children*, New York: Vintage Books (1974 edition).
Hesse, M. B.
    1966 *Models and Analogies in Science*, Notre Dame, Indiana: Univ. of Notre Dame Press.
Holmberg, A.
    1969 *Nomads of the Long Bow: The Siriono of Eastern Bolivia*, Garden City, New York: The Natural History Press.
Hopen, C. E.
    1958 *The Pastoral Fulbe Family in Gwandu*, London: Oxford University Press.
Kaye, B.
    1960 *Child Training in Ghana*, Legon: Institute of Education, Child Development Monographs, no. 1, University College of Ghana.
Kenyatta, J.
    1939 *Facing Mount Kenya*, London: Secker and Warburg.
Klima, G. J.
    1970 *The Barabaig*, New York: Holt, Rinehart and Winston.
Kuper, H.
    1965 "The Swazi of Swaziland" see Gibbs (ed.).
Leacock, E.
    1971 "At Play in African Villages" in *Natural History*, Special Supplement on Play, (December).
Leis, P.
    1972 *Enculturation and Socialization in an Ijaw Village*, New York: Holt, Rinehart, and Winston.

LeVine, R. A. and B. B.
  1966 *Nyansongo: A Gusii Community in Kenya*, Six Culture Series, Volume II, New York: John Wiley and Sons.
Mackay, R.
  1974 "Conceptions of Children and Models of Socialization" in *Ethnomethodology* (R. Turner ed.), Harmondsworth, England, Penguin Edition pp. 180-193.
Maier, H. W.
  1969 *Three Theories of Child Development*, New York: Harper and Row.
Malinowski, B.
  1944 *A Scientific Theory of Culture*, New York: Oxford University Press, 1960 edition.
Marshall, L.
  1965 "The !Kung Bushmen of the Kalahari Desert" see Gibbs (ed.).
Matson, G.
  1931 "Somali Game" in *Journal of the Royal Anthropological Institute*, London, 61:499-511.
Mead, M.
  1930 *Growing Up in New Guinea*, New York: Dell Publishing Company.
Messing
  1961 *The Highland-Plateau Amhara of Ethiopia*, Ann Arbor: University Microfilms.
Monroe, P.
  1906 *A Textbook in the History of Education*, New York.
Norbeck, E.
  1971 "Man at Play" in *Natural History*, Special Supplement on Play, (December).
Ottenberg, P.
  1965 "The Afikpo Ibo of Eastern Nigeria" see Gibbs (ed.).
Peshkin, A.
  1972 *Kanuri Schoolchildren: Education and Social Mobilization in Nigeria*, New York: Holt, Rinehart, and Winston.
Piaget, J.
  1962 *Play, Dreams and Imitation in Childhood*, New York: W. W. Norton and Company.
Powell-Cotton, P. H.
  1931 "A Mancala Board Called Songo", in *Man*, London, 31:133.
Raum, O. F.
  1940 *Chaga Childhood*, London: Oxford University Press International African Institute, 1967 edition.
Roberts, J. M.; Arth, M. J.; Bush, R. R.
  1959 "Games in Culture" in *American Anthropologist*, 61:597-605.
Roberts, J. M.; Sutton-Smith, B.
  1962 "Child Training and Game Involvement" in *Ethnology*, 1:166-195 (April).
Schapera, I.
  1930 *The Khoisan Peoples of South Africa*, London: Routledge and Kegan Paul.
Schwartzman, H.
  1974 "Re- metaphorizing' the Study of Children's Symbolic Play Activity", Paper presented at the 53rd Annual Meeting of the Central States Anthropological Society, Chicago, March 27-30.
Sears, R. R.
  1947 "Influence of Methodological Factors on Doll-Play Performance" in *Child Development*, 18: 190-197.
Shimahara, N.
  1970 "Enculturation—A Reconsideration" in *Current Anthropology*, 11:143-154.

32

Spencer, F. C.
    1899 *Education of the Pueblo Child* (A Study in Arrested Development), Columbia University Contributions to Philosophy, Psychology and Education.
Stenning, D. J.
    1965 "The Pastoral Fulani of Northern Nigeria" see Gibbs (ed.).
Steward, J. (ed.)
    1946-51 *Handbook of South American Indians*, Washington, D.C.: Smithsonian Institution, Bureau of American Ethnology, Bulletin 143.
Sutton-Smith, B.
    1972 *The Folkgames of Children*, Austin, Texas: University of Texas Press.
    1974 "Towards an Anthropology of Play" in *The Association for the Antropological Study of Play*, Newsletter, Volume I; Number 2, Fall, (condensed version of paper presented for the Symposium on Recreation at the State University of New York, Brockport, August, 1974).
Sutton-Smith, B.; Roberts, J. M.
    1970 "The Cross-Cultural and Psychological Study of Games" in *The Cross-Cultural Analysis of Games* (G. Luschen ed.), Champaign, Illinois: Stipes, pp. 100-108.
Sutton-Smith, B.; Roberts, J. M.; Kendon A.
    1963 "Strategy in Games and Folk Tales" in *Journal of Social Psychology*, 61:185-189.
Turnbull, C. M.
    1961 *The Forest People*, New York: Simon & Schuster.
Turbayne
    1970 *The Myth of Metaphor*, Columbia, South Carolina: University of South Carolina Press.
Wagley, C.
    1964 *Amazon Town: A Study of Man in the Tropics*, New York: Alfred A. Knopf.
Wagner, R.
    1975 *The Invention of Culture*, New York: Prentice-Hall.
Whiting, B. (ed.)
    1966 *Six Cultures: Studies of Child Rearing*, New York: John Wiley and Sons.
Whiting, J. W.; Child, I. L.
    1953 *Child Training and Personality: A Cross-Cultural Study*, New Haven: Yale University Press.

SPORT AS ART
Some Reflections on Definitional Problems in the Sociology of Sport

Richard Carlton
The University of Guelph

"There is a certain kind of behavioral scientist who, at the least threat of an exposed ambiguity, scurries for cover like a hermit crab into the nearest abandoned logical shell."

(Kaplan, 1964:71)

The systematic construction of definitions is no longer widely regarded as a productive form of theorizing, at least amongst North American sociologists. To many, "definition" connotes little more than an arid semantic exercise. To the contrary, it will be argued here that the development of adequate theoretical definitions is a rewarding, even indispensable task which merits continuing attention in sport, as in many areas of sociological enquiry.

Definitions, Theory and Research

The current lack of interest in theoretical definition can be seen, in part, as a legacy of the operationist debate: we have now virtually adopted in practise that kind of operationism which failed to win acceptance as a formal articulation of research method. To the extent that sociologists have increasingly recognized the need for adequate and articulate operational definitions, a corresponding requirement for explicit theoretical definitions has been neglected. Yet, in our day to day work, it is the battery of theoretical concepts, however weakly defined, which continues to furnish both the criteria for operationalization and the ground of intelligibility and interpretation for our observations.

One might argue that the observational procedures carried out within any enquiry *are* the definitions of the terms to which they might be linked, but the logical and practical difficulties of this strict operationist perspective have been so thoroughly exposed that most social scientists still prefer to regard their procedures as operationalizing *something* (Bierstadt, 1959). The need for adequate theoretical concepts remains widely admitted, if not well served.

Two sociologists exploring the hypothesis that participation in school sports is positively related to academic achievement may well elect to identify "sports", as opposed to other activities, by means of slightly different field procedures (i.e. operational definitions) and may encounter concretely different sports in the schools chosen for study. The generalizability, and ultimately much of the worth of their studies, however, hinges upon our assumption that they are basically studying "the same thing," even though they may choose to "get at it," so to speak, in quite different ways. We suppose, reasonably, that both researchers are providing information about a distinctive category of activities, popularly known as "sports", which may be expected to show some common attributes. It is on this account that we would view the two studies as related, or as contributing to a "common" field. We read and think in this way, even though we do not often make our assumptions explicit.

Lack of attention to definition may also be rooted in the uncritical appropriation of the covert classificatory schema of our language, which have delineated so many of the "substantive" fields of sociological inquiry. Many of these, it might be argued, lack conceptual integrity in that they do not explore any single aspect or area of social life *capable of sociological definition*. The very notion of a "substantive" field could, and perhaps should be seriously questioned.

In terms of publication, teaching and conferences, which might be taken as external evidence of activity, the sociology of sport is becoming a very lively field indeed. Yet, if one were to ask any of the participants, "What is it that you are studying? What is this activity called sport, which is found in every culture but is different everywhere we find it? By what distinctive external criteria can we recognize sport?" I doubt that our reply would yet be very satisfying. Certainly no consensus can be found in the literature. Without an answer to this apparently naive question, the positivist would argue that we cannot say what range of cases our theories are supposed to encompass.

A review of theoretical literature in the sociology of sport strongly suggests a decline in concern for 'tight' classification schemes. While many of the earliest essays and papers aimed at circumscribing the field through precise definitions and classification, and much debate at conferences was given over to such problems, these worries have gradually given way to the more productive reporting of concrete comparative and experimental research, which has not waited upon any definitional consensus. The establishment of research traditions is clearly, in itself, one strategy for cumulatively specifying the meaning of a concept such as sport. Nevertheless, we would argue that it can be useful to review definitional problems formally from time to time, to assess classification and boundary difficulties arising out of field research and to refine certain elements of our "working consensus" through the injection of new ideas or further distinctions. This conceptual clarification or enrichment is basic to the development of theory. Such is the aim of the reflections which follow: they begin with a recognition that much has already been accomplished in articulation of the definitional problems, which are no longer novel, and aim not to conclude but only to stimulate further effort at conceptual mapping.

Sport: A Definition in Difficulty

Considerable effort has already been made to define sport. Yet the outcomes, to date, have been mutually conflicting, somewhat inconsistent with popular usage, and certainly problematic in terms of research utility. Some writers have suggested that the essence of sport is "competition", yet it is clear that there are many sorts of competition—war or scholarship examinations are two examples—which we do not speak of as "sports". Likewise, there are activities such as skin diving—commonly thought of as a "sport", which can be carried on in a completely non-competitive setting.

The concept of "game" has been cited by many (Loy, 1968) as central to the notion of sport, yet there are many sports such as weight-lifting, which are manifestly not "games", while games such as parchesi would hardly qualify as sports, by any definition. In the same way, one can see that the notions of "play", "leisure" or "recreation" are not coextensive with even our simplest apperception of sport.

Some efforts at definition have consisted merely of classifying particular games and sports according to their reliance on chance or skill, and according to

35

the presence of competitive and game elements but the result is entirely culture-bound, and only points to the accidental character of these properties in particular sports.

Through persistent effort, Kenyon and his collaborators (1966, 1968, 1969) have developed a more complex set of criteria which have gained very wide currency and which are either cited or paraphrased in many recent expositions, including those of Loy (1968), Olsen (1969) and Suits (1971). Consensus amongst these theorists is that sport can be identified with reference to three major criteria: (1) characteristic socio-cultural organization, or "institutionalization", (2) game-competitive or non-utilitarian motivation, and (3) a substantial element of skill-refined gross physical activity. In spite of the developmental and heuristic value of this approach, it could be argued that most recent empirical inquiry owes little in the way of theoretical formulation to such definitions, and may already have disclosed underlying problem areas.

One such persistent difficulty clearly has to do with the cruciality of the gross motor activity factor. Although this element is most often cited as the "specific difference" which delineates sport within a larger genus such as games, contemporary "sport sociology" is almost wholly indifferent to the kinetic dimension. To this extent, what passes for "sport sociology" is frequently only the sociology of complex organizations, of leadership, of collective behaviour or of some other conceptually—i.e. theoretically—integral area, to which the element of physical activity is entirely accidental and irrelevant. This suggests strongly that we have not yet succeeded in constructing a theoretically meaningful classification, as we have, for example, in categorizing bureaucracies or primary groups. Another way of illustrating the problem is to point out that research in the latter areas tests propositions both specific and universal to the class of phenomena in question, whereas most current research in the sociology of sport focuses upon propositions accidentally testable in some sport situations but specific and generalizable to another overlapping category of action or actors.

Of considerable interest, in this regard, is an atypical research report which appeared almost a decade ago in the British Journal of Sociology. The investigators, Norbert Elias and Eric Dunning (1966) attempted an analysis of group dynamics in football, guided by conventional small group theory. Their conclusion, surprisingly, was that such theories simply did not fit: "Confronted with the study of sport groups *in vivo*, small group theory failed us." Their inference from this apparent failure is even more provocative, however. The researchers concluded that "the distinguishing features of this type of group" necessitated distinct modifications of the general theoretical framework for small groups. In short, they confronted the possibility that sport groups might be sociologically *distinctive*, not merely accidentally identifiable through the presence of gross physical activity, as has been assumed by the bulk of recent researchers. It is clear, moreover, that the conceptualization of sport represented by our textbook definition, above, offers little guidance as to what these sociologically relevant differences might be.

A second problem increasingly evident in the research literature has to do with what is variously termed the 'lusory' or non-utilitarian element of conventional definitions. Almost invariably, writers and researchers have interpreted this with reference to the motivations of individual actor-participants, often in an occupational context. Ingham and Loy (1973) suggest that "the expressive frame of sport is maintained, therefore, if participants engage in sport out of expressive concerns". Anderson, et al (1969) argue that sport "must bear the stamp of play and competition and the essential interest for the participant should not be financial advantage". Not only within our own culture, in the research treatment of professional commercial and spectatorial involvements, but in comparative work, with the necessary imputation of ideal-typical motivational constructs, the reduction of the definitive criterion to an attitudinal variable poses a considerable barrier.

In view of these sorts of difficulties, then, it may prove worthwhile to attempt further refinement of our conceptualization and definition of sport, which we will approach through a reconsideration of art and play forms.

Sport as Art: Toward a Reconceptualization

Reviewing the activities popularly characterized as "sport", in diverse cultures, one agrees immediately that *gross physical activity* is an ever-present factor. Yet this element is inadequate, if taken alone, since it may also be found in many other areas such as work or military enterprise. If one then asks what distinguishes running or fighting *qua sport*, from the same activities carried out by a courier, soldier or hunter, it would seem that the difference might indeed lie in the absence of instrumental or utilitarian elements, as has conventionally been argued. The courier runs in order to get from A to B, and his arrival at B is presumably *instrumental* to some other activity, such as relaying a message. By contrast, the athlete, runs *for the sake of the running* and may indeed arrive back at A if he is using a circular track: his running is valued intrinsically rather than extrinsically.

Now it might appear that we are returning here to the level of the actor and his motivations, but this need not be the case. Either the courier or the athlete may be personally motivated by rewards which are "extrinsic" (salary, health, prestige) or "intrinsic" (satisfaction in the activity per se, as expressive, exhilarating or efficient). Both elements may be present in the way that a single actor defines his activity, and indeed, two participants might well be quite differently motivated within the same event. A professional hockey game, for example, might involve players who play primarily "for immediate personal satisfaction" and others who compete essentially "for the money". Analysis at the level of participant motivation will never effect meaningful classifications, even for activities as diverse as work and sport.

On the other hand, there is a contextual definition of any activity which is independent of participant motivation. A competitor in a weight lifting contest may view his participation as predominantly utilitarian—a way of earning a living or of acquiring prestige, but the lifting of heavy concrete or metal "weights" is not socially viewed as "useful", nor causally efficient. As a matter of fact, the weightlifter invariably puts the weights right back on to the floor or mat from which he lifted them in the first place. All sports possess a large measure of non-utilitarian character, which presupposes only a degree of normative consensus governing participant conduct rather than specific participant motivations.

What may appear to be the same activity may be very differently defined in a different socio-cultural context; two men may be sawing logs but if one is sawing in a situation intended to be productive of firewood while the other is a participant in a log-sawing contest, we call the former "work" and the latter "sport". This is not to say that the logs cut in the course of the contest may not ultimately be burned, but this utilitarian element is viewed as irrelevant or accidental to the socio-cultural meaning and normative structure of that activity. Utility, like deviance, can be construed as a normative situational quality arising out of audience-shared definitions rather than actor motivations.

Where this sort of problem has been most evident in research and discussion is in respect of 'professional' sports. Tension has rightly been perceived, precisely where the symbolism of the activity could be undermined by the constraints of the "business" setting, which is after all a condition of the occurrence of the sporting event, but not of its structure or meaning. When there is suspicion of "fixing", however, or when the workmanlike behaviour of the "pro" inhibits the spectator in imputing qualities of agression, exhilaration or involvement which are somehow essential to the expressive meaning of the event, then the "sporting" character of the event gives way to an occupational one.

Classification through a residual category built upon the exclusion of material utility, however, is clearly inadequate, even when attained at a structural rather than motivational level. It will be important to identify the sociological genre of sporting activities; a task well begun in Simmel's work on play.

While it is true that the work of Georg Simmel is occasionally cited in the literature on sport, there has been virtually no systematic effort to explore his sociology of play as a source of insight in these areas. Simmel defines "play" in terms of the primacy of formal properties of behaviour, emancipated from the significance of content.

> This complete turnover, from the determination of the forms by the materials of life to the determination of its materials by forms that have become supreme values, is perhaps most extensively at work in the numerous phenomena that we lump together under the category of *play*. Actual forces, needs, impulses of life produce the forms of our behavior that are suitable for play. These forms, however, become independent contents and stimuli within play itself or, rather *as* play. (1950:40)

For Simmel *social* play or "sociability", for example, designates any activity in which sociation (social interaction) is implemented and explored for its own sake, rather than for the sake of the content. Some content remains, of course, but it is selected and fashioned according to the needs of formal development. Thus, sociability is a play-form of social interaction, in which the "arts" of co-quetry, conversation, or partying retain the dynamics but not the content of social life in sexual, ethical, or other dimensions.

From this point of view, sociability is a play form of sociation, abstracting and stylizing the characteristic forms of social interaction, just as the plastic arts are play forms of sense experience, drawing upon and finding their idiom in the cognitive and affective modalities of perception.

The relation of art to play, defined in this way, did not escape Simmel:

> In both art and play, forms that were originally developed by the re-
> alities of life, have created spheres that preserve their autonomy in
> the face of these realities. It is from their origin, which keeps them
> permeated with life, that they draw their depth and strength . . . The
> forms in which this process results gain their own life. It is freed
> from all ties with contents. It exists for its own sake and for the sake
> of the fascination which, in its own liberation from these ties, it dif-
> fuses. (1950:40)

Here, as elsewhere, popular usage is revealing. The expressivity of art de-rives in part from the emancipation of form from content, and it is this which lends to art a certain timelessness. Thus we speak of photographic "art", as dis-tinguished from a snapshot or newsphoto, when the instantaneity, or some other formal quality of the process—grain, chiaroscuro or monochromatic effects—are emphasized or enjoyed for their own sake: the content clearly comes to serve the interest of the media or form. The "art" of conversation, like the art of the painter, accentuates formal considerations as over against the "subject matter" and we use the term analogously when we refer to the "art" of the craftsman. The "art" of welding denotes the process or form of the activity without refer-ence to the content, i.e. irrespective of what is being welded. The notion of art then, implies a preoccupation with form.

When we refer to this dynamic exploration or manipulation of form for its own sake, we use the term "play". When we enjoy the motion of light on water, for example, attending to the formal aspects of movement or the medium of light itself rather than the content—waves—we speak of the "play" of the light on the water. The child who "plays" house, the boy who "plays" hockey, the violinist who "plays" music are all creatively engaging in art under the forms of sociability, sport or aesthetics. Thus, play is the dynamic aspect of art, or, con-versely, art is the idiomatic, aesthetic—expressive, cultural stylization of a play form.

Sport, as a play form of tactility, motion and vertigo is an art; in so far as kinetic play forms are contained within interactional frameworks drawn from social life, but detached from the instrumentality of their content, sport may also be a form of sociability. Thus springboard diving or gymnastics are sports, but could hardly be construed as sociability. Diving and gymnastic contests, however, are clearly situations in which social relationships such as competition or cooperation are engaged and enjoyed for their own sake.

Since both sport and sociability are "play forms," we find in both an emphasis on "good form", and an effort to prevent the undertaking from succumbing to the threat of content. Neither the party-goer nor the athlete can afford to take content too seriously, since the "play" quality of the activity is thus jeopardized. The advice of the experienced conversationalist to "avoid politics and religion" is directly analogous to such admonitions as "its not the winning but the playing, that counts". Sportsmanship and etiquette are the ethics of play.

Originally, much social play involved a sociability built on everyday activities of the hunt, agriculture, war or transport. Elaboration of play forms in games or contests was facilitated by the simultaneous emancipation of kinetic play forms from task skills and functional linkages. Discus throwing, for example, has become an 'art' rather than a combat skill, and as such is more malleable material for the social play of athletic contests.

It is this aesthetic-expressive element alone which seems able to account for the depth and inclusiveness of *spectatorial involvement*, to which the real motives and rewards of physically active participants must be irrelevant. This is everywhere true of the arts which are delimited in their expressivity not by participation, but rather, by a community of shared idiom, experience, sentiment and interpretation. Thus, we speak of "folk", "popular", or "national" art forms, having reference not to creative artists or performers alone but to an aesthetic community comprised largely of spectators or consumers.

Clearly, productive participation has been and remains an expectation for particular age and sex groupings in various societies. North American male youth are expected to participate in some athletic games, for example; to abstain is virtually a breach of character imputing a lack of "manliness". Similarly participation in dancing or exhibitions of combat skills has often been seen as mandatory for whole classes of individuals in other societies. Nevertheless, the arts take on a communicative role which sets them apart from pure self-expression on the one hand, and from utilitarian activities on the other. In a very real sense, it is the audience, real or implied, which constitutes art, and not art which "finds" an audience. Small groups may well gather to "perform" for their own satisfaction—whether this is for an evening of chamber music or an early morning game of "shinny", but the meaning of the activity and the canons of appreciation derive from some larger reference group, present or not.

A recent student newspaper which I happened upon almost accidentally while in the midst of these considerations, gives an accurate, if not very original account of the role of a school football fan:

40

"The players are out there to prove something and you have to give them a chance to do so . . . I watched the last game with as much anxiety as if I myself was in there playing. To be a true fan, you have to feel the excitement and emotion of the players. You have to let the players know that you are behind them all the time. (*The Double-Blue*, 1971)

Thus, the "fan" not only participates vicariously in the activity of the game—which must be symbolically meaningful for him—but must be caught up in the kinds of collective behaviour through which audiences develop a shared response to the spectacle and through which in some situations they may even interact with performers. This sort of spectatorial participation is not essentially different from that of the theatre audience. Indeed, the element of theatre is an important component of many sporting events in which heroes, villains, comedy, retribution, catharsis, fate or other tragic and dramatic elements may be highlighted. It is no accident that every successful sports writer has a sharp eye for what Robert Ezra Park used to call the "human interest story".

In sum, precisely because sport is expressive rather than instrumental, it is not necessary to *perform* in order to have a *sport* experience, any more than it is necessary to sing, play, write poetry, paint or sculpt in order to have some other sort of aesthetic experience. Sport, then, exhibits a strong and clear continuity with the other arts in the import and primal character of spectatorial involvement.

Kinetic Play

As an art form, kinetic play may be expected to exhibit varying degrees of patterning, from relatively 'free forms' to highly stylized and rigidified rituals. The raw material of kinetic play is common to other than human species, and the analogy suggested by terms such as "horseplay" is also appropriate to the spontaneous humming, chanting, running, jumping or arm-swinging of children. At the other end of the spectrum, we have the highly structured persistent cultural patterning of springboard diving or gymnastic figures and routines, identified as 'sports' within the larger domain of 'sport'. Few sociological studies focus upon the symbolism of the kinetic element per se, which is seen almost as an accidental quality of sport situations. Both Beiser (1967) and Goffman (1961), however, have suggested ways in which the expressive components and kinetic play elements can move to the centre, rather than the periphery of analysis. In different ways, both argue that the exploration, maintenance and enhancement of self in sporting activities can be understood in large part as a function of the symbolism attached to body-movement. The fighter, the golfer, the quarterback and the goalie are expressing something of themselves and to themselves through their stylized 'acting out' of kinetic play forms. Although social play, with expressive role allotment is also present in such situations, the languid grace of aquatic figures, the apparently relaxed and contained power of the golf swing, the raw physical aggression of a tackle or a body check are all expressive of important physical, affective and sexual elements which may be closer to genotypic than phenotypic, more akin to Cooley's (1902) primary social substratum than any culturally diversified secondary learning.

Kinetic play, or perhaps more properly, kinetic art forms, if we are to take explicit account of cultural patterning, may also become the surrogate content of 'serious' social interaction, where sport becomes a medium for the expression of social solidarity or conflict. The use of wrestling bouts to settle boundary disputes among the Ifugao (Frederickson, 1969), or the many forms of trial by athletic combat illustrate the molding of kinetic play to other social purposes.

In activities such as exercise or therapy, outcomes which are accidental to kinetic play forms may be exploited, and the expressive symbolism may be radically undermined. Therapeutic activity is inherently instrumental. Cycling, for example, is commonly regarded as sport when it is removed from the context of utilitarian transport to a setting in which the expressivity and exhilaration of effort, motion and kinetic expression are given free rein. When therapy or exercise becomes the prime consideration however, it is not only convenient but somehow appropriate to remove the wheels, at once so expressive and so functional. The "exercycle", like the rowing bench, is a "prop", a technological eunuch, which in an introverted way provides the minimal conditions for specific physical activities, while depriving those activities of their external efficacy and meaning. Unlike sport, therapy and exercise are no longer characterized by exploration of form for its own sake: like work, the normative structure of these activities reflects the suppression of aesthetic elements in the interest of efficiency. Therapy, for this very reason, predictably lacks the spectatorial appeal of sport.

From this discussion it is clear than an argument might be made for kinetic play forms as the definitive criterion of sport. From this perspective, sport might be redefined as an art from of kinetic play, most frequently developed within a context of the broader-ranging social play forms or 'sociability'.

Some Research Implications

By way of conclusion, it is possible to suggest how the bent of current research might be shifted through an emphasis on the art and play elements of sport. First, such theorizing should provide a healthy counterbalance to the prevailing functionalist orientation in sport sociology. Following Merton's (1949) popularization of Pareto's (1965) work on latent utility, sociological researchers have been ingenious in relating sport to social ends such as skill learning and maintenance, to culturally relevant socializing functions or to the career significance of avocational to vocational pursuits. Increasingly, however it may be necessary to conclude, with Elias and Dunning (1966) that there can be a tolerable lack of utility or purpose, manifest or latent, in many areas of social structure, particularly those characterized as play. Emphasis on the kinetic and social

42

play elements of sport could bring an alternative set of considerations to the fore.

Secondly, attention to the distinction between *sociability* and *kinetic play* ought to clarify a great deal of the overlap between research specific to sport, of which there is very little, and research generic to social play such as game forms, of which there is a great deal. For better or worse, sport sociology seems bent on following the route taken by sociology of work: a strongly applied bias oriented to the solution of "Human relations in sport" problems, and the maximization of organizational efficiency and productivity. In large part, then, sport sociology has involved a pattern of replication in which conventional studies of leadership, morale, occupational violence, or formal organization frequently pass for innovative research, breaking ground in the 'new' field of sport sociology. Our research needs to articulate meaningfully the distinguishing and unique qualities of sport activities, if we are to have a genuine sociology of sport; for this reason we are far from finishing with the problems of definition and conceptual mapping.

Finally, sociologists probably have a great deal to learn from their anthropological colleagues if they are to locate or develop the theoretical tools requisite to the study of artistry in sport. Although the literature of sociology, back to Veblen (1899) and beyond, has pointed to the symbolism in sport, little headway has yet been made in exploring either the relative autonomy of play forms, or the integrity of the kinetic, social, linguistic and technological expressive components.

Perhaps these considerations of sport as art will provoke some reanalysis of the conventional classifications, and will aid us, in some small way, in charting more imaginative, unpredictable and rewarding paths of inquiry.

REFERENCES

Anderson, H., Bo-Jensen, A., Elkaer-Hausen, H., and Sonne, A., "Sports and Games in Denmark in the Light of Sociology," in Loy, J. W., and Kenyon, G. S., *Sport, Culture and Society*, New York, The MacMillan Company, 1969.

Beisser, A. R., *The Madness in Sports*, New York, Appleton-Century-Crofts, 1967.

Bierstedt, R., "Nominal and Real Definitions in Sociological Theory," in Gross, L. (ED.) *Symposium in Sociological Theory*, New York, Harper and Row, 1959.

Caillois, R., "The Structure and Classification of Games" in *Diogenes*, 12, Winter, 1955, pp. 62-75.

Cooley, C. H., *Human Nature and the Social Order*, New York, Chas. Scribner's Sons, 1902.

Elias, N. and Dunning, E., "Dynamics of Group Sports with Special Reference to Football," in *The British Journal of Sociology*, December, 1966, pp. 288-402.

Frederickson, F. S., "Sports and the Cultures of Man" in Loy, J. W. and Kenyon, G. S., *Sport, Culture and Society*, New York, The MacMillan Company, 1969.

Goffman, E., "Fun in Games" in *Encounters*, Indianapolis, Bobbs-Merrill Co., 1961.

Ingham, A. G. and Loy, J. W., "The Social System of Sport: A Humanistic Perspective," in *Quest*, Monograph XIX, January 1973, pp. 3-23.

Kaplan, A., *The Conduct of Inquiry*, San Francisco, Chandler Publishing, 1964, pg. 71.

Kenyon, G.S., "A Conceptual Model for Characterizing Physical Activity," in *Research Quarterly*, 39, 1, March, 1968, pp. 96-105.

Kenyon, G. S., "A Sociology of Sport: On Becoming A Sub-Discipline," in Brown, R. C. and Cratty, B. J. (Eds.), *New Perspectives of Man In Action*, New Jersey, Prentice-Hall, 1969, pg. 168.

Lopreato, J., *Vilfredo Pareto*, New York, Thos. Y. Crowell Co., 1965, pg. 15.

Loy, J. W., "The Nature of Sport. A Definitional Effort" in *Quest*, Monograph X, May, 1968, pp. 1-15.

Merton, R. K., *Social Theory and Social Structure*, New York, The Free Press, 1949, pg. 19 ff.

Olsen, A. M., "Sociology of Sport in Relation to Physical Education and Sport Theory," Paper Given at the International Workshop on the Sociology of Sport, Macolin, Switzerland, 1969.

Suits, B. "The Elements of Sport," Paper Given at the Third International Symposium on the Sociology of Sport, Waterloo, Canada, 1971.

The Double-Blue, Toronto, St. Michael's College High School, 1971.

Veblen, T., *The Theory of the Leisure Class*, New York, The MacMillan Co., 1899.

Wolff, K. H., *The Sociology of George Simmel*, New York, The Free Press, 1950, pg. 40 ff.

SPORT AS RITUAL: A THEORETICAL APPROACH

Scott Kilmer
York University

The approach used in this paper for comprehending sport is a ritualistic one, hence the dynamics of myth and ritual shall be briefly discussed in order to achieve a base for such a ritualistic analysis. "The function of myth is thus held to be the validation, or justification of cultural beliefs and practises . . . Myths are said to be taken seriously in the sense that they deal with subjects of the most importance to native life and constitute primitive man's beliefs as to the cosmic significance of his rites and customs." (Bidney, 1967, 289-90, 291) Myth thus serves as a means for validating important cultural practices as a base for human belief systems. "By myths we mean the value impregnated beliefs and notions that men hold, that they live by and for." (Young, in Bidney, 1967, 210)

As with beliefs, myth is laden with underlying emotions, which are brought out by the aspects which myth itself delves into. "The most significant myths and legends emerge out of recurrent problems of adjustment to our physical and socio-cultural world." (Bidney, 1967, 210) Adjustment, especially when it is of a social nature, is very often rife with emotion—thus even at a conscious level of analysis (the analysis of myth as conscious tales which may be analyzed in the same manner as stories) myth will often be laden with emotion. At an unconscious level of analysis of myth, this emotional quality is often further enhanced. "Myth does not reveal the whole of a people's culture and design for

44

living, though what is embedded in tradition often leads to knowledge and truth lost to the conscious mind of a people." (Lessa, in P. Maranda, 1972, 71) As emotions have been postulated as existing basically in the unconscious mind (although surfacing to the conscious mind occasionally), they cannot often be understood in a cause/effect relationship by the person experiencing them. The same has been said of myth, that much of mythical truth is lost to the conscious mind of a people, so perhaps both myth and emotion lie on rather similar, unconscious planes of thought.

Perhaps here an analogy will help to elucidate matters. The analogy is that of the bifurcation of behaviour into active and passive realms. 'Pure' intellectualizing can be seen as being a rather passive realm, a realm of the conscious mind, a realm of relative non-involvement. "There is a kind of intellectual remoteness necessary for the comprehension of any great work in its full designs and its true proportions." (Samuel Johnson, in J. Thompson, 1970, 42) In contrast to this, beliefs entail very active involvement. "Myth is linked with the rules and norms and actual behaviour of the society in which it is accepted: and this is an intrinsic part of its definition. People believe in it, take it for granted, act upon it, and cite it as an ideal or a possible basis for action. It is the *belief* and *action* dimension that counts." (Berndt, 1973, 83)

Here the discussion of ritual shall begin, in order to comprehend some of its relationships to myth. Ritual may be seen as being the action side of myth—"ritual is the routine of worship." (Encyclopedia Brittanica, 1911, 370) As such, ritual consists of sacred ceremonies and their routines, with the routines being seen as consecrated acts which contain great mystical powers. Ritual acts are an escape from the profane, everyday world into the sacred, due to these mystical, magical attributes. The acts which are performed during the ritual event are generally stylized and repetitive, as it is feared that they may lose their magical power if stylization is altered. The rules for stylization, once accepted by a given cultural system, are then adhered to fixidly, and can be used as an excellent basis for an in-depth analysis of the rite itself. The stress for analysis should be placed on the segment of the rite which contains the most emotional involvement. "The intensest emotions of a community are discharged in a representative ritual which thus becomes the relevation of the inmost desires, strivings, and necessity of the group mind, the expression in action of thoughts that cannot be uttered adequately in words." (E. O. James, 1933, 36)

Here the conception of ritual as the acting out (and thus the concretization) of symbolic ideas should shed further light on ritual. Ritual serves to objectify and concretize the idea of group solidarity, as common sentiments are expressed and manifested in group rituals. As these common sentiments are expressed through group, communal participation, the rituals are transcendental experiences for the individuals involved in the rituals, as this group sentiment replaces and transcends the individual, profane existance. Thus ritual exists on a higher-order plane than does normal, everyday life. "The participants in the rite are convinced that the action actualizes and effects a definite beatification, brings about an order of things higher than that in which they customarily live." (Huizinga, 1967, 14)

As ritual events exist on this high level, they contain a great degree of power—and such power is often intensified through the use of drugs (beer, peyote, magic mushrooms, etc.) or through the sacrifice of a symbolic object (goat, chicken, person, etc.). This often allows the participants in the ritual (whether they are directly involved in the ritual or are merely observers) to relate themselves even further to the ritual, as they thereby reach a deeper level within their own minds. And as many of those participating in the ritual thus reach a similar level in their minds, ritual events can serve as a corporate catharsis. "Gluckman sees the ritual enactmentof conflicts of interest as a form of catharsis that banishes the threat to unity imposed by the conflicts . . . The occasions (that allow for license on rules of moral behaviour) are principally ritual events, and they are often the same as those during which expressions of hostility are allowed or prescribed." (E. Norbeck, 1967, 198; article by Evans Pritchard, 216) Ritual events can be seen from this perspective as group activities in which aggression is allowed to surface—with the degree of symbolism involved in this aggression varying greatly cross-culturally. By serving as an outlet for aggression ritual keeps internal tensions from breaking up the society, and can be seen as actually transforming them into socially integrating forces.

A brief resume of myth and ritual shall be attempted here, before moving on to the relationship between sport and ritual. "The essential truth of the myth lies in the fact that it embodies a situation of profound emotional significance, a situation, moreover, which is in its nature recurrent, and which calls for the repetition of the ritual which deals with the situation and satisfies the need evoked by it . . . If we turn to the living myth, that is the myth that is believed in, we find that it has no existence apart from the ritual." (Lord Raglan, in Sebeok, 1971, 123, 126) Ritual deals with mythic themes, it takes these themes and illustrates them in group form. Ritual takes mythic ideas away from the realm of pure passive thought and places them in the realm of active social phenomena. This is why men such as Lord Raglan (and the many others who believe in the primacy of ritual over myth) stressed the great importance of ritual within society. "Ritual has been, at most times and for most people, the most important thing in the world." (Raglan, in Sebeok, 1971, 133) Ritual takes many of the ideas incorporated in myth and applies these themes to social events, thus allowing for their dissemination.

Sport, especially when it occurs as a large scale event (such as American football, South American soccer, etc.), has all the trappings of myth and ritual. "The world of myth (and ritual) is said to be a dramatic world, a world of conflicting powers, and mythical perception is impregnated with these emotional qualities." (Bidney, in Sebeok, 1971, 11) Large scale sporting events create a dramatic atmosphere, where conflicting powers meet head-on in a very emotional setting. And this setting itself contains a sacredness which sets such events apart from the profane world. This sacredness has been labeled by Huizinga as the "Magic Circle", and is extremely relevant for the comprehension of sport. For the sporting event occurs within a specified area, and the social events happening within this area become endowed with special qualities—as they occur inside the Magic Circle on sacred ground.

The events which occur inside the Magic Circle bring a temporary, limited perfection into an otherwise imperfect world. Here the analogy of sporting rules with ritual's stylized actions should clarify matters. Rituals across the world contain stylized, repetitive acts which change slowly over time for fear of losing their magical attributes. The same dynamics also hold for sporting rules, as once such originally arbitrary rules become accepted in a given sporting event, they are rigidly adhered to and change very little over time. The following example illustrates the dynamics underlying sporting rules and their use inside the Magic Circle. Recently in Ontario, the National Hockey League has come under fire from the government for being too violent and thereby influencing youngsters to become more violent. Clarence Campbell, president of the N.H.L., retorted with the following; "Violence is a way of life in the N.H.L." (Toronto Star, February 9, 1975). He believed, and in all probability he was correct, that violence was an integral part of hockey's rules, and that by changing such rules, the sport would lose many of its supporters. As long as such violence occurs within the Magic Circle, it is socially acceptable.

But the Magic Circle has more than just spatial dimensions, such as a hockey arena or a football field—it also has temporal dimensions, as the following hockey example further illustrates. In the recent Russia/Team Canada hockey series, the Russians were winning the sixth game by one goal late in the game. The Canadians were trying hard to tie the game (which was being played in Russia), but the horn blew, ending the game and breaking the temporal dimension of the sixty minute Magic Circle. A Canadian player, however, refused to listen to the horn, and began to punch a Russian player after the game had ended. The next day the Russian coach issued a statement to the papers stating that the Canadian player should be arrested and sent to jail for accosting a Russian citizen. The Magic Circle of the hockey game had been broken and the players were then in the profane world, where one is arrested for punching people. The event was cleared up and the Canadian player was not arrested, but the seriousness of the Russian coach's actions was a good illustration of the temporal aspect of the Magic Circle.

"Arenas are the concrete settings in which paradigms become transformed into metaphors and symbols." (V. Turner, 1974, 17) The actions that occur within the arena are full of symbolic meaning, as Eldridge Cleaver points out. "Our mass spectator sports are geared to disguise, while affording expression to, the acting out in elaborate pageantry of the myth of the fittest in the process of surviving . . . (Sport is) the basic cultural ethic, hammered and sublimated into national-communal pagan rituals." (Cleaver, 1972, 85) Large scale sporting rituals are symbolic validations of group norms throughout the world, with only the types and methods of symbolization differing.

This validation is enhanced by the great power which is at the base of such sporting rituals—whether this power be the power of an eight-hundred horsepower engine, the power of 100,000 people chanting in unison, or the power of hitting a baseball four hundred feet. This power is unleashed in accordance with the rules of the sport, where the rules themselves contain the basic symbolism of the sport. The unleashed power acts out these rules and moves them from the realm of pure thought into the realm of action—in the same manner that ritual does for mythical symbolism.

This power is often enhanced in the same manner that occurs in ritual throughout the world—through the ingestion of drugs and the sacrifice of symbolic objects (as previously discussed). The consumption of alcohol during sporting events, especially in the United States, occurs amongst the fans as expected behaviour; as does the personal sacrifice of the sporting participants' physical bodies. The following example, as it is an extreme one, should help to support these points. The example is that of auto racing—of men driving machines on the edge of existence. Auto racing attracts extremely large crowds around the world, and in America it is the second largest spectator sport (Purdy, 1963, 138). Drinking alcohol is one of the favorite pasttimes of auto racing fans, and it is openly encouraged by the track owners who sell it at concession stands. This drinking, in conjunction with the roaring engine noises of the racing machines, gives the fans the feeling of power. And this power is further enhanced by the sacrificial aspects of the sport itself, as death on the asphalt track occurs with grim regularity. Ken Purdy points out that "Grand Prix driving is the most dangerous sport in the world. It is one of the riskiest of man's adventures. In one recent year the mortality rate was 25%." (Ken Purdy, 1963, 23) From this perspective, auto racing may be seen as being the most extreme example of the sacrificial aspect of sporting rituals, but other sporting rituals also contain this sacrificial aspect, though it is often of a more covert, symbolic nature.

What is the purpose of all this power, and why is the power in such ritual sporting events often so great? Jung gives a partial answer in the following: "Whenever the magical aspect of a rite tends to prevail, it brings the rite nearer to satisfying the individual ego's blind greed for power." (Jung, 1958, 198) As such sporting rituals occur in front of extremely large audiences, (crowds at stadiums of over 100,000 people, audiences of millions via television) the power needed to satisfy such a large audience of egos must be immense. This power often reaches an extremely high level, as exemplified by the power of life and death in auto racing, and can be seen as often being beyond the control of mere rationality. Otherwise, why would a rational person take such great chances as an auto racer does or why would a rational person sit and watch an event in which he knows death may occur at any moment? The answer to this is that ritual is not based in rationality, as Leach points out in the following: "Ritual is often viewed as a nonrational means to achieve culturally defined ends; its symbols are characterized as condensed, containing multiple meanings." (Leach, in Lessa, 1972, 333) Sport as ritual contains such condensed symbolism—for the action occuring within the Magic Circle of sporting events is full with the tenseness of victory and defeat within a compressed arena of both time and space.

REFERENCES

Berndt, C. and R.
    1973 *The Barbarians*, Aylesbury, Bucks, Hazell Watson and Viney, Ltd.
Bidney, David
    1967 *Theoretical Anthropology*, New York: Shocken Books.
Cleaver, Eldridge
    1972 *Soul on Ice*, New York: Dell Pub. Co.
Encyclopedia Brittanica
    1911 New York
Firth, Raymond
    1973 *Symbols, Public and Private*, London: Allen and Unwin, Ltd.
Harris, N.
    1971 *Beliefs in Society*, Aylesbury, Bucks, Hazell Watson and Viney, Ltd.
Huizinga, J.
    1967 *Homo Ludens*, Boston: Beacon Press (Orig. 1955).
James, E. O.
    1933 *Origins of Sacrifice*, London: John Murray Pub. Co.
Jung, C. G.
    1958 *Psyche and Symbol*, Garden City, N.Y.: Doubleday and Co., Inc.
Lessa, William A. (ed.)
    1972 *Reader in Comparative Religion*, New York: Harper and Row.
Luschen, Gunther (ed.)
    1970 *The Cross Cultural Analysis of Sport and Games*, Champaign, Ill.: Stipes Pub.
        Co.
Maranda, Pierre
    1972 *Mythology*, New York: Penguin Books.
Norbeck, Edward
    1967 "African Rituals of Conflict" in Middleton, ed., *Gods and Rituals*, New York:
        Nat. Hist. Press.
Purdy, Ken
    1963 *All But My Life* (The Life of Stirling Moss), New York: E. P. Dutton and Co.,
        Inc.
Sebeok, Thomas (ed.)
    1971 *Myth, a Symposium*, Bloomington, Indiana: Indiana Univ. Press.
Thompson, J.
    1970 *The Rise and Fall of Maya Civilization*, Norman, Okla.: Univ. of Okla. Press.
Toronto Star
    1975 Toronto: February 9
Turner, Victor
    Dramas, Fields, and Metaphors, Ithaca, N.Y.: Cornell Univ. Press.

THEORETICAL CONSIDERATIONS AND A METHOD FOR THE STUDY OF PLAY[1]

Elizabeth C. Mouledoux
Loyola Campus, Concordia University
Montreal, Quebec

In 1971, Sutton-Smith, having completed with his associates a comprehensive two volume survey of the literature on play and games[2] made the following evaluative summary:

> Consider, for example, hide and seek, ring-a-roses, solitaire, chicken, bingo, football, zero-sum, wooden leg, criscom, simuload. No one has yet successfully incorporated these into a single theoretical system, despite the fact that the category label "game" is still applied to all of them. [Avedon and Sutton-Smith 1971: 3]

Such judgments of theoretical underdevelopment in the field of play are common, and yet I have found that there exists a sizable fund of fruitful theoretical material which is referred to only superficially, if at all, and remains unassimilated and unused in both theoretical and empirical publications. The neglect, or perhaps worse, the superficial misrepresentation of previous work in literature reviews[3] is exemplified by the work of Roger Caillois (1961). Taking exception to the above-quoted statement, I would like to propose that there is available— in French since 1958, and in English since 1961—in Caillois' work on play, a comprehensive theoretical system which successfully incorporates all the variety of games to which Sutton-Smith alludes.

Caillois' theory has several important qualities which have gone unnoticed, though they deserve commendation. First of all, his theory of *play* is derived from empirical documentation, both historical and observational, on play itself. In this it is unlike many, or perhaps most, contemporary theories of play which merely represent attempts to transpose play phenomena into the terms of theories derived from other realms. Examples include attempts to apply psychoanalytic, information-processing, cognitive, role-, or learning theories to play. Invariably, in such cases only those aspects of play which fit the preconceived theory are considered, and unwieldy play phenomena are ruled out on some grounds or simply ignored. Caillois' theory, however, is inductive, derived from play activity itself, and thus open to the whole range of recorded and observable phenomena.

---

[1] The research project referred to in this paper was supported in 1974-75 by a research grant from the Loyola (College) Research Committee.

[2] The two volumes referred to are Avedon and Sutton-Smith (1971) and Herron and Sutton-Smith (1971).

[3] See, for example, the reviews of Berlyne (1969), Gilmore (1971), Klinger (1969), Millar (1968) and Singer (1973).

A second value of Caillois' theory is its combination of clarity and openness. The basic terms and relationships of the theory are described with sufficient clarity and detail to serve as a basis for empirical research. The theory provides a clear framework, an orientation and a classification, while being open to appropriate modifications and extensions. It is a theory on which one can build. Its openness, too, is of the nature that it allows for the possibility of asking questions on all levels of discourse. Being problem-oriented rather than methodology-oriented, and requiring no narrow theoretical or disciplinary allegiances, it is eminently suited for the study of play, which cuts, as it does, across all the conventional disciplinary lines in human studies.

The final point I would make now in this brief introduction is to comment on the value for theory of Caillois' basic terms. These are the four basic types of play: competition, chance, vertigo, and mimicry (which can also be combined in certain specified, theoretically relevant ways). An important quality of these basic concepts, that is, his types of play, is their dual nature, in referring to, and being defined in terms of, both the formal qualities or structure of the games or play activities included in the type, and at the same time in terms of the nature of the personal experience (or basic human tendency) for which the type of play allows expression. Thus the terms are applicable equally and simultaneously to the play activity or game as a socially and historically transmitted object and as a personal experience and expression.

This dual character adds a flexibility in understanding complex phenomena which more specialized one-dimensional theories lack. Thus some of the seeming dilemmas and contradictions of play can be resolved with a theory like Caillois'. One example is the problem presented by spectator sports. Caillois points out that the form of a game can allow for more than one basic experience, for different players, or for the same player at different times. Thus such a game as hockey which is a game of *competition* for the players may be looked upon as a game of *mimicry* (simulating the experience of another, in this case, the hockey player) for the spectators. In a similar fashion, differences in personal experience with the same game may be accounted for. For example, skating may at one time provide an experience of *competition* in skill with another skater, but at another time the skater may abandon himself to the experience of *vertigo* in skating.

Over the course of several years, using student observers from a developmental psychology course, I have developed a way of studying play which depends primarily upon Caillois, is supplemented with concepts and classifications from Piaget (1962) (with reference to young children) and, to a lesser extent, from Peter and Iona Opie (1969), Sutton-Smith (see Avedon and Sutton-Smith, 1971) and Parten (1929). For the theoretical orientation of students, Caillois (1961), Piaget (1962, 1969) and Huizinga (1950) are most used. Appended to this paper is the "Master Outline for Play Observations", which, supplemented by the various outlines, charts, and forms to which it refers, has been developed for the instruction and guidance of student observers. These materials give them the theoretical orientation and skills needed to observe and record behavior in natural settings and to classify and describe conceptually the data so obtained.

This research project has allowed theoretical and methodological considerations to proceed together, with adjustments as needed from one to the other. To date, infants and children of all ages, in a variety of natural environments, have been observed at play. More recently, interviews and questionnaires have been used with older children and adults. A file of play forms and games in the Montreal area is being slowly built up, and recorded in such a way as to allow for a variety of comparisons among age, sex, language, and ethnic groups, and types of neighborhood. At the same time, the uses and limitations of a number of theories, Piaget's and Caillois' in particular, are being explored.

In the remainder of this paper I will discuss some characteristics of play which a comprehensive theory must take account of and which present unsolvable problems for certain kinds of approaches. I have found that specialized theories and methods are unable to cope with the full range of play phenomena. Some of these limited approaches nevertheless yield useful information and insights, while others prove detrimental to an understanding of play as an integral and complex phenomenon in its own right.[4]

The first characteristic which will be noted is that play is an activity which is relevant to the whole life span. In spite of its changing aspect, there is something recognizable and agreed upon as play from early childhood throughout adult life, and even in young infants and some animals. Theories with a developmental bias, which is common particularly in psychology, have viewed play primarily as a childhood phenomenon, thus obscuring its character in adult life and in culture.

Piaget, with his developmental orientation, provides an example of the limitations suffered by such an approach. Piaget can thus speak of "adult play, which ceases to be a vital function of the mind when the individual is socialized" (1962; 168). Within his theory, play is a function of immaturity; so "symbolic play is merely egocentric thought in its pure state" (1962: 186), and symbolic play is represented as declining after its peak at age four. Piaget can derive from his theory that "games with rules . . . are almost the only ones that persist at the adult stage" (1962: 146), despite common experience to the contrary.

Referring, on the other hand, to Caillois, we see that the emphasis is reversed, in that the full variety of play forms only appears with the achievement of a certain maturity. The animal, infantile and early childhood forms are not

---

[4]Berlyne's (1969) review provides a clear example of the destruction of play as an area of study due to a behavioristic, biological and reductionist orientation. Berlyne concludes his review of play with the statement, "In sum, the foregoing lends little support to the view that *play* is a useful category for psychology . . . it looks as if psychology would do well to give up the category of *play* in favor of both wider and narrower categories of behavior." (1969:843)

denied or ignored, but they are seen as simpler, basic, rudimentary forms. An analogy may be made with language, whereby we might say that while animals and young infants vocalize and communicate with sounds, they do not have a language. While the three-year old child has language, it is vastly different from that of the older child and again from the full variety of forms, functions, and meanings found in the language of a mature person in a linguistically rich culture. It might be added that the shift of emphasis from childhood to maturity does not preclude the full developmental study of childhood forms of play, or of animal forms, but rather, I believe, enhances it since the full range of possible forms can be kept in mind. Moreover, it avoids the error of denying the obvious facts of play in adult life, or of regarding these as infantile remnants.

A second characteristic to be noted is that play and games are recorded in all historical and cultural milieux, revealing similarities that extend over broad ranges of time and place, as well as variations. Bibliographies prepared by Avedon and Sutton-Smith (1971) present a rich source of information gathered by historians, anthropologists and folklorists relevant to this assertion. In their study of play the Opies (1969) very nicely, if unsystematically, include data and discussions of how childhood games persist and how they change, raising incidentally some interesting questions about the "conservatism of childhood" and thus indirectly the neglected question of continuity in human nature. Both Huizinga and Caillois question the implications of evidence of repetition and recurrence of play forms, and, contrariwise, evidence of differences in the forms, the quality and the cultural context of play in different times and places.

A comprehensive theory of play must be open to the evidence, which is already considerable, of both variation and persistence. Structuralists such as Piaget emphasize the universals in form, ignoring variations in content and meaning of play activities, and questions of the possible relationship between form and content or meaning. Piaget makes a dichotomous distinction and takes as an assumption what should be open to exploration and evidence; that is, he asserts that the structure of play is an inevitable outcome of the structure of the child mind, while content varies with the child's natural and social environment (1962: 157). It is of interest in this context that the anthropologist O. F. Raum in 1953 attributed to the structuralist influence among social anthropologists the decline of anthropologists' interest in, and contribution to, the study of play and games in the recently preceding decades (in Avedon and Sutton-Smith, 1971: 12). Another deterrent to a broad understanding of play is posed by environmentalists and behaviorists who refuse to pursue the implications for human nature of the evidence of persisting similarities in play in widely varying environments. As a result, they magnify differences in individuals and in social groups and neglect continuities.

A third characteristic of play is that it is an activity engaging the whole person. For a comprehensive theory, distinctions of the cognitive and the affective aspects of a play activity are admissible only as temporary abstractions for analytical purposes; the theory must be able to integrate both these aspects at a higher level of discourse.

Piaget's specialized cognitive emphasis leads generally to a lack of appreciation of the attractions and pleasures of play. For example, Piaget's exercise play, defined as functional repetition of an activity for its own sake, seems to overlap with activities which Caillois would describe as *vertigo* (sliding, swinging, twirling, jumping). However, Piaget's system does not include any concepts which can account for the pervasive attraction for both children and adults,for the type of play which consists of "an attempt to momentarily destroy the stability of perception and inflict a voluptuous panic upon an otherwise lucid mind" (Caillois, 1961: 36). For similar and other reasons, games of *chance* are also ignored by Piaget. J. L. Singer (1973) recognizes Piaget's limitation in respect to the affective component, and in fact takes this weakness as a point of departure in offering his approach as a correction. However his aproach is again a fragmented and partial one. The emphasis is on the affective component and on individual personality, and though the cognitive aspect is vaguely represented theoretically, it is unrelated to his research method. Singer in this work limits himself to imaginative play and, given his level of analysis, it is doubtful that he could deal with a broad range of play forms.

A fourth characteristic to be noted is that every play activity is simultaneously individual and social. Even when an individual plays alone, play is part of a social experience. For example, when a child is engaged alone in imaginative play, he pretends to be other persons and to do things about which he has heard, read or has seen, and he uses the common language in his imaginings and monologue. A single person playing a game of solitaire is using a socially transmitted play form. On the other hand, when persons play in a group, a game like football with strict rules, or a ritualized traditional singing game, there is nonetheless personal experience for the players, with individual variations in skill, improvisation, meaning, and feeling.

Play, in other words, has that two-fold tendency which Dilthey (1954) has described in discussing the relationship of individuals to philosophy, art, religion, law, and economy. In these relationships he speaks of "the two-fold tendency in the formation of psychological concepts" such that individuals are both "particulars under a universal, as cases under a rule," and "they are also joined to this rule as parts in a whole." (Dilthey, 1954: 4)

A comprehensive theory then must be able to deal with the individual, personal dimension, the social dimension, and to repeat, the historical dimension, which has been discussed earlier. The dual or "two-fold tendency" of Caillois' concepts noted earlier makes his classification and theory particularly suitable for the treatment of all three of these dimensions.

It is possible to describe any theory in terms of its relevance to one, two or all three of the essential dimensions. Some specialized theories, like Piaget's, in effect bypass all three by functioning at such a level of abstraction as to make all three facets of human experience irrelevant. Piaget (1970) acknowledges this quality of his theory himself, stating that

> Structuralism calls for a differentiation between the *individual sub-ject*, who does not enter at all, and the *epistemic subject*, that cogni-tive nucleus which is common to all subjects at the same level. (1970: 139)

Piaget's lack of interest in culture (and by implication, history) has already been noted.

The final characteristic to be noted in this paper is that play, while de-finably distinguishable, presumably, from other cultural forms, shares much with art, religion, language and other forms. In our research experience this has been reflected in the problems of observers, and respondents, who report difficulty in deciding whether or not some activities involving handcrafts, music, dramatics, art, religious festivals, family and social events, *et cetera*, should be recorded as play.

The relationship of art and play in childhood has been discussed by Sir Herbert Read (1967). Read, in stating that play is a form of art, points out that he is reversing Margaret Lowenfeld's argument that art is a form of play. He points to a possible resolution of the distinction by quoting Hautlaub's sugges-tion that "play becomes art the moment it is directed to an audience or a spec-tator" (Read, 1967: 194).

The relationship of play and religion is another fruitful area of investiga-tion. Hugo Rahner (1967) discusses the shared elements of play and religion, drawing on writings about play from antiquity and the early Church. Huizinga (1950) both begins and ends his celebrated book on play with the famous quota-tion from Plato which, he states, "identifies play and holiness" and "exalts the concept of play to the highest regions of the spirit" (Huizinga, 1950: 19). He relates play to ritual, sacrament, mystery and liturgy, finding in all of these, common elements which lie at the basis of man's potentiality for culture and civilization. Caillois, too, discusses play in relation to the sacred, and more spe-cifically, considers some types of play experience, as in mimicry and vertigo, in relation to some types of religious experience.

Consideration of the general interrelationship of play and a whole range of cultural forms is best represented in Huizinga's work. He develops in the cen-tral portion of his book (1961), a discussion of "play elements" as expressed in language, art, war, poetry, knowing, myth, and philosophy. Caillois' congeniality in general with this viewpoint may be summed up by quoting his statement: "What is expressed in play is no different from what is expressed in culture" (1961: 64).

While Cassirer (1944) does not include play among art, myth, religion and language as symbolic forms, its inclusion might be fruitfully argued. For one thing, the often noted and problematical "freedom of play" may most easily be understood in the same terms in which Cassirer presents the argument of man's uniqueness from the rest of nature:

> No longer in a merely physical universe, man lives in a symbolic universe. Language, myth, art and religion are parts of this universe. They are the varied threads which weave the symbolic net, the tangled web of human experience. (1944: 43)

Another encouragement to exploring play as a symbolic system comes from Piaget's identification of the emergence of true play, that is, symbolic play in the second year of life, with the emergence of what he calls the symbolic processes which include, in addition to symbolic play, deferred imitation, language, the mental image (representative memory), and drawing (Piaget, 1969).

It must be cautioned that the existence of shared elements in play and other cultural or symbolic forms does not by any means imply that they are the same or interchangeable. It has already been noted that Read appeals to a possible difference in aim of art and play. Huizinga's suggestion with regard to sacred rites and play is not contradictory to this view. Huizinga suggests that "if ritual proves to be formally indistinguishable from play" there is still the question of "how far such sacred attitudes as proceed within the forms of play also proceed in the attitude and mood of play". Incidentally, he expresses surprise that "anthropology and comparative religion have paid so little attention to the problem" of distinguishing play and ritual. (Huizinga, 1950: 20). In any case, the question of distinctions among the various cultural or symbolic forms is a matter for exploration and does not have to be solved in neat and simple definitions before research begins.

In conclusion, the writer has found that certain characteristics of the complex phenomenon of play require attention in research efforts and place demands on the kind of theory which can be used in directing general research on play. Caillois' work has proven most suitable for the many reasons noted in this paper. It is interesting that Caillois' translator in 1961 referred specifically in his introduction to the methodological value of Caillois' typology, but to the writer's knowledge it has not been used heretofore. It is to be hoped that Caillois' neglected work will receive more of the attention which it deserves.

Appendix

Master Outline for Play Observations

Before beginning a set of observations for a particular problem, check the relevant items among the array on the general outline below:

Background information
Observer's Name:

Date/s:
Time/s of observation:
Place of observations
    (1) Type Home/Street/school playground/city playground/Nursery school/ Classroom/Other
    (2) Specific locale: Address if possible/Name of school (if approp.) Name of city, or suburb, or section of city, etc.
Subjects: Age/s
              Sex/es
              Language used in play
              Other languages
              Ethnic group
Other (Special conditions):

Summary of Play Descriptions

Name of Game (or Roles):
Duration of Episode/or Average duration of brief episodes.
Objects Used:
Objects Constructed:
Chants, Rhymes, Songs, Dialogue:
Spontaneous Speech Activity:
Recurrence: When, How often played, seasonal?
Rules (or role prescriptions):
Rule, or role, variations, known to player:
Oher names for same game:
Other play or play-like activities liked by subject/s:

Classifications

1. Piaget's Developmental (structural, age-related) classification. See outline #1 for detailed descriptions of categories:

    a.   Exercise or practice play (three subtypes)

    b.   Symbolic play
         (1) Simple imitative and pretending play (5 subtypes)
         (2) Symbolic combinations (4 subtypes)
         (3) Ordered symbolic combinations
         (4) Symbolic constructions

    c.   Rule games
        Source: Traditional _____ Spontaneous _____
        Mode: Physical _____ Mental _____
        Degree of each factor: Chance _____ Skill _____

Competitive _____ Co-operative _____
Intermediate _____ Team _____ One per side _____
Central person _____ Individual _____

2. Caillois' Classification (based both on *structure* of the game, and on the *basic human tendency* or need satisfied in the experience of the game)—See Outline #2 for detailed descriptions of categories.

    A. Competition
    B. Chance
    C. Vertigo
    D. Mimicry
    E. Combinations of the basic four types

3. *Manifest content.* Express the theme of the play in ordinary language. This categorization is particularly applicable to Mimicry (symbolic play) and combined types which include Mimicry, such as traditional games of childhood. For examples of possible terminology refer to the Opies (1969, Table of Contents).

Summary Descriptions, Ratings and Comparisons Relevant to Play Research

1. *Degree of Mastery and Challenge.* (skill, discipline, training, meeting self-imposed challenges). See Outline #2, Item #III, and Instruction Form #1)

    A. Games rated on a continuum:
        Paidia _____ Ludus

    B. Some play-like activities, not classifiable as one of the basic (or combined) types, may be classified in terms of Paidia and Ludus.

2. *Social dimension*

    A. *Relation to other players*

        (1) For young children use *Partens* (1929) social classification, as follows:
            (a) unoccupied behavior
            (b) solitary play
            (c) onlooker behavior
            (d) parallel play
            (e) associative play
            (f) cooperative play

(2) Degree of social involvement—applicable to older children and adults. See Caillois Outline #2, P. 3.

B. *Relation to society*

    (1) *Social or collective symbolism* (language, rules, gesture, knowledge, custom, morals, songs, roles, music, rhymes, chants)

    (2) *Coherence* (order, intelligibility) *versus privatism* (idiosyncratic, Personal, unintelligible, egocentric)—especially applicable to symbolic play of young children.

    (3) *Realism versus imaginativity* (in Mimicry)

        (a) *In situations*—Rate from naturalistic imitation of immediate life situations *to* imaginative transformations with fictional characters, far-way places, other times, unusual situations.

        (b) *In use of objects*—Rate from realistic correspondence between objects used and their pretended use to imaginative substitutions and constructions.

    (4) *Source*

        (a) Whether spontaneous or traditional

        (b) Source of characters and situations:
Television _____ films _____ books and stories _____
history _____ cultural events _____ folklore _____
personal life _____ Other _____ (describe)

    (5) Variety in types of play, content, characters and sources—can be applied in comparative, longitudinal or long term studies.

3. *Relation to other cultural forms*

A. *Public versus private*: Are activities engaged in privately, as individuals, within the home, with private facilities? Or are activities engaged in publicly, as part of a community, neighborhood, ethnic, religious, group? (latter would include feasts, festivals, celebrations related to important events and anniversaries in the group's tradition, as well as neighborhood block parties, reunions of large extended families, etc.)

Note that there are areas of uncertainty due to contemporary elements of commercialism and government-owned public facilities. Some activities can be carried out among large numbers of persons and remain entirely private. The crucial factors are tradition and relationship to a stable cultural or institutional grouping.

B. Play elements experienced in *institutional forms* in society (see Caillois, 1961, p. 54, his chart is reproduced in Instruction form #2)

C. *Socially-condoned corruptions of play* (activities which have the formal appearance of play, or include play elements, but in which there are violations of essential play characteristics. (See Caillois, 1961; his summary of play chracteristics and chart including examples of corruptions of each basic type of play are presented in Instruction form #2)

D. Play activities in varying relationships with other *symbolic cultural forms*.

   E.g., Plastic Arts, Handcrafts, Music, Drama, Knowledge (scholarship, science); Religion, Poetry, Stories (fiction, fantasy, legend, etc.), and so on.

4. *Affective component*—judgments of feeling and mood accompanying play episodes. Note that these components are applicable both to *individuals* and to play *groups*. Note also that aspects of this component are implicit in other classifications and dimensions of play listed elsewhere in this outline. Some of these are noted briefly below.

   A. Affect as a part of other classifications:

      (1) Caillois' Classification: Each of the four basic types is in part clearly defined in terms of a basic affect. Different types of feeling are expressed in the different types of games, competitive, chance, vertigo and mimicry. The variety or the relative emphasis on various types displayed by either an individual or a social group may be taken as a means of describing affect.

      (2) Manifest content. If noted over a long-term of study, a preponderance of one or several basic themes may be justified as an indicator of feeling tone in individuals and social groupings.

      (3) Corruptions of Play (see item (3) on page 47). These corruptions are defined in part in terms of the un-play-like overindulgence in extremes of the basic satisfactions which the basic types of play

provide, and violation of one or more of the essential characteristics of play. Examples in one popular game, hockey, are violence incorporated as a part of the game; emphasis, even in children's leagues, on winning more than on sportsmanship, the neglect of family and other obligations by hockey TV spectator addiction (a corruption of Mimicry); and others.

Corruption of play forms in individuals and in groups can be described and theoretically related to studies of individual personality and the character of cultural groups.

B. Other dimensions of affect

(1) Additional affective components related *theoretically to play*; which may be rated by observers, e.g.:
   1 — Joyfulness (smiling, laughter)
   2 — Aggressivity (hostile actions and expressions)
   3 — Self — forgetfulness and absorption in play versus self-concern and self-consciousness
   4 — Degree of interest and concentration
   5 — Other

(2) Some affective temperamental or personality traits, not directly related to play theory, could for research purposes be included in play research.

REFERENCES

Avedon, E. M., and Brian Sutton-Smith, Editors
    1971 *The Study of Games.* New York: J. Wiley and Sons.
Berlyne, D. E.
    1969 *Laughter, Humor and Play.* In The Handbook of Social Psychology, G. Lindzey and E. Aronson, Eds. 2nd edition, 3: 795-852. Reading, Mass.: Addison-Wesley Pub.
Caillois, Roger
    1961 *Man, Play and Games.* New York: Free Press. (Translation by M. Barash of Les Jeux et Les Hommes. Paris: Gallimard, 1958).
Cassirer, Ernst
    1944 *An Essay on Man.* New Haven, Conn.: Yale University Press.
Dilthey, Wilhelm
    1954 *The Essence of Philosophy.* Chapel Hill: The University of North Carolina Press. (Translation by S. A. Emery and W. T. Emery of Das Wesen der Philosophie. 1907).
Gilmore, J. B.
    1971 *Play: A Special Behavior.* In Child's Play. R. E. Herron and Brian Sutton-

Smith, Eds., pp. 31–325. New York: Wiley and Sons (Republished from Current Research in Motivation, R. N. Haber, Editor. Holt-Rinehart, 1966).

Herron, R. E. and Britan Sutton-Smtih, Editors
  1971 *Child's Play*. New York: J. Wiley and Sons.

Huizinga, Johan
  1950 *Homo Ludens: A Study of the Play-Element in Culture*. Boston: Beacon Press. (First published, 1938).

Klinger, Eric
  1969 *Development of Imaginative Behavior: Implications of Play for a Theory of Fantasy*. Psychological Bulletin 72: 277-298.

Millar, Susanna
  1968 *The Psychology of Play*. Middlesex, Eng.: Penguin Books.

Opie, Iona and Peter Opie
  1969 *Children's Games in Street and Playground*. Oxford: Clarendon Press.

Parten, M. B.
  1929 *An Analysis of Social Participation, Leadership, and Other Factors in Pre-School Play Groups*. Unpublished Ph.D. thesis, University of Minnesota.

Piaget, Jean
  1962 *Play, Dreams and Imitation in Childhood*. New York: W. W. Norton (Translation of La Formation du Symbole Chez l'Enfant. 1945)

Piaget, Jean
  1971 *Structuralism*. Harper Torchbook Edition. New York: Harper & Row. (Translation by C. Maschler of Le Structuralisme. 1968).

Piaget, Jean   and Barbel Inhelder.
  1969 *The Psychology of the Child*. New York: Basic Books.

Rahner, Hugo
  1967 *Man at Play*. New York: Herder and Herder.

Read, Sir Herbert
  1967 *The Art of Children*. In The World of the Child, Toby Talbot, Editor, pp. 191-236. New York: Doubleday (First published in Education through Art, 1943).

Singer, J. L.
  1973 *The Child's World of Make-Believe: Experimental Studies of Imaginative Play*. New York: Academic Press.

CHAPTER II

Ethnographic Studies of Children's Games in Traditional and Acculturating Societies

Introduction

The sine qua non of anthropological research on play has been the description of children's games. By 1890, ethnographic descriptions of games from around the world were sufficiently numerous for Tylor and Culin to conduct comprehensive comparative studies. John M. Roberts and his associates have, more recently, drawn on this huge literature for comparative analyses. But the problems which have plagued the cross-cultural reports on play apply as well to games.

First and foremost has been the lack of game description in context. All too often games are described as wooden, static artifacts of culture. Field workers describe the rules and implements of play, but fail to flesh out this skeleton by further describing the players, their motives, antecedent and surrounding conditions of play, variations in rules and structure over time and intra-culturally, and the relationships between games and other playforms. Scheffler's review of game research in Mexico illustrates this problem very well. It also shows a refreshing change in more recent research where a number of investigators have placed games in their broader social and cultural contexts.

A second problem, closely related to the first, is the conflicting view of games as folklore and games as "folklife." Many field workers have arrived on the scene as a culture is undergoing acculturation and change. The tendency has been to elicit game descriptions from the memory of older informants rather than through observation. Games are thus viewed as vanishing folklore tied to the past. This approach is perfectly legitimate and the resulting descriptions are extremely useful in studies of social structure, diffusion, and integration. They are also vital to the archaeologist attempting to reconstruct the past. But games as folklore should be sharply differentiated from descriptions of games as they are currently being played. Lancy's research bridges these two approaches, describing games as remembered by informants but no longer played, as well as, contemporary games in their contemporary settings. Rosenstiel carefully points out the historical nature of her work in describing the games of Motu children as they existed *prior to 1945*. Ager, Farrer and Storey all describe the contemporary games of traditional societies, and attempt to show how these games might differ from those played prior to modern times.

Ager, Farrer, and Blanchard (in Chapter III) all found that introduced games are altered in significant ways by the host culture. Their studies and others based on acculturating societies add immeasurably to our understanding of the processes of cultural change. Lancy found that children's games were among the first institutions to be drastically changed after the Kpelle established contacts with Western society.

A third problem concerns the relationships of games to play. Games, because they are structured, tend to be both more permanent and more amenable to collection than other playforms. As Schwartzman and Barbera (Chapter I) show "play as a game or sports activity" is an often-used metaphor in the ethnographic literature. Having collected all the games for a society, the ethnographer contents himself with the notion that he has described children's play. Or, worse, ethnographers impose rules and fixed structure on play activities that lack them so that they resemble games. Ager, Lancy, and Storey all refer to non-game play activities in the societies they studied. These non-game activities may indeed be patterned and quite stable over time, but are not games by any widely used definition. Developmental psychologists, notably Piaget, can be credited with some influence here. There seems to be a shift from descriptions of children's games to descriptions of childhood, viewed as a developmental process. Variation in games played as a function of age was found for the Kpelle (Lancy) and is also a prominent finding in von Glascoe's (Chapter III) work.

A final problem concerns the extent to which investigators have been willing to assume that games are significant in training and socializing children. In its most basic form this assumption has led to a kind of "game" where the investigator collects a game then tries to match it to some feature of adult behavior which the game "teaches." Sutton-Smith deplored this tendency and warned that "Evidence for the effect of particular games on particular learning are few," (1971; 256). Lancy's research found little evidence of learning effects from games. Games as training devices deserves to be treated as an hypothesis rather than an assumption and much more stringent rules of evidence must be invoked in this area in future.

REFERENCES

Sutton-Smith, Brian. In Herron and Sutton Smith (Eds.) *Child's Play*. New York: J. Wiley, 1971.

THE ROLE OF TRADITIONAL GAMES IN THE PROCESS OF SOCIALIZATION AMONG THE MOTU OF PAPUA NEW GUINEA

Annette Rosenstiel
William Paterson College of N.J.

Games play an important role in the socialization process in all societies. They provide insight into those things which are considered important in a given society, and may either imitate or provide physical preparation for life situations (Tylor, 1871: 72-81: 1899: 305-308).

To Huizinga (1950:52), all play has meaning, and all life is, in essence, play, since it involves social interaction and role playing, which are also basic components of the voluntary activity which we call play. He goes on to say that play is a phenomenon that is integrated into culture, and that the factor of play is an integral part of the cultural process (Huizinga, *op. cit.*, 53, 172). Starting with the anthropological concept of duality in community structure, he discusses play as a preparation for role learning and social interaction in life.

Games are organized forms of play, in which the dualisms of adult life are recreated symbolically or in microcosm, and may act as preparation for full-scale adult activity.

This paper is concerned only with traditional children's play and games, and their function in the socialization process of the Motu of Papua New Guinea, in the period preceding intensive European contact. However, in order to understand fully the role of children's play and games in the traditional Motu socialization process, it is necessary to understand the basic patterns of the culture itself, and the physical environment in which it functions. I shall describe the culture as it existed prior to 1945, when extensive changes were brought about by modernization and war. Consequently, all descriptions are in the ethnographic present (Rosenstiel, 1953).

The Motu, a Papuo-Melanesian people, inhabit a group of eighteen villages, scattered over the southeastern coastal area extending thirty miles to the north and south of Port Moresby, the administrative capital of Papua. This is the so-called "dry" area of Papua, because of its comparatively low rainfall, which ranges from 40 to 100 inches a year, as compared with 450 inches a year recorded elsewhere on the island. From May to November, the region is swept by the full force of the Southeast Trade winds, and is scorched by the almost vertical rays of the sun. At that time, it is a brown, barren-looking place. But, with the coming of the Northwest monsoons, the dry, volcanic soil takes on new life: gardens bloom, and the countryside is ablaze with brilliant tropical flowers and fruits. It is during this period that the major rainfall of the year takes place.

It would have been impossible for the Motu to depend upon crops alone for subsistence. Since the soil is shallow and infertile, a particular plot can produce a crop only once in five to seven years. Also, because of the tropical climate, food spoils quickly. Therefore, garden produce cannot be stored for any length of time due to lack of facilities. The basic diet of taro root, breadfruit and pawpaw is supplemented by wallaby and wild pig, as well as by the marine life which abounds in the coastal waters, and by turtles, as well as by the greatest of sea delicacies, the dugong or sea-cow, a mammal. Hunting and fishing are carried out on a communitywide, cooperative basis, with specific rules governing the distribution of the catch.

But Motu subsistence activities revolving around the gardening and hunting cycle are secondary in importance to the vast network of social and religious ramifications attendant upon the organization of the annual *hiri*, or trading expedition to the Gulf of Papua, during which thousands of pots made by the Motu are transported hundreds of miles overseas, to be exchanged for sago and wood, which are basic to Motu survival. Sago, a starch, is needed as a food supplement, and wood is required for the building and repair of the *lakatoi*—the outrigger canoe which is the major means of water transportation. Sometimes, extremely bad weather makes it impossible for the Motu to undertake the *hiri* for several years in succession. At such times, the overconcentration of rainfall often destroys garden crops as well, leading to severe famine and hardship.

The belief in spirits permeates the Motu's entire existence. There are evil spirits that lurk abroad at night; hence the Motu are mortally afraid to go out after dark. Other evil spirtis are believed to cause sickness and death. The Motu are particularly afraid of the *vata*, invisible sorcerers who are supposed to be able to club a victim to death, restore him to life by incantation, and then let him die permanently several days later.

The Motu environment is thus harsh and difficult. For example, even the wood used for garden fences must be brought from twelve miles inland, and the traditional *rami* (grass skirts) of the women must be imported from Hula, twenty miles down the coast. Medicine and sorcery come from the Koita, another tribe in the immediate vicinity.

Confined to his own immediate area, and to his own lineage group for subsistence, the Motu would soon starve, dwindle and die out. They have learned, however, to live in a state of peaceful coexistence even with previously hostile neighbors. The Koita, traditionally an enemy of the Motu, now share their villages, and the Motu and Koita have agreed to exchange with each other the results of their hunting, fishing, gardening and pottery-making activities, in accordance with a prearranged plan.

The stability of Motu culture has been maintained through the establishment of an essential social cohesion which is reinforced in all phases of the culture, beginning with the earliest integration of the Motu child into the life of the community. The games analyzed in this paper were first described in the early nineteenth century and later were observed by the author during her field work in the area around Port Moresby during 1944 and 1945. It is not possible in a paper of this length to discuss all the games played by the Motu children, but this study will analyze various types of games and play. Our primary concern here is only with the traditional games which serve to reinforce the stability and continuum of the culture. As a basic part of the socialization process (Roberts and Sutton-Smith, 1962:167), they represent steps in the child's mastery of his physical, social, and valuational environment.

Games of physical skill provide a first introduction to achievement, as well as to many of the basic skills needed for survival. Since they involve no strategy among the Motu, they do not engender conflict (Roberts and Sutton-Smith, *op.*

cit: 180-181). They reproduce life situations in microcosm, a necessary modification, since the child is incapable of performing these acts on an adult level.
Most important from the point of view of this writer is the fact that

> . . . through these models society tries to provide a form of buffered
> learning through which the child can make enculturative step-by-step
> progress toward adult behavior.
>
> (Roberts and Sutton-Smith, *op. cit*: 182-183)

The emphasis on physical skills in the organized games of the Motu sub-
stantiates Sutton-Smith's finding that these games are the major form of play
among children in tropical regions, in subsistence-level cultures with no class
stratification and a low level of political integration as well as an undeveloped
judicial system—peaceful people, among whom the socialization of children follows a permissive pattern. (Sutton-Smith, 1972).

Of the three groups of games identified by Roberts and Sutton-Smith
(1962:166), namely, physical skill, strategy, and chance, traditional Motu games
fall into the first category, for most of the organized play of Motu children is
focused around the development of skills needed in adult life. The games presented for consideration in this paper perform the integrative functions which
Sutton-Smith has identified as basic to what he terms "relatively static societies".

From infancy, the Motu child is exposed to the continuity of social interaction. Swinging in a *kiapa* on the verandah of his home, or from the branch of a
tree while his parents work in the garden, or suspended on his mother's back by
a tump line, or riding pick-a-back on his father's shoulders, the child is free to
watch the activities of his parents, his siblings and others, and gradually to internalize and to imitate the behavior he observes. As they grow older, girls learn
gardening, pottery making and household skills from their mothers, and boys
learn hunting and fishing skills from their mother's brother.

Other than the basic division of labor, there is no social distinction between the sexes. Since there are no secret societies, there is no need to entirely
exclude women or girls from particular social activities, nor men from others.
There is no preference for children on the basis of sex: girls and boys are equally
desired. There is an equality in group play, also, mirroring the adult attitudes.
Girls and boys play together in some group games.

Because the sea plays a paramount role in Motu life, Motu children learn
to swim even before they learn to walk. Children also learn to build and sail
small *lakatoi*, and hold miniature races while the men are away on the *hiri*, thus
developing assurance in the water, and competence in handling the craft which
are to be so important to them in adult life.

There are group water games, such as *paroparo* (little fish), a girls' game in
which two circles are formed in the water, one inside the other. The object of
the game is for the inner group to try to penetrate the outer circle successfully

by swimming under water. The goal of the outer circle is to prevent this, while beating the water and singing, and by using body blocking tactics to prevent them from achieving their goal. However, should the inner circle succeed in penetrating the outer circle, the inner group then becomes the outer group, and the outer group becomes the inner group. The two groups then reverse their roles and the game begins again.

The games are non-competitive. In each case, the goal is to improve the skill of the individual. No prizes are awarded. There is no restriction on the number of times a child can try. Since the game is a microcosm of adult society, the inept child may find that he loses status among his peers as a result of repeated failures, or extreme clumsiness. In these group games, there are no real victors. If one group achieves its goal, it merely changes places with the other group and tries to keep them from achieving that goal in their turn, as we can see from the earlier example.

The Motu child requires a well-developed sense of balance, for his daily life involves going up and down ladders to his home, which may be as high as ten feet from the ground, or in the sea, and maintaining a precarious balance on the wide-open deck of a wind-swept, wave-tossed *lakatoi*. In the game of *manu-manu* (little bird), one girl, holding a stick as a balancing rod, stands on a long wooden plank which is raised off the ground by her peers, who carry the plank to and fro while she sings and dances on it. In *evanena* (looking down the pole), two rows of boys face each other and make a platform of arms similar to a "fireman's carry." A small boy stands on the arms of the last two boys, and walks forward on the arms of the other boys. As he progresses, the last two boys rush forward to the front of the line, so that it continues to extend even as the boy walks forward, and the game continues until the walker tumbles off. Both of these games develop balance and sure-footedness, and dispel fear of heights.

To develop keen eyesight and coordination of eye and muscle, even before they can handle a full-sized spear, boys from the age of 5 to 8 learn to "throw the kurukuru." *Kurukuru*, a tall, spiny grass used for thatching, often grows to a height of almost six feet, on abandoned garden plots. To play this game, a boy pulls down the leafy part of the grass to expose the spiny shaft, which is then flexed and aimed. Using each other as targets, the children develop great dexterity, hitting each other at a distance of as much as forty feet. Although this is basically a boys' game, small girls often play it also, imitating the actions of the boys. Later, when they become proficient, the boys play *kabele* (hit it), a game in which one boys throws a coconut, and another tries to spear it in flight.

In *barikau* (cat's cradle or string figures), we find an excellent preparation for the adult occupation of net making, which requires an ability to twist and weave cord. Different names are given to the different string configurations, and in learning to make and identify the string figures in *barikau*, children become consciously aware of some of the concepts and values of the culture. The vocabulary of *barikau* is illustrative of this. Each string figure is named for some significant cultural item, and is consequently related to the cultural concept governing its use. Examples of this include the figures called *lahia* (fire), *bava* (crab), *vaga* (sorcerer), *doa* (boar's tusk), *komada* (surf), *asi-asi* (double canoe), and *manu* (bird).

Many games are in direct imitation of the activities of adult life: birth, feeding, widowhood, pot and basket making, fishing, and sailing. At eight to twelve years of age, boys are already adept at handling the fish spear, using a toy spear about two-thirds the size of the adult spear. Thus, when they are ready to accompany their fathers on fishing and hunting expeditions, the small boys have already acquired those characteristics of fearlessness, poise, and visual and muscular coordination which will be necessary during their entire adult life. They know the social and ceremonial significance of the objects which they have seen and played with since early childhood.

Throughout his formative years, the Motu child's energies are focused through play activities upon accepted customs and values, thereby assuring the cultural continuity of the society. The first and most spontaneous reaction of the child to its varied social heritage, is that of imitation, and so in the beginning, it is prepared through play activities for the life it will lead in adulthood. As the child grows older, play and work alternate, and each eventually assumes its relative position in daily adult life. It is obvious, therefore, that as far as the Motu child is concerned,

> . . . play is the most adequate introduction to life, and imitation the indispensable medium by which . . . culture is made continuous, preserved, and may become the basis of further accumulation and increase. (Miller, 1928:151)

The games described above are indicative of the stages of muscular and social maturation through which Motu children pass, and all of them are functional, that is, they serve a definite "cultural purpose" (Sutton-Smith, 1974:11). Sutton-Smith believes, however, that the significance of games in general often goes beyond their function as a tool for socialization, and that they may even serve as a challenge to the existing social system. The games described in this paper are not of the type which work toward the inversion of existing cultural norms; rather, they act to reinforce the *status quo*. Games that have been introduced through culture contact more nearly reflect the conditions of conflict and tension which have been engendered as a result of alien cultural influences. However, in this paper I have restricted myself to a description of the traditional games which work toward maintaining the equilibrium of the culture. Even here, it is certainly possible to recognize some role inversions which occur as a part of a number of these games. In the underwater swimming game, for example, in which there is an automatic reversal of role, as the inner circle breaks through the outer circle, and in *manumanu* and *evanena*, as the child falls from the raised playform or the arms of his co-players, only to be replaced by another child.

Games and play are therefore an important aspect of the Motu socialization process. They help to form the basic features of personality (Linton, 1945: 17, 33), and to develop physical and mental attitudes and capabilities, as well as the values which help the Motu cope with the variety of environmental situations in which he finds himself and they serve as guide for action in adult life.

REFERENCES

Huizinga, Johan, *Homo Ludens*. Boston: The Beacon Press, 1950. (Orig. 1938).

Linton, Ralph, *The Cultural Background of Personality*. New York: Appleton-Century-Crofts, 1945.

Miller, Nathan, *The Child in Primitive Society*. New York: Appleton, 1928.

Roberts, J. M. and Brian Sutton-Smith, "Child Training and Game Involvement," *Ethnology* 1, 1962: 166-185.

Rosenstiel, Annette, *The Motu of Papua New Guinea. A Study of Successful Acculturation*. Ann Arbor, Michigan, University Microfilm. (Ph.D. Dissertation, Columbia University), 1953.

Sutton-Smith, Brian, *The Folk Games of Children*. Austin: University of Texas, 1972.

Sutton-Smith, Brian, "Towards an Anthropology of Play," *TAASP Newsletter*, 1(2), Fall, 1974: 8-15.

Tylor, Edward B., *Primitive Culture: Researches into the Development of Mythology, Philosophy, Religion, Language, Art and Custom*. London: J. Murray, 1871.

Tylor, Edward B., *Anthropology: An Introduction to the Study of Man and Civilization*. New York: D. Appleton, 1889 (orig. 1881).

THE STUDY OF TRADITIONAL GAMES IN MEXICO:
BIBLIOGRAPHICAL ANALYSIS AND CURRENT RESEARCH

Lilian Scheffler
Direccion General de Arte Popular.
Ministry of Education. Mexico.

STUDIES OF GAMES IN MEXICO   .

In our country, studies concerning traditional games and play have been few compared to the studies of other areas of Folklore. Since the end of the last century until today we have registered fifty seven studies including books, theses, and articles (besides some mention in ethnographic monographs of more or less importance that will not be considered here).

Of the fifty-seven studies mentioned above, seventeen are very small articles of merely descriptive character or in which games are considered just as a minimal part of the development of children's life. The other forty may be divided into four groups to make our analysis easier, according to the subject they treat: 1) children's games, 2) games of physical skill, 3) games of chance, and 4) miscellaneous.

1) *Children's games*

In the first place we have the studies about games made by the pioneers in this field. Frederick Starr, at the end of the last century in his *Catalogue of a collection of objects illustrating the Folklore of Mexico* (1899) makes a compilation of different aspects of folklore, including a certain number of children's games, and some adult amusements that he collected in our country.

Second, I will mention Ruben M. Campos' book *El Folklore Literario de Mexico* (1929) in which he includes a section dedicated to the games that the mothers played to amuse little children during the twenties. Zingg in his article "Juegos y juguetes de los ninos tarahumaras" (1932), comments on the way in which games reflect the norms of the culture of a group. Garcia has two articles: "Juegos Infantiles" (1929) and "Juegos de Ninos" (1932) in both of them he gives examples of games played by children of different ages.

I will next consider the studies with historical and comparative approaches. First the studies made by Vicente T. Mendoza: "Origen de los juegos mexicanos" (1939), "Origen de tres juegos mexicanos" (1943a) and "Un juego espanol del siglo XVI entre los otomies" (1943b); in these three articles the author is concerned basically with the Spanish origin of some children's games played in Mexico and the transformation they have suffered with the passing of time.

It is important to mention Mendoza's book: *Lirica Infantil Mexicana* (1951) in which he gives different examples of children's games pointing out the place in the country where they are played. He also makes a classification of the games according to their complexity.

Another important study is the book *Links into Past* (1953) of Cecilia Gil de Partearroyo, in which she analysizes historically and comparatively different versions of singing games that are played by Spanish speaking children of Mexico and part of the southwest of the United States. The games are divided in ten categories according to the theme they treat. She is also concerned with the origin of the games, and gives parallel versions of the same games in other parts of the world, pointing out their persistence and annotating the importance of Spanish, African and Anglo-Saxon elements that came together with the traditions of the Indian population.

A third book of interest in this field is Francisco Moncada's: *Asi juegan los ninos* (1962), which is a collection of games and includes the words, music, and a description of each one of the games. He also gives the characteristics of the informants who gave him the data and organizes the games according to complexity.

We next have studies focused according to psychological theory. For example, the MA thesis of Mariana Morillo: *Estudio psicologico comparado sobre los intereses recreativos de un grupo de ninos y un grupo de ninas* (1963) in which she studied the ludic interests of girls and boys from 11 to 13 years old using questionnaires and analysing the way in which play helps the child to identify himself with the role of the adult. She emphasizes the differences that exist in the area of game preference between the sexes.

Michael Maccoby in "El juego como expresion caracterologica y cultural" (1966a) and "La guerra de los sexos en una comunidad campesina" (1966b) with the data that he obtained in a mestizo town in the state of Morelos, proposes that in analysing children's—and also adult—games, consideration be given to the unconscious attitudes about authority, the differences between the sexes and the social character of the community.

Of recent publication we have the studies made by Margit Frank Alatorre and Antonio Alatorre in the magazine *Artes de Mexico* (1972). She gives some examples of lyrical poetry used by children, and analysizes them emphasizing their non-logical character and the form in which they play with the absurd. She is also concerned with the origins of the games and their persistence through time, making comparisons with examples from different epochs in Spain and America. Antonio Alatorre, on the other hand, according to memories of his childhood makes a description of different aspects of children's lore, such as songs, games, religious chants and especially singing games.

2) *Games of Physical Skill*

We will consider here all those studies that treat with games that imply any form of motor activity, and in which this activity is decisive for the objectives of the game itself.

a) *Ball Games.* In pre-Hispanic times ball games were intimately related to religious aspects of the culture; they were truly ritual games, through which the group thought that the natural forces of the world continued their course. Not celebrating these games could produce the extinction of the whole of humanity and also through these games the group obtained magical benefits for all the members of the community (Lopez Austin: 1967).

Some of the ball games that exist today in Mexico are derived from those of pre-Hispanic times, even though they have lost their ritual meaning. For example the "hulama" and the "pelota mixteca." About the first one we have Alfredo Ibarra's article "Juegos y deportes en Mexico" (1942) in which he mentions the antecedents of this game, with descriptions of the way the "hulama" was played in the State of Sinaloa during the forties.

Isabel Kelly in "Notes on a west coast survival of the ancient mexican ball-game" (1943) studies the "hulama" that is played in Nayarit, Sinaloa and other places of the occident of Mexico. She deals with the form in which the balls are made, the indumentary of the players and the characteristics of the game itself. Also Armando Franco in his article: "La pelota mexicana" (1964) describes the game of the "hulama" and one called "la pelota de brazo", the difference consists only in the size of the ball used. Both games were played until the sixties in some places of the State of Culiacan.

Arturo Oliveros (1972) studied the "hulama" that is played in Mazatlan and Sinaloa. He proposes, following Huizinga, that through play man "re-creates" himself and even though the original sense of the game has been lost, it really persists as the spiritual need of a group which wants to mtaintain a link with its past.

Referring to other types of ball games, Beals & Carrasco in "Games of the Mountain Tarascans" (1944), describe three ball and stick games similar to hockey that were played in two towns of the State of Michoacan among the Tarascans, and they point out the similarity of these games with other ones of the same type in North and South America. Jose Corona Nunez (1942) describes a ball game, also of the Tarascan group, that was played with a ball of fire and a stick during 1916 and 1920.

We also have another descriptive article by Ursulino Rueda Saynez (1942) in which he speaks about two ball games that were played in Juchitan, State of Oaxaca. To finish with the studies that refer to ball games I will mention William Swezey's article "La pelota Mixteca" (1972) in which he refers to the similarity of this game to the pre-Hispanic ball games and gives a detailed description of the rules of the game, the players, the type of glove they use, based on observations made by himself in the states of Oaxaca and Puebla.

b) *Races*. We will consider here the studies that refer to the races that are run among the Tarahumara and Tepehuanes groups. Carolos Basauri in "La resistencia de los Tarahumaras" (1926) describes this game which he considers the more typical sport of the Tarahumaras. He notes the rules of the game, the active participation of spectators and the bets that are made in favor of one or another of the players. Francisco Plancarte in his article "Ariweta" (1958) describes these same races, the ones in which men participate and others in which women are the runners and remarks on the economic importance of the races and the magical protection that is given to the players.

More recently, two authors have focused on the races: John G. Kennedy (1969) and Campell W. Pennington (1970). The first one, besides giving the description of the game, points out the role that witchcraft and fraud have in this game. He analyzes the race as an important economical activity, as a force for social cohesion and as a channel through which the group sets free its agressive impulses. The second author demonstrates that the race was introduced in the Tarahumara group at the end of the XVII or beginning of the XVIII century, replacing another rubber ball game that the Jesuits described as the most important of that group during the time of the conquest. He also points out parallels with races in other parts of the world.

3) *Games of Chance*

This type of game as Caillois (1958) says, reveals the favor of the destiny, the player is a passive one, he does not use his natural dispositions, the resources of his intelligence or his skill, he just waits the verdict of luck.

a) *Lottery*. In the first place Alfonso de Medina (1943) describes the environment of the places in which the lottery was played in Mexico City during the thirties. Jose G. Montes de Oca (1932) also speaks about this game, of the places where it was played, about the people who went there, and also gives some poetical examples of it.

Besides refering to the game and the environment that surrounds it Jose J. Nunez y Dominguez (1932) is concerned with the European origin of the lottery, the time in which it was established in Mexico and the importance that it had until the thirties. An anonymous author, probably a newspaperman, in "De las polakas pueblerinas o las loterias de cartones" (1934) speaks about the gradual disappearance of this game in Mexico City and its importance in the fairs of the small towns.

Another game very similar to the lottery is called "Coton Pinto" and is still played in the State of Oaxaca, it was described by Gustavo Varela Rojas (1942), giving also twenty poetical examples that were used in the game.

b) *Patolli*. From the studies that treat this game of pre-Hispanic origin, (very similar to the Spaniard "Quince" that is played on a board with dice), we have an article written by Alfonso Caso (1925a, 1925b), in which he describes the *patolli* game, its representations and rules, as this game was played during the twenties in two towns, one of Totonaco speaking people, and the other of Nahuatl speaking people of the Northern highlands of the State of Puebla.

The *patolli* game was also observed in the Tarascans of Michoacan by Beals & Carrasco, who describe it together with other games of this area in their article "Games of the mountain Tarascans" (1944).

c) *Others*. Vicente T. Mendoza has also a contribution on games of chance, an article titled "El juego de naipes en el Folklore de Mexico" (1948) in which he points out the Spanish origin of the cards and gives a list of verbal expressions related to this type of game.

We will also mention a Master's thesis of Susanna Pellon: *El juego de azar en Mexico* (ensayo de interpretacion psico-social) (1954) in which she tries to do a psychological analysis of the game of chance in Mexico since the pre-Hispanic time until the present, showing a relationship between the psychodynamics of the game and the so-called "Mexican character."

4) *Miscellaneous*

We include here Evangelina Gonzalez' article (1950) about different aspects of folklore in a town in the State of Tlaxcala, in which she includes seven versions of games that are practiced especially during the wakes of dead children.

Finally we will mention Munro S. Edmonson's article "Play, Gossip and Humor" (1967) that is of a general character and in which he analyzes historically and comparatively the ludic activities of the Indian groups of Middle America, such as verbal games, sports, ball games, games of chance and the toys that are used by the children, giving examples from pre-Hispanic and native cultures of the area.

BALANCE OF THE STUDIES OF GAMES IN MEXICO

Through the previous analysis we can appreciate that 55% of the studies that have been made in Mexico about games are of the descriptive type or mere collections of play activities.

22.5% of the analyses that have been made are of the historical or comparative type; 10% are represented by studies in which psychological theory have been used, and the remaining 10.5% is divided between those who have made the intent to relate the games to other aspects of culture and the two classifications that have been done for children's games according to their complexity.

In reference to the Indian groups the Tarascans and the Tarahumaras are the ones who have the largest number of studies, and the Zapotec, Nahua, Otomi, and Totonaco have only one study for each one of them.

CURRENT RESEARCH

Since the creation of the Direccion General de Arte Popular in the middle of 1971, under the Ministry of Education, studies about games have been increased through the work of one of its Departments, the Department of Investigation of Popular Traditions that is directed by the Anthropologist Gabriel Moedano. This Department conducts research also on folk narratives, dance, music, drama, folk medicine and arts and crafts.

The Department has fifteen researchers, all of them anthropologists, except for three of them who are still studying Anthropology.

We began to work on a Pilot Project on the subjects cited above, in the State of Tlaxcala, located in the central part of Mexico. The research was done mainly in the area of the mountain La Malinche which still has a population who speak the Nahuatl language. This project took place from 1972 to 1974 and included bibliographical research and field work in several towns of the area.

Concerning our subject of traditional games we have had the following results: several articles concerning children's games; others about wake games that are especially played when little children die; and a reconstruction of games that were played in older times (obtaining the data from old people) to compare with the ones that children play today.

We also issued a monograph titled *Traditional Games from the State of Tlaxcala* in which an analysis is made of children's games, wake games, adult games and amusements and the relation of games to dance; because we have found that the people in the area call "games" to the dances that are presented during the different "fiestas" that are celebrated during the year.

All the articles written about games will be included in a Bulletin that is going to be published two or three times a year beginning this year, and the monographs are going to be published separately.

This year we have initiated two more projects, one in the State of Guanajuato and the other in the Mixtecan coast area of the State of Oaxaca; in both projects we will conduct similar research.

Because these projects are just beginning we have only made some surveys in which we have collected general data about the subjects we are interested in. Later, based on these data, we will select the communities that will be studied in an intensive form. Afterwards we will prepare articles that will be published in the Bulletin mentioned above and also monographs about games that we think will be ready for the following year.

REFERENCES

Alatorre, Antonio.
  1973 "De Folklore Infantil." *Artes de Mexico*. Ano XX. No. 162. p. 35-46.
Basauri, Carlos.
  1926 "La Resistencia de los Tarahumaras." *Mexican Folkways*. II. No. 4, p. 40-47.
Beals, Ralph & Carrasco, Pedro.
  1944 "Games of the Mountain Tarascans." *American Anthropologist*. Oct.-Dec. Vol. 46. No. 4, p. 516-522.
Caillois, Roger.
  1958 *Teoria de los Juegos*. Barcelona. Editorial Seix Barral, S.A.
Campos, Ruben M.
  1929 *El Folklore Literario de Mexico*. Mexico. Talleres Graficos de la Nacion.
Caso, Alfonso.
  1925a "Un antiguo juego Mexicano: El Patolli." *Revista de Revistas*. Mexico. Marzo 8. No. 774, p. 40-41.
  1925b "Un antiguo juego Mexicano: El Patolli." *El Mexico Antiguo*. Marzo. II. No. 9. p. 203-211.
Corona Nunez, Jose.
  1942 "El juego de pelota entre los Tarascos." *El Nacional*. Mexico. 6 de Septiembre, p. 3, 6.
Edmonson, Munro S.
  1967 "Play, Gossip and Humor." in *Handbook of Middle American Indians*. Vol. 6: Social Anthropology. University of Texas Press. p. 191-206.
Franco R., Armando.
  1964 "La Pelota Mexicana." *Rumbos*. Suplemento cultural de *El Diario de Culiacan*. Sinaloa, Mexico, 27 de diciembre. Ano I, No. 12, p. 3 (an).
Frank Alatorre, Margit.
  1973 "El Folklore Poetico de los Ninos Mexicanos." *Artes de Mexico*. Mexico. Ano XX. No. 162, p. 5-30.
Gil de Partearroyo, Cecilia.
  1953 *Links into Past,* a folkloric study of Mexican children relative to their singing games. Mexico, Editorial JUS.
Gonzalez, Evangelina.
  1950 "Recoleccion folklorica en San Juan Totolac, Tlaxcala." *Anuario de la Sociedad Folklorica de Mexico*. Mexico. VI. p. 539-553.

Ibarra, Alfredo.
    1942 "Juegos y Deportes en Mexico." *Anuario de la Sociedad Folklorica de Mexico.*
        Mexico. I. p. 41-49.
Islas Garcia, Luis.
    1929 "Juegos Infantiles." *Mexican Folkways.* Mexico. V. p. 78-85.
    1932 "Juegos de Ninos." *Mexican Folkways.* Mexico. p. 63-74.
Kelly, Isabel.
    1943 "Notes on a west coast survival of the ancient Mexican ball-game." *Notes on
        Middle American Archaeology and Ethnology.* Carnegie Institution of Wash-
        ington. Nov. 10. No. 26.
Kennedy, John G.
    1969 "La carrera de bola de los tarahumaras y su significacion" – *America Indigena.*
        Mexico. Enero. Vol. XXIX. No. 1, p. 17-42.
Lopez Austin, Alfredo.
    1967 *Juegos Rituales Aztecas.* Mexico. Universidad Nacional Autonoma de Mexico.
        Instituto de Investigaciones Historicas. (Serie Documental, No. 5).
Maccoby, Michael.
    1966a "El juego como expresion caracterologica y cultural." *Revista de Psicoanalisis,
        Psiquiatria y Psicologia.* Mexico. Fondo de Cultura Economica. Mayo-Agosto.
        No. 3, p. 7-24.
    1966b "La Guerra de los sexos en una comunidad campesina." *Revista de Psicoanali-
        sis, Psiquiatria y Psicologia.* Mexico. Fondo de Cultura Economica. Septiem-
        bre-Diciembre. p. 54-76.
Medina, Alfonso de.
    1934 "Aspectos de la metropoli de hoy: Las tablitas, algo 'Made in Mexico'." *El
        Ilustrado.* Mexico. 26 de Abril. Ano XVII. No. 888, p. 16-17.
Mendoza, Vicente T.
    1939 "Origen de dos juegos mexicanos." *El Nacional.* Suplemento Dominical. Mexi-
        co. 10 de Septiembre. p. 11.
    1943a "Origen de tres juegos mexicanos." *Anuario de la Sociedad Folklorica de
        Mexico* (1941). Mexico. II. p. 77-89.
    1943b "Un juego espanol del siglo XVI entre los otomies." *Anales del Instituto de
        Investigaciones Estaticas.* Mexico. Universidad Nacional Autonoma de Mexico.
        Vol. III. No. 10, p. 59-74.
    1948 "El juego de naipes en el folklore de Mexico." *Almanaque de Prevision y Se-
        guridad.* Monterrey, N. L., Mexico, p. 133-136, 138, 140, 144.
    1951 *Lirica Infantil de Mexico.* Mexico. El Colegio de Mexico.
Moncada Garcia, Francisco.
    1962 *Asi juegan los ninos,* recopilacion de juegos Infantiles. Mexico. Editorial
        Avante.
Montes de Oca, Jose G.
    1932 "Las Loterias." *El Ilustrado.* Mexico. 28 de Septiembre. Ano XV. No. 802,
        p. 28-29.
Morillo Safa Preciado, Mariana.
    1964 *Estudio psicologico comparado sobre los intereses recreativos de un grupo de
        ninos y un grupo de ninas.* Tesis. Mexico. Colegio de Psicologia. Universidad
        Iberoamericana.
Nunez y Dominguez, Jose de J.
    1932 "Las loterias de figuras en Mexico." *Mexican Folkways.* Mexico. VIII, p. 87-
        106.
Observador.
    1934 "De las polakas pueblerinas o las loterias de cartones." *El Ilustrado.* Mexico.
        Ano XVIII. No. 901. p. 16-17.

Oliveros, Arturo.
    1972 "Sobrevivencias del juego de pelota prehispanico." *Religion en Mesoamerica.*
        XII Mesa Redonda de Antropologia. p. 463-469.
Pellon, Riveroll, Susanna.
    1954 *El juego de Azar en Mexico* (ensayo de interpretacion psicosocial). Tesis.
        Mexico. Facultad de Filosofia y Letras. Universidad Nacional Autonoma de
        Mexico.
Pennington, Campell W.
    1970 "La Carrera de bola entre los Tarahumaras: Un problema de difusion." *America Indigena.* Mexico. Enero. Vol. XXX. No. 1. p. 15-40.
Plancarte, Francisco.
    1958 "Ariweta." *Boletin Indigenista.* Boletin del Instituto Nacional Indigenista,
        Mexico. Junio No. 60, p. 2-4.
Rueda Saynez, Ursulino.
    1942 "El Tapu y el Guipi." *Itsmo.* Mexico. 31 de Enero. Ano II. Tomo II. p. 4-6.
Starr, Frederick.
    1899 *Catalogue of a Collection of objects illustrating the Folklore of Mexico.* London. (Publications of the Folklore Society, Vol. XLIII).
Swezey, William R.
    1972 "La Pelota Mixteca." *Religion en Mesoamerica.* XII Mesa Redonda. Mexico,
        Sociedad Mexicana de Antropologia. p. 471-477.
Varela Rojas, Gustavo.
    1942 "Costumbres Oaxaquenas: El Coton Pinto." *Anuario de la Sociedad Folklorica de Mexico.* Mexico. III. p. 123-135.
Zingg, Robert M.
    1932 "Juegos y juguetes de los ninos tarahumaras." *Mexican Folkways.* Mexico.
        VII, p. 107-110.

FIELD STUDY: CHILDREN'S PLAY IN BALI

Kim Susan Storey
Hampshire College

My study of children's play took place in a small village called Piliatan in
Bali, Indonesia. The Balinese, both adults and children, are deeply involved in
religious ceremonies which include magnificent displays of dancing, a highly developed *Gamelan*—a percussion orchestra, and many theatrical performances.
The children are part of the work activities, participating in irrigated rice agriculture, the carving of wood for sale, dances for tourists, and household chores.
When children are involved in a working world, what forms does their play take?
Does their play differ from the leisure activities of adults? Would play even be
necessary in such a society as Bali? Questions of this kind formed the background for three months of research on children's play in Bali.

During my first two weeks in Piliatan I saw children engaged in a working world; except for a few odd games, their leisure activities consisted of sitting, staring aimlessly into space, eating, and talking quietly. Rather than playing at adult chores, they actually swept, raked, shoveled, planted, and carried rice and water on their heads. Children not yet five years old had the responsibility of caring for babies. It was only after two weeks passed that I observed children at play.

Later it became apparent that during those first two weeks of little play activity, there had been a hiatus in festivals and performances. Then occurred a temple festival, called an *odalan*, in celebration of a temple's anniversary of consecration. The children's play activity increased during this festival, and during all subsequent festivals. Festivity in the village seemed to give sanction for children to engage in their own play forms.

I found it useful to divide Balinese children's play into three main categories:

I. *Games*, which have predetermined rules and involve competition
II. *Imitation Play*, which involves close replication of adults and their activities.
III. *Pastimes*, which are forms of play that are relatively unstructured and lack competitive elements.

I. Games

Games were played before school, during recess, and at other moments of the day when the children had free time. There seemed to be game seasons, during which the children's preference would turn toward one or two games. These games would continue anywhere from a few days to a few weeks, until some others took their place. Thus there was not much diversity of games in the play areas at any one time, despite the fact that the children had a large repertoire.

I recorded twenty-eight games, many of which are similar to those played by our children. Twenty-four of the games emphasized physical skill, such as one in which players try to hit one stone with another. Many of the physical skill games involved chasing and tagging. The other four games emphasized strategy, such as one in which a player attempts to glean the location of a hidden stone from the facial expressions of his opponents.

Within the games recorded, three types of relationships among players became apparent:

1. *It Figure versus the rest of the group*, as in Keep Away or Monkey in the middle
2. *Each Player For Himself*, as in Hopscotch
3. *Team versus Team*, as in Softball

Of the twenty-eight games, twelve had an "It Figure", eleven had "Each Player For Himself", and five had "Teams". Thus, games with an "It Figure" and those with "Each Player For Himself" outnumbered "Team" games twenty-three to five.

I think the reason for these preferences is that within the game structure the children are able to assume superior or inferior positions depending on the outcome, and, as opposed to the case with the "Team" game, this position does not have to be shared with other players. This is reflective of the Balinese caste system in which social status is highly stratified, with corresponding modes of conduct. Within the game structure the children learn that different positions in the game require different ways of behaving. Children in Bali are casteless until puberty, and the status exploration in their games prepares them for positions they are to assume in the adult social order. In addition, children assume positions individually, and in "It Figure" games this position is in direct contrast to that of the other players. This situation is uncommon in adult life, in which outcomes are usually shared with an extended family, and group loyalty is strictly regulated. Thus these games may also function as a device for change in the society. Within the play structure children are able to explore various possibilities which otherwise might not have been explored within a rigid society.

Four of the twenty-eight games recorded were based on a mythical story theme, such as one which involves the mythical Bird Ga-Ga. In this game one child, the Bird Ga-Ga, hides his head, while one of the players takes the Bird's egg and hides it. When the Bird discovers that the egg is missing, he runs in search of it. The game is also played with Bird Ga-Ga tied by coconut fibers to a tree. The Bird tries to tag one of the players as they run and sing around him.

Though the children were able to perform mythical story games when I requested, they did not by preference play them. This movement away from mythical story games is a result of acculturation. The Balinese, affected by a great influx of tourists, are becoming more competitive in their desire for money and material possessions. The frequency of harvests has increased, leaving less time for the post-harvest festivities, during which the children formerly played mythical story games. In addition, the children now attend school, which further reduces available play time. As a result of the increasing competitiveness of Balinese society, the children prefer more competitive games, rather than those based on mythical stories.

II. Imitation Play

The children's imitation play reflected adult activities, and increased in frequency during times of festivity. The activities imitated were temple festivals and performances, and those work activities in which the children did not have a major role.

One temple festival event that was imitated was a cockfight. This was for men only, and children were not really allowed into the spectator circle. But on the sides of the cockfighting ring a group of children peeked. They then imitated the scene inside the ring. They flapped their arms like wings, and hit each other in groups of two or three, running back and forth as the cocks did. Then two boys climbed on top of another, perhaps in an attempt to equalize strength. But that did not work too well, and the game ended as all collapsed. This imitation game was repeated for the next few days in the school yard.

Another temple festival event imitated was a cremation. This was a huge joyful sendoff of the soul to higher and better worlds, and with the potential for reincarnation. The cremations were costly, and their preparation demanded much time and effort in making elaborate decorations. During the ceremony the children were let out of school. The body was placed in an animal-shaped coffin, and put into a huge colorful tower, which was twirled around and around to confuse the bad spirits, and then set on fire to burn in magnificent splendor as everyone shouted with pleasure.

Much of the children's time was spent watching the preparations and attending the cremations, rather than imitating these activities. However, I did observe two occasions when cremations were imitated. On one occasion a baby was placed on a bicycle representing the cremation tower, and the bicycle was twirled around and around. The children shouted with pleasure as if they were sending off a soul to the other worlds. On a second occasion, children paraded around carrying a box in imitation of a coffin. One child carried a live bird, something often done at cremations, and another banged a pan, in imitation of Gamelan music.

An important location for the children's imitation games was the courtyard adjoining the housing compound, where the *Ketjak* Dance (Monkey Dance, for which the village is famous, took place. These dances were performed on the average of one morning every one or two weeks. Decorations for the dance were elaborate, with many bamboo and banana leaf decorations hung all over the courtyard. After the performance, the courtyard full of decorations became the playground for the children. Two play scenes I observed are as follows:

1. A group of about six boys, seven and eight years in age, gather in the courtyard. Some of the decorations are made into a ring so as to form a headdress. Two boys put the headdress on, face each other, and bow as if two kings greeting one another. They have pretend fights imitating the monkey fight of the Ketjak Dance. A bamboo pole is used as a charging pole as three boys charge in fun at another boy, all collapsing in laughter. The play scene concludes in much roughhousing, shouting, and laughter.

2. A group of boys, seven and eight years in age, run around the play area, beating each other over the heads with bushes. This is in

imitation of the fight scene in the Ketjak Dance. The boys then proceed to sprinkle red confetti—also part of the dance—over all the children playing hopscotch. There is much shouting and laughter.

In addition, while the actual Ketjak Dance was performed, children stood in the back, imitating the movements of the dancers, and quietly following along with the chanting.

In addition to cockfights, cremations, and Ketjak Dances, Balinese festivals include numerous performances of dance, music, drama, and shadow puppet shows. Many of the performances that I observed occurred at night. All children, whether they walked or were carried, attended the performances along with the adults. The performances took place in an open-air pavilion, which was surrounded by tropical plants, enveloped in darkness, and dimly lit by oil lamps. The villagers crowded in, and there was always a group behind stage getting another point of view. They socialized among themselves before a performance began. During a performance attention wandered. Some of the children fell asleep in their parent's, grandparent's, or child-caretaker's arms, lulled to sleep by the Gamelan music. Both children and adults would sit through five or more hours of performance. They nodded to the music, watched some parts and missed others, sometimes slept and sometimes socialized.

It became apparent that both Balinese children and adults had seen all the performances many times, so missing some parts was not important, because the dance was understood as a whole. The Balinese viewer, adult or child, could anticipate every movement and every sound.

The children imitated the performances they observed:

1. After a *Barong* Dance performance, a boy about nine years old performed for his two friends a section of the dance, imitating the high leg lifting movements characteristic of the dance.

2. After a *Wayang Kulit* (Shadow Puppet) performance, a boy used his fingers as puppets, making them talk and fight. His speech was characteristic of that used for a performance.

3. After the *Gamelan* (Percussion Orchestra) accompanied a dance performance, a group of children banged cans and hummed in imitation of Gamelan music.

Thus, through the children's imitaton play the importance of performance in Balinese life became apparent. The performances functioned for both adult and child as not only entertainment, relaxation, and a chance for social gathering, but also as a learning situation for the acquisition, appreciation, and sustainment of Balinese culture. The performances which were so much a part of the children's lives naturally carried over into their imitation play. In their imitations the children were able to rehearse aspects of the performances which they might be performing in adult life. They obtained great delight out of imitating adults as closely as possible. In addition, the adult's participation in leisure activities gave sanction to the children to rest from their work activities and engage in their own play forms.

The children participated in most work activities. The few in which the children did not have a major role were imitated in preparation for adult life. One of these activities was the management of the *warungs*. Warungs are the little food stalls set up on the side of the street. One can have meals or drinks prepared there, or buy food to take home. The warungs are usually run by married women with families, and are used as their major source of income. Children not able to participate in the management of the warungs, imitate it:

> Ketut, a seven year old girl, sits in front of a little table. On the table are little bits of vegetables and fruit. There are banana leaves to wrap the food in, and bits of newspaper to be used as money. All is set up to resemble a real warung. A little girl pretends to buy fruit, and Ketut wraps it up nicely in a banana leaf for the customer. The customer wanders off and Ketut, having no more customers, decides to eat some fruit.

III. Pastimes

Children's pastimes were leisure activities which involved much flexibility of action, and which lacked competitive elements. Some of the children's pastimes were inactive, as they sat talking, eating, picking lice out of each other's hair, or just staring. However, I did observe many active pastimes. Among these were play with toys such as kites and pinwheels of bamboo and flowers, play with recreation equipment such as a seesaw and a slide, and play which involved movement skill such as somersaults, hopping, jumprope, and climbing trees.

One of the children's favorite pastimes was playing with animals. Though the children imitated animals—the cocks in a cockfight and the monkey in the Ketjak Dance—these animals were always from rituals and performances. The domesticated animals which served no ritualistic function were not imitated, but rather they were played with in what we would consider cruel fashion. Dogs were kicked around, and I observed a little boy shooting dogs with a sling shot. Children were given lizards to play with, and pulled off heads, tails, and feet while the adults looked on in laughter. A number of times I observed children playing with baby birds. They played catch with one, bounced it up and down, and squeezed it until it squeaked. Sometimes the bird was mutilated until it finally died. All this cruelty was accepted by the Balinese. They were amused at my horrified response.

In Bali children are not allowed to crawl, the act of crawling being seen as a beast-like activity. The canine teeth are filed in an elaborate tooth-filing ceremony, for fear of their beastly influence. Dogs are of the lowest possible form and are given no respect. Thus the Balinese belief in the beastly influence of many animals manifests itself in the children's play with animals.

While in Bali, I did not observe any fantasy play, in which a child relies on inventiveness rather than imitation. This may have been my inability to recognize such play. However, it has been shown that if adults are strict, then children's play is usually very imitative, whereas if adults are flexible in their roles and interactions with children, then play involves fantasy, and is not a replication of adult models. Thus fantasy play may not exist in Balinese culture, which is highly stratified and strictly regulated. On the other hand, in spite of a rigid social structure, much permissiveness was allowed the children. Privacy was not respected, and children had access to almost everything, such as cupboards, drawers, and mothers' purses. In addition, though the children participated in work activites, during their leisure time they were free to come and go as they pleased. Further research must be done to determine whether imagination play exists in Bali.

Thus, though Balinese children were involved in a working world, and participated in many adult leisure activities—the festivals and performances—they did engage in their own play forms. The adult play forms did not sufficiently accommodate the special needs of children. The children's games, imitation play, and pastimes were necessary and important in the children's development.

THE PLAY BEHAVIOR OF KPELLE CHILDREN DURING RAPID CULTURAL CHANGE

David F. Lancy
Learning Research and Development Center
University of Pittsburgh

Introduction

The Liberian town of Gbarngasuakwelle stands at the crossroads of two drastically different cultures. On the one side is the traditional Kpelle culture which, like many West African societies, includes slash and burn subsistance cultivation, a magico-religious system made up of various secret societies and dominated by medicine men called Zo's and a rich variety of craft technologies. On the other side, since early 1973 the town has been linked to the modern, urbanizing sector of Liberia by an all-weather road. New roles, customs and artifacts have been introduced into the town at a rapid rate. In this paper I will examine one feature of the society, play, as it has been more traditionally practiced and as it is changing under the influence of westernization.

The paper is organized into three sections. In the first section, I will breifly describe the various traditional Kpelle playforms; in the second section, I will discuss the relationships between play and work or technology and; in the last section, I will describe the changes that are occurring in playforms and the implications of these changes for other areas of the society.

Traditional Kpelle Playforms

Initially, I elicited the names and categorical relationships of all playforms practiced or known by my informants in Gbarngasuakwelle. This procedure yielded over 90 playforms grouped into eight major categories. These categories were:

      (1) *Nee-pele*, make believe.
      (2) *Sua-Kpe-pele*, hunting play.
      (3) *Pelle-Seng*, toys.
      (4) *Pele-Kee*, games.
      (5) *Polo*, story telling.
      (6) *Mana-Pele*, dancing.
      (7) —————— , musical instruments.
      (8) *Kpa-Kolo-pele*, adult play.

Further discussion will be limited primarily to the categories in which children are the principal participants, namely numbers one through five.

The taxonomy served as a guide to further elicitation and observation. My intention was to obtain descriptions in context of the various playforms. Make-believe play involves the conscious dramatization of some real-life and usually adult activity by children aged four to seven. An example would be a little scene I witnessed where four children played at "blacksmith." One boy is the smith, and another boy acts as client. Differently shaped and sized sticks represent hammers, a rock represents the anvil, and a piece of bamboo partially slit along its length represents the tongs. The smith pounds away at a flat piece of wood putting it into and out of the "fire" and the finished "machete" is then given to the client who takes it into the jungle to "cut brush."

Hunting play is quite similar to make believe play in that actual situations are dramatized. But now certain features of reality are greatly abstracted and rules are added, as in a game where the object is to shoot arrows into a target. The bow and arrow is a hunting weapon and the target may be called by the name of an antelope, but the hunt is reduced to the moment of shooting. Rules specify that each player stand behind a line while shooting and he is given only four arrows to shoot. Turns are taken in rotation and so on.

The variety of games is quite large. Almost all are played in groups of three or larger and they tend to be ranked in complexity. A good many of them involve tricks of one sort or another. Generally speaking, younger children play games with simpler structures and tend to be the victims or dupes of tricks. They are almost never taught to play games but rather watch slightly older children at play and when they have acquired the rules, they join in. Hence, there is a developmental progression in game play. From age seven to age twenty, the games played change with every jump of three to four years. Children play the games of their age set, but also observe the next older set at play and copy, at first poorly, these more complex games.

Tiang-kai-sii is a simple counting game with stones, played by children aged eight to eleven. Ten or twenty-five stones are laid out in a line and the child, holding his breath, must touch each one in succession with his finger saying as he goes Tiang-kai-sii-taang (one), Tiang-kai-sii-verre (two), etc., to ten or twenty-five. If he misses a stone or a phrase another player makes the attempt. From twelve to fifteen children play Kpa-keleng-je. Ten stones are placed in a line. One player points to the first stone and say, "Is this the one?". The other player, whose back is turned, says "Yes, if you miss the stone, you will break your thigh." The first player again points to the first stone and says "Is this the one?". The second player answers "No, continue." The first player then points to the second stone and asks the question. This time the answer is "Yes". Then he points to the first stone, the answer will be "No," he points to the second stone, again the answer is "No," then to the third stone and now the answer should be "Yes" and so on for all the stones. If the player whose back is turned misses, they exchange places and the game begins again.

There are relatively few traditional toys as such—dolls for girls and tops for boys. In actuality, however, any object that a child plays with becomes in that instance a toy. Therefore, toys are important in make-believe and hunting play and in some games that model reality. Stories also model reality in a number of respects, but unlike other playforms, which reduce reality to a more abstract form, stories expand reality into the realm of fantasy. In stories, animals talk to each other and to people; men have access to magical powers; there are spirits in human form like witches, boogeymen and so forth. Stories are told by males exclusively from the age of nine upward. There are four types of stories and these tend, like games, to have a developmental component. One story form, for example, is told only by young boys, another only by older boys and men.

An interesting game which has some similarity to stories is called Kolong. Kolong are paired phrases. One member of a team gives the first (or stimulus) phrase of the pair and the opposing team must supply the complementary (or response) phrase. If they succeed they gain a point and it becomes their turn to offer a stimulus phrase. If they fail, the first team gains a point and may now offer another stimulus phrase.

Adult play refers to the custom of adults to gather after work to drink and gossip on a porch or inside someone's house. Two games are associated with adults, however, these are gbang, a gambling game in which cowrie shells are used like dice in craps and malang, the well-known African board game with seeds, which is elsewhere known as wari or mancala. I won't describe the game because it is well documented (see, for example, Culin, 1971), but the Kpelle have evolved a variety of forms of the game and each form demands various intricate strategies for successful play. Teenage boys are taught to play the game by their grandfather or some other kinsman who is greatly senior to them in years. These older men own the game boards which are elaborately carved and hence rather costly. Now I shall examine the roll of these playforms in training or preparing children for adult work.

The Function of Play in Adult Work

When I went into the field, I carried the explicit hypothesis that play was the equivalent for the Kpelle of an education system. In other words, I hoped to demonstrate direct links between information acquired in play and demands to utilize that same information in some type of adult work. Alas, I was unable to do so. Using a variety of techniques including controlled experiments, I was unable to demonstrate that any belief, concept, physical or cognitive skill is learned exclusively in play. On the other hand, I didn't find that play has no relationship to work. They are, to use a favorite anthropological term, "integrated." While I can't propose a general model of how play and work are integrated in Kpelle society, I can offer some specific instances.

Make-believe play seems to be one step in an alternatively collapsing and expanding process. A child of three spends hours observing a blacksmith at work. A child of four brings his stick down on a rock repeatedly and says he is a blacksmith. A child of eight weaves with his friends an elaborate reconstruction of the blacksmith's craft, all in make-believe. The child of ten is a blacksmith's helper in reality; he fetches wood for the forge and no more. At twelve he begins learning the actual skills of smithing, adding a new one every few months or so. At eighteen he is a full-fledged blacksmith with his own forge. Parallel patterns can be observed for virtually every class of work.

In hunting play, the child gradually moves from play to serious hunting but again the transition is far from direct. He has played at trapping for a number of years. But when he learns to trap, his father or older brother will assist and guide him in the slow and complex art of making dozens of different traps, in recognizing the signs of the 40 plus animal species, which are trapped and hunted, and then in combining these two skills into effective trapping.

Many games involve counting or seriation or the use of mapping and projective geometry. These skills are perhaps practiced in game play but are not exclusively learned in play. Parents teach their children to count and gradually give them greater and greater responsibility in marketing where they learn to add, subtract, multiply, and divide. Children learn applied geometry in watching, then helping to lay out farm plots, fences, and paths and in building houses. It is very difficult, therefore, to separate out what is learned in game play from the skills acquired in watching, listening, and doing various tasks. It seems most reasonable to assign games a practice rule. By repeating certain operations over and over in the course of the game, knowledge of them is solidified. This practice may not be available if a child's exposure to geometry is limited to helping build a house every other year or so.

Stories and Kolong are most certainly related to court disputes. Adults are frequently involved in court disputes and the penalties for losing a case are severe. Winning depends less on the facts of the case than on one's ability as orator, town historian, and debater. As mentioned above, stories vary considerably in content and structure. Children are exposed to important underlying beliefs or ethos of the culture in these stories. Equally important, in telling certain types of stories, there is great emphasis placed on the use of dramatic gestures and other oratorical devices. In one type, there is actually a debate built into the story where the teller must defend his interpretation of the story against alternative explanations offered by members of his audience. In the game of Kolong, the response parts of the paired phrases are actually proverbs. Children do not normally use proverbs in conversation but by playing the game they acquire a store of them which will be later used when they appear as adult litigants in the courts.

The next section will deal with changes in the play practices of children which have occurred over the last few years and also with the declining role of play in the integration of the culture.

Changes in Play and Their Impact on the Town

The children of Gbarngasuakwelle have made two discoveries that, over night, revolutionized their play practices. These are the wheel and the ball. The wheel comes in many manifestations. It may be on a small car made out of wires or carved out of wood; it may be an old tire propelled by two sticks; a piece of vine tied in a loop; a bicycle wheel; even a broken lantern with a round base. During the observation period, wheel rolling was the most frequently observed play activity of boys aged 6 to 18. Even when the wheel was a loop of vine, it symbolized the automobile because boys invariably made engine noises as they rolled their wheels. Wheel rolling as "car driving" was one example among many of the new types of make-believe play. One of the most interesting I witnessed could be labeled "presidential entourage." President Tolbert rides past the town on many occasions enroute to his ranch. He and his aides travel at high speed in one or two limousines, preceded and followed by police cars that keep their sirens blasting the entire time. People, and especially children, hearing the sirens run out to the road side to watch and wave flowers. One day a group of boys reproduced the spectacle. One boy walked in front of the procession making siren-like noises. Another boy, the oldest and tallest of the group, walked behind in his best impression of "stateliness." He was followed by two boys waving scraps of cloth which symbolized the small national flags always flown from the limousines. Other boys walked behind, also erect and dignified and, along their "route," the remaining boys stood waving flowers and shouting greetings to

"President Tolbert."

Make-believe play follows closely on the heels of new social customs. The older school boys erected a flag pole outside the "school" on September 25, 1973. From that day on, the children would "pledge allegiance" to the flag as it was raised every morning before filing inside. On September 29, 1973, I witnessed two boys make a miniature flag pole out of bamboo, cut a scrap of cloth into a rectangle, attach it to the pole with string and then run it up and down the pole saluting and mumbling something that approximated the "pledge allegiance."

I saw very little make-believe of complex adult skills such as weaving and blacksmithing. Informants, when questioned about nee-pele, would describe various forms in the past tense, indicating that long before, say, leatherworking, ceased to be practiced, children had given up imitating it in their play.

Changes in hunting are reflected in hunting play (sua-kpe-pele). Gun and dog hunting now predominate and the various forms of group hunting and bow and arrow hunting have disappeared. Thus, bow and arrow and net-hunting games are gone from the play repertoire of young boys, only to be replaced by play centering on the slingshot (actual) and the gun (modeled). Trapping is also waning mainly because young boys and men find gun hunting more exciting. Geleng-gbe, the boys secret society where initiates were taught medicines to lure animals into traps is no longer active. Older men complain that their sons aren't interested in learning to trap, preferring instead to go to school.

The play of very young children (i.e., under the age of seven) seems to be fairly stable. They imitate their parents and spend a great deal of time in hiding play and other traditional games. Slightly older children, however, are going to school and this has an effect on their play behavior. For example, a modern analogue of tiang-kai-sii is a game where two boys take turns writing numerals in the sand at rapid speed, with their fingers. One boy writes "one," the other boy erases it and writes "two," the first boy erases the two and writes "three" and so on. This is an example of new forms of drawing play (loo-pele). School children are much more likely than their same age counterparts not attending school to draw pictures in the sand, or write letters or words in the sand. Still older boys are turning to imported games, there is one "Ludo" (an English board game with dice) and one "Checkers" game in town and these are both constantly in use by a shifting group of boys aged 13 to 18. These foreign games seem to compete directly with traditional games as participation in them has fallen off sharply in recent times. The case of Malang is quite interesting. As I pointed out, boys learn the game from older men, primarily because these men own the game boards and have stored in memory the various strategies for successful play. The ludo and checkers boards on the other hand are owned by young men (both less than 25). Thus, these games represent not only new playforms, but also make boys less dependent on older men and, perhaps, less respectful of them as well. This is only a small instance of a transfer of the authority base away from the town's elders to young men who are partially literate and, more importantly, have lived at least part of their lives outside the town in more westernized settings. One result of the abandonment of traditional playforms by school children aged 10 to 18 is that certain games will be lost to the society forever. As I showed earlier, games tend to cluster with certain age sets. Children learn new games from the next older age set. If one set abandons the games it traditionally plays, then the next younger and subsequent age sets will have no avenue for learning these games.

I've never heard adults more critical of children's behavior than when they're playing ball. Part of the reason is that adults resent the change represented by the ball game but also the ball, careening on its course, often strikes people or houses. In town, boys kick around large gourds, cans, and, if any are available, small rubber balls about seven inches in diameter. They've developed a number of games that derive from soccer. One of these is for a boy who is "it" to try and kick the ball at any one from a group of boys who are running around him and trying to avoid being hit. If a boy is hit he becomes "it" and kicks the ball until he hits someone. The second game is played by two boys who try to dribble the ball around each other. A third game is played between two houses and with one or two boys on a side the team trys to block it. Next to wheel-rolling, ball games constituted the most frequently observed play activity of boys.

Ball play not only divides young from old in the sense that old people have never, nor are ever likely to play with balls, but it also divides school children from children not attending school. The soccer field and the one regulation sized ball belong to the school. Soccer must also be played on a relatively flat surface, which means on the field or in town and it must be played during daylight. Children not attending school spend all day on the farm where a flat playing surface is impossible to find so they don't have any opportunities to engage in ball play. I found evidence, therefore, of a growing gap between the play behavior of children in school as against children not attending school.

The ball and wheel seem to be deeply rooted in more elaborate contexts. Soccer is the national sport of Liberia; all the public schools have soccer teams and the ability to play the game, understand the rules and so forth seems to go hand-in-hand with becoming a student and learning to read and write and do arithmetic. Significantly, there are no games that involve throwing or batting balls, only kicking. Similarly, wheel rolling is tied to the automobile which represents not only a powerful and expensive symbol, but also connotes the excitement of a trip to the capital city, Monrovia. I introduced the American game of frisbee into the town to see how a new playform, not buttressed by elaborate symbolism would be received. Women now use plastic buckets with circular lids to carry around their possessions. The buckets wear out before the lids do so there were a fair number of these lids to be found lying around. The lid approximates a frisbee in shape and size so on four successive evenings I used one of them to teach four boys (aged 10 to 13) how to toss a frisbee. Then, for two weeks, my assistant and I monitored children's play for evidence of the game. Since my demonstration had attracted a substantial audience each time, I had reason to believe that the idea had been widely difused. What I found was that for four days after the demonstration there was sporadic frisbee tossing, primarily by the boys I had taught, but after that I found no sign of it.

Changes in story-telling and kolong are not yet very great. Foreign elements do not seem to have crept into the stories to any appreciable degree. Boys tell traditional stories in school, at the request of the teacher (he is Kpelle). But they don't tell stories in the evening which is the normal story-telling time, rather, they read their textbooks and do homework. Story-telling by children not attending school and by men also seems to have declined as has kolong although the extent of the decline is difficult to estimate.

Prima-facie evidence suggests that there has been an overall decline in time allotted to play. In a society where everyone works on the farm in cooperative work parties, as the number of laborers available declines, the amount of work that falls on to those remaining must increase (assuming no increase in productivity which is the case here). More time spent in work probably means less time for play. This has in fact been happening. Men, young men especially, have been leaving the town in increasing number to seek wage employment to purchase luxuries. Their families stay at home and are expected to make the usual size rice farm. The men periodically do participate in tree-felling and burning, but they are lost to the family working unit at other times. Children who are in their working years, especially boys aged 8 to 13, are going in increasing numbers to school, thus, they too, are lost to the working unit for at least two-thirds of the weekly work period. The burden of farming then is falling increasingly on women, young children and older people. The later two categories, in particular, appear to be working more and playing less as time goes on.

The bearers and practitioners of traditional Kpelle culture are declining in number and are confined more and more to those who are middle aged or old. The paradox as I see it is that the increasingly high cost of energy, raw materials and labor in industrialized countries, means that the returns for participating in that sector of Liberia that is highly westernized are already beginning to diminish. These older people then have become the repositories of a store of invaluable information on how to adapt successfully without outside assistance in what must be considered a marginal ecological zone. To the extent that traditional playforms act to link the development of children to the technology of their parents, the loss of these playforms may indeed be disastrous.

REFERENCES

Culin, S.
  1971 *Mancala, The National Game of Africa*. Reprinted in The Study of Games, E. M. Avedon and B. Sutton-Smith (Eds.), New York: J. Wiley.

THE REFLECTION OF CULTURAL VALUES IN
ESKIMO CHILDREN'S GAMES

Lynn Price Ager
The Ohio State University

In recent years there has been a surge of interest and research focused on the relationship of games and culture. One major result of cross-cultural surveys and culture-specific studies of games has been the discovery that in any society, games are integrally related to major cultural institutions such as religion (Lambert, Triandes, and Wolf 1959), levels of subsistence activity and social complexity (Roberts, Arth, and Bush 1959), and child-rearing customs (Roberts and Sutton-Smith 1962). Games are an important part of children's activities in many societies, and it is therefore of interest to study the roles and values of a society as they are perceived by children and acted out in games and play. Also, since games are viewed as mechanisms of socialization by many scholars, we may be able to learn *which* norms and values are learned in games or expressed in games. This paper is based on my research into the relationship of games and values in an Eskimo village,[1] but I believe the hypothesis that games are an expression of cultural values is a generally applicable one and can apply both to traditional societies and those undergoing acculturation.

I define a game as a play activity which has explicit rules, specified or understood goals (winning is not necessarily one of them), the element of opposition or contest, recognizable boundaries in time and sometimes in space, and a sequence of actions which is essentially "repeatable" every time the game is played. (I do not consider "competition" and "two or more sides" necessary for a definition of game.)

Games have been classified into four primary categories, based on the dominant or characteristic mode of contest present: games of physical skill, of chance, of strategy (Roberts, Arth and Bush 1959), and memory-attention (Eifermann 1971).

Values are used here as Clyde Kluckhohn defined them:

In the broadest sense . . . (one) may usefully think of values as abstract and enduring standards which are held by an individual and/or a specified group to transcend the impulses of the moment and ephemeral situations. From the psychological point of view, a value may be defined as that aspect of motivation which is referable to standards, personal or cultural, that do not arise solely out of an immediate situation and the satisfaction of needs and primary drives.

---

[1]This research was supported in full by the National Institute of Education grant number NEG-00-3-0104. Drafts of this paper were read by Daniel Hughes, Ojo Arewa, Allan Tindall, and Margaret Landis. Their reactions were appreciated.

A value is a selective orientation toward experience, implying deep commitment or repudiation, which influences the 'choice' between possible alternatives in action. These orientations may be cognitive and expressed or merely inferable from recurrent trends in behavior. A value, though conditioned by biological and social necessity, is in its specific form arbitrary or conventional.

Values, then, are images formulating positive or negative action commitments. They take distinctive forms in different cultures, tend to persist tenaciously through time, and are not mere random outcomes of conflicting human desires. (Kluckhohn 1958, quoted in Lantis 1959, p. 37).

My research into children's games took place during eight months in Tununak, an Eskimo village on Nelson Island, along the Bering Sea coast of Alaska. This area of southwestern Alaska has been one of the last to be exposed to the outside world, primarily, I think, because of its lack of commercially exploitable resources. No gold prospectors, whalers, or fur trappers have descended on this area in hoards as they have in so many other Eskimo communities in the past. Itinerant Catholic missionaries have been in varying degrees of contact with Nelson Islanders since the 1890's, but their influence was a gradual one, as evidenced by the fact that shamanism as a viable religious practice has disappeared only within the memory of middle-aged informants. Anglo-American school teachers have been teaching in Tununak since the 1920's, and earlier in the century a Northern Commercial Company store was operating for awhile. But compared to many other Alaskan Eskimo coastal communities, Tununak has been pretty much left alone by the outside world until the past two decades. Here, men still hunt and fish to supply the staples of their family's diet; and the people still all speak Yupik, their native tongue, as their first, and sometimes only, language. Dog teams were replaced by snow machines within the past nine years, and the last semi-subterranean house was abandoned for a "modern" plywood frame dwelling only about six years ago. Electricity was brought to the community four years ago, but there is still no indoor plumbing or running water. After completing 8th grade in the village Bureau of Indian Affairs school, some students leave to attend regional high schools, but higher education is a relatively new goal, still rarely fulfilled. Even the young people who do graduate from high school often return to live in Tununak rather than move to metropolitan areas in the state where they can find jobs.

What the culture of Tununak was like prior to contact I can only surmise from ethnographies of other southwestern Alaskan communities, since I am the first anthropologist to carry out ethnographic research on Nelson Island. The closest communities for which we have good information are on Nunivak Island, about 20 miles across the Etolin Strait from Nelson Island, where Margaret Lantis conducted ethnographic fieldwork beginning in 1939 (Lantis, 1946). My discussion of Eskimo values is based on my own observations in Tununak as well as on published reports of other ethnographers, particularly those of Lantis (1959). Games mentioned are those I saw played or ones informants told me used to be played, and these were all classified according to the categories mentioned on page 80. The relationship between games and values is one I perceived through analysis. An emic approach to this subject was not possible under the particular field conditions I encountered.

The Eskimos of Nelson Island are classified as Bering Sea hunters and fishermen (Oswalt 1967). They derive most of their subsistence from the ocean—primarily fish (salmon and herring) and seals, with walrus, white whale, and sea lion from time to time. As hunters, they place a high value on hunting, hunting skill, and hunting achievement. This overwhelming fact of their lives, that their very survival depended on a hunter's ability to find, kill, and retrieve game, has dominated every aspect of their culture and cannot be overstressed. It has been only recently that a cash economy has affected in any major way the subsistence patterns of these people, and government aid of various kinds now provides them with economic security should their traditional means of getting food fail. A man's prestige, however, is still measured to a great extent in terms of his hunting skill. It is no surprise, therefore, that we find games of physical skill to be overwhelmingly preferred to other types. Of 39 games recorded for the village, 25 were games of physical skill. Games which require dexterity, strength and endurance are quite obviously functional in a society so dependent upon these qualities in its members, both male and female. The significance of this type of game is further apparent when we discover that games of physical skill and games of memory-attention were the *only* kinds played in the traditional culture. None of my informants reported "old time" games of chance or strategy, and Lantis (1946) reports that there were none on Nunivak Island, although games of chance have been reported for aboriginal groups of Eskimos from other areas. Success in games depended exclusively on one's own skills. This was true in real life as well. Economic pursuits were individual for the most part (Oswalt 1963: 100,121), although sometimes partners might hunt or set fish nets together and divide the spoils. Self-reliance and independence were valued personal traits (Lantis 1959). Individual self-testing games are by far the most popular among Eskimos today, and so far as I can determine, have always been. Old games such as dart throwing, juggling, tag, and contests of strength, such as broad jumping, wrestling, and foot racing, tested the ability of the individual. Many new games which have been adopted by the Eskimos are also essentially individual tests— marbles and jacks are two examples. A good memory was also a valuable personal asset in a hunting culture (Nelson 1969), for it is of positive survival value to remember one's own experiences in emergencies, the experiences of others in similar situations, to remember landmarks on an almost featureless terrain, to remember animal habits which help one predict their behavior. *Remembering* helps the hunter and may even save his life. Two games which test children's memory are storyknifing (Oswalt 1964; Ager 1974), and string figures.

Emphasis on individuality in achievement, both in real life and in games, has fostered a spirit of competition among Eskimos. But mitigating the disruptive aspects of aggressive competition is the social morality of the group. It is realized, or at least used to be, that the group was the only insurance an individual had. If one man had a run of bad luck in hunting, his family would not go hungry if he had relatives and friends to provide for him in emergencies. Thus, there was a high value on group survival (Lantis 1959; Nelson 1899: 294), which led, in the most extreme situations, to sacrifice of individuals for the good of the group (e.g. infanticide and elimination of the old and infirm in periods of starvation). The kind of competition in games I saw was one in which everyone tried to do his best but not at anyone else's expense. (Senengutuk 1971: 145). Consistent with the idea that one man's gain is not necessarily another's loss is the custom of giving prizes. In the old days, the winner of one game put up the prize for the next, so the only real winner, materially, was the winner of the last game played. Today in Tununak, when games are held on the 4th of July, *everyone* who plays receives a prize. On a game night organized for the children in the community hall, no prizes were given at all. In addition, there are games of individual skill which have no element of real competition, such as storyknifing and string figures, and thus have no criteria for winning. These two games may be played in groups in which each participant tries to tell her best stories or make many string figures and be able to make them very quickly (so contest is present but minimal), or they may be played alone and are therefore sometimes only amusements because the element of opposition is lacking. The lengths to which we go, in our own society, to encourage a winning spirit in players can be seen on any summer Saturday afternoon at little league baseball games. Parents and players boo "bad" calls by the umpire; those who strike out sometimes cry; and the losing team goes home depressed. Coaches admonish the players to be good sports because "winning isn't everything," but the very fact that we feel it necessary to verbalize such a concept is some indication that it is not ingrained.

The high value placed on non-aggression within the group is reflected in the lack of malice in games and sports among the Eskimos. Even in the most painful contests of endurance and strength (such as mouth pulling, finger pulling, and other trials between two individuals), participants do not become angry at one another because of the discomfort each is inflicting on the other. (Contrast this with our own sports, such as boxing and hockey). Eskimo losers are good sports. They leave laughing; the audience laughs when someone loses or looks funny or makes a mistake; and participants in many games derive much amusement from playing. (I should mention here that laughter is not *always* an indication of amusement. In some instances, laughter in Eskimo culture is a means of concealing shame or hurt feelings.) Humor is greatly valued among all Eskimos reported in the literature (Lantis, 1959; Nelson 1969). The children show this when they play, too. Even cheaters do not evoke an angry response but an amused one. The other players yell "cheater" good naturedly and laugh;

in fact, the cheating is blatant when it occurs, as if done to amuse oneself and the others. Although the subject of this paper is children's games, I might note here that nearly all adult games I witnessed were also occasions for humor.

Another value in Eskimo society is what Lantis calls the "devaluation of possessiveness" (1959). In general, there is very little, if any, emphasis in games upon equipment. One of the favorite games in Tununak is called "Lapp game." It resembles baseball in that a ball is hit with a bat, but the bat need only be a handy piece of wood. In another popular game which has been introduced, marbles, the children bring one marble to the game and leave with that same marble. The game they play has no provisions for winning another player's marble. They do know a game in which the object is gain possession of others' marbles, but they rarely play it. In all my months there, I saw the "winning game" of marbles played only once; a novice player who had lost his marble sat off to the side waiting for the game to end so his marble would be returned. When it was explained that it would not be returned, he was incredulous. It appeared to me that since this game was so rarely played, the children (who played marbles in little groups throughout the village almost every day for the entire summer of 1974) were indeed expressing a preference for the non-winning game. They enjoyed the contest of skill, but did not seem to enjoy taking each others' marbles as prizes.

What I have said so far applies to the traditional cultural values which survive today. But what about the changes taking place in Eskimo society as a result of contact with Anglo-Americans? As I see it, many values are just now beginning to change in Tununak, and the full effect of modernization will be felt there within the next decade (it has been felt already in other, less isolated, villages). Because of the changes Eskimo culture is making to adapt to modern technology, economy, and life-styles, many individuals now find that it is becoming increasingly important to be well educated in order to cope with the complexities of Anglo-American culture. What we see now in the game repertoire is still a preponderance of games of physical skill, but these, along with memory-attention games, are no longer the only kinds played. Games of strategy (chess, checkers), games combining chance and strategy (board games, card games), and sports such as basketball and football which combine physical skill and strategy have been adopted by the children and the adults. The relationship of games of strategy to cultural complexity has been discussed by Roberts, Arth, and Bush (1959). Following their line of thinking, we can say that acceptance of games of strategy is consistent with new values regarding competence in coping with the complexities of modern life, particularly since the recent settlement of the Native Land Claims with its complicated legal and economic significance for the natives and the new demands on community leaders to formulate long range plans and goals for the group.

A final point I wish to make with regard to the games is that children actually play very few formal games in their total play activity (Oswalt 1963).

Sutton-Smith and Rosenberg (1971: 44-45) have suggested that the trend away from formal games to informal play activities among Anglo-American children may be explained by the changes in the society they live in—a society increasingly permissive and more informal in social relationships, particularly in relationships with parents. If this is true, we could suggest that it may apply cross-culturally as well: one reason for the relative scarcity of formal games compared to informal play activities among Eskimo children may be the value of equality in their society (Senungetuk 1971: 45). Eskimo culture is noted for its lack of rigid, formal, hierarchically ordered social realtionships, which is consistent with their emphasis on essentially equal standards of living for everyone and lack of formal authority in leaders. Their preference for the unstructured and the permissive may help to explain the children's preference for informal play. Interestingly, if they adapt completely to modern western civilization, they will have to introduce *more* formal organization and structure in their social organization, so perhaps we will see an increase in the number of formal games played in the future.

In summary, I think we can see that the traditional hunting complex requiring individual initiative, memory, and physical strength fosters values which are expressed in the *types* of games traditionally played by Eskimo children, i.e. those games of physical skill, particularly the self-testing variety, and games requiring both dexterity and memory-attention, such as string figures. The cultural value placed on individuality and self-reliance but without disruption of group unity and solidarity is expressed in *attitudes* in games, that is, pleasurable competition in some games but absence of humiliation for the losers and the humor which envelops game playing. The general lack of emphasis on material possessions is reflected in players' careless attitude toward game equipment and in minimal emphasis on prizes in competitions. New values associated with competence in the complex modern world may be related to increasing interest in games of strategy, where the emphasis is on testing the mind rather than the body. Finally, infrequency of formal games can tell us something about values as well. In Tununak, formal games are less frequent than informal play activities, and this may be a reflection of the high value placed on informal, permissive relationships in social relations.

The hypothesis that important cultural values will be reflected in children's games has been shown to be a workable one in the community I studied. It remains for other investigators to discover if cultural values find such clear expression in the games of other societies.

REFERENCES

Ager, L. P.
    1974 *Storyknifing: An Alaskan Eskimo Girls' Game.* Journal of the Folklore Institute XI: 3. Indiana University.

Eifermann, R.
  1971 *Determinants of Children's Game Styles*. Israel Academy of Sciences and Humanities, Jerusalem.
Kluckhohn, C.
  1958 The Scientific Study of Values. In *3 Lectures*. University of Toronto Installation Lectures, pp. 25-54.
Lambert, W., L. M. Triandis, and M. Wolf
  1959 *Some Correlates of Beliefs in the Malevolence and Benevolence of Supernatural Beings: A Cross Cultural Study*. Journal of Abnormal Psychology 58: 162-169.
Lantis, M.
  1946 *The Social Culture of the Nunivak Eskimo*. Transactions of the American Philosophical Society 35: 3: 155-323.
  1959 *Alaskan Eskimo Cultural Values*. Polar Notes 1: 35-48.
Nelson, E. W.
  1899 *The Eskimo About Bering Strait*. Bureau of American Ethnology, Eighteenth Annual Report. Washington, D.C.
Nelson, R. K.
  1969 *Hunters of the Northern Ice*. University of Chicago Press, Chicago.
Oswalt, W.
  1963 *Napaskiak*. University of Arizona Press, Tucson, Arizona.
  1964 *Traditional Storyknife Tales of Yuk Girls*. Proceedings of the American Philosophical Society 108: 4: 310-336.
  1967 *Alaskan Eskimos*. Chandler Publishers, San Francisco.
Roberts, J., M. J. Arth, and R. R. Bush
  1959 *Games in Culture*. American Anthropologist 61: 597-605.
Roberts, J. M., and B. Sutton-Smith
  1962 *Child Training and Game Involvement*. Ethnology 1: 2: 166-185.
Senungetuk, J. E.
  1971 *Give or Take A Century*. The Indian Historian Press, San Francisco.
Sutton-Smith, B., and B. G. Rosenberg
  1971 Sixty Years of Historical Change in the Game Preferences of American Children. In *Child's Play*, R. E. Herron and B. Sutton-Smith, eds., Wiley and Sons, New York, pp. 18-50.

PLAY AND INTER-ETHNIC COMMUNICATION

Claire R. Farrer*
University of Texas-Austin
Mescalero Apache Indian Reservation

This paper is a report of an on-going research project. I would like to acknowledge the financial support of the Whitney M. Young, Jr. Memorial Foundation and the courtesy of Mr. Wendell Chino, President, Mescalero Apache Tribal Council, for allowing me to live and work among his people.

This paper makes two points: first—free play is a valuable, though largely neglected, tool for anthropologists, folklorists, and educators; second—research cooperation between social scientists and the people we study is becoming essential in the contemporary situation.

I am currently living and working on the Mescalero Apache Indian Reservation in southcentral New Mexico. This reservation was closed to research workers for close to twenty years prior to my being allowed to work there beginning in 1974. Over a year's negotiation preceded permission being granted me to do my work. It is *still* closed without special Tribal permission. Ours is a business agreement: I am allowed to do the research which will form my Ph.D. dissertation in anthropology and folklore in return for services I can provide which the Tribe needs. Specifically, I write graded reading materials, based upon Apache traditions and life-style, for first through sixth grade pupils in the reservation school. Additionally, as the situation has developed, I serve as an educational consultant for the Tribe. Our agreement further stipulates that I will not publish nor publicize information about the Mescalero people without first submitting the data to the Tribal Council for approval—and this paper has been through the Council. Should any royalties accrue, they will be divided equally between the Tribe and me. Further, my project is an applied one which, if the results are consistent with the report I'm giving today, will provide additional benefit to the people through increasing the communication between non-Indian teachers and Indian children. This is not to say there are no theoretical applications—quite the contrary, as will become obvious.

The point to which I am alluding is that we who study living populations as anthropologists—or as behavioral scientists in general—have entered a new era which finds those people we study taking a more active part in our research, from the design through to the result stages. This, I believe, is particularly true in the American Southwest where there is a new consciousness of both ethnic identity and power, as well as pride, among Native Americans and Spanish-speaking groups. While it necessitates changes in our basic orientation, I personally believe the new liaison produces data which are more reliable. At the same time, the liaison vastly increases rapport. My work is a case in point.

Since September 1974 I have been developing a technique that utilizes the free play of young children as a tool to improve communication between teachers and children from other than mainstream American backgrounds. For the purpose of my study, young children are those between the ages of 3 and 9 years. The inter-ethnic component is between non-Indian teachers and Native American children, specifically Mescalero Apache children. While I have data from other ethnic groups, these will not be considered because of time limits.

The guiding hypothesis of the study is that the free play activities of young children replicate the communication system they have been taught by their parents and, therefore:

1. Observation of free play activities will yield insights into values and how children have been taught to learn allowing,
2. Classroom teachers to re-structure teaching techniques and, if necessary, the physical environment of the classroom to take advantage of the pre-existing, culture-specific communication patterns and, thereby,
3. More effectively communicate with children in their charge.

The investigation of the hypothesis and its corollary propositions required what I've called an ethnography of a playground. One segment of that ethnography, a game of tag, I'll discuss here.

First, however, let me remind you of standard, mainstream American tag games. When predominantly Anglo-American children play tag there is an initial period of negotiating who will be "it." The game proceeds in lines with the rectangular or square playground being utilized in a grid pattern of horizontal, vertical, and diagonal avenues. Rules are negotiated too. I often hear, "That's not fair!", or, "Janie's cheating!", or "You can't *do* that!". Tag, for mainstream American children, involves one's own personal space in which the child is encapsulated—even when several are involved in running from the "it" individual, each runs by him/herself. Touching another, other than in a tag move, is deemed an impediment to rapid progress. Tag is usually played with one's friends and is often an indicator of who likes whom.

Tag play at Mescalero, in contrast, is initiated in one of two ways: either children run from the building yelling "Not it!" and proceed to the tag area or they spontaneously break into a tag game as the result of one child tagging another on the jungle gym. The tag area for Mescalero Apache children is the jungle gym. I've not seen tag played on the ground. There are chasing games and "games" where one child will run up to another to hit, kick, or offer verbal abuse for a past wrong, real or imagined; but these are not tag games. However the game is initiated, a group of children—as few as three or as many as eight—will begin circling the jungle gym by moving left hand and foot to the left, then sliding the right hand and foot to the left to a position by the left ones which, in turn, move again. In other words, they stand on the lowest level of the jungle gym with their hands holding onto the next higher or second higher bar, depending upon their size. From this position they race around and around. Movement is to the left, clockwise. Oftentimes the children's bodies touch as they race around. However, a tag occurs only when the "it" person touches another's head (the preferred tag spot), shoulder, arm or leg in a deliberate movement. Bodies may be in continuous contact, but a tag is effected only when a child removes his/her hand from the bar and touches a particular place on another child.

At all times verbal interaction is minimal, even when the game isn't being played by the rules. For instance, occasionally a child will circle to the right, causing momentary confusion. Perhaps the counter-clockwise circling will last for one complete tag round, but not often. Usually counter-clockwise movement—or going through the bars of the jungle gym in a linear fashion—forces the game to disintegrate or causes it to stop momentarily so it can begin again "properly". When a child does go through rather than around, or when an "it" child moves around counter-clockwise, there is no verbal correction. The others either allow the abberant movement or stop the game. There is, however, much giggling and laughter while the game is in progress—little, if any, verbal interaction but much vocalization.

How the game is played obviously differs from standard Anglo-American tag. It is a round game, not a linear one. Bodies may touch during play. There is no calling out of corrections or amendments to rules during play. It is recognizable as tag, but still it is very different. Each of these differences is predicated on an aspect of standard, adult, Mescalero behavior. The children are replicating, or acting out, basic tenets of the culture. They stress in their play the importance of contact, circularity, and learning by observation. They are making statements about standard communication patterns: when it is appropriate to speak and when to remain silent; to whom one speaks; and in what manner; and whether "speech" is verbal or non-verbal. Thus, play is metacommunication.

Circularity is of paramount importance for the Mescalero Apache and this is readily evident in the play of children. It could be argued that playing on a jungle gym changes the form of the game. It's difficult, even for an agile child, to move through the bars of a jungle gym quickly in a linear fashion. It's much easier to go around and around on a jungle gym. However, I maintain the jungle gym was *chosen* as the accepted arena for tag precisely because it lends itself to a circular game. Circles are important to the Mescalero Apache people. Their traditional homes, whether tipi or brush arbor, were circular. Dance patterns are circular and, incidentally, move clockwise. Tribal decisions are made by consensus; each speaks until no one has more to say. The circle pattern is egalitarian as is the society. No one is the obvious leader in a circle. And unless you see the beginning of the game or an actual tag, no one is obviously "it" in Mescalero tag.

In standard Anglo-American tag, a touch is a tag. In Mescalero style tag, bodies may touch throughout the game. Indeed, the children usually group themselves so that their bodies *must* touch. A tag, then, has to be a specific movement of a hand to one of the few specific places I've already ennumerated. Touching is likewise common to adult Mescalero Apache people. When friends are speaking, they frequently stand side by side with arms touching. During meetings, pow-wows, or church services one's personal space is only what one is physically occupying. There are no bubbles of encapsulated space which one claims as one's own. If it is crowded, people sit with bodies touching at hips, arms, and shoulders: comfortable for the Mescalero but too intimate for Anglos. When chairs were set up for the choir last Christmas for the annual pageant, they were placed much closer than normal in Anglo situations and much closer than they need have been, since space was no problem. Choir members' shoulders often touched. When the women dance, there is just enough space between them so one's foot won't kick another's; but shoulders often touch during side-by-side dances. To be close to another is to be involved in the event. Touching in tag identifies the participants in the game and excludes others who may be on the jungle gym at the same time but not part of the tag game.

In Mescalero style tag mistakes are not called out; rules are not negotiated. Similarly, Mescalero Apache parents rarely correct their children in public. Children are expected to behave properly by observing and copying their older siblings, cousins, and parents. When a child misbehaves, he is ignored, if the infraction is slight. If the infraction is more serious, he is physically restrained or removed from the scene. When a child goes through the jungle gym linearly or moves counter-clockwise, the group will often go along for a short period of time or the game will stop. All this occurs without verbal interaction. But children simply won't play with those who don't play properly. The deviant is effectively, and nonverbally, removed from play. Children are again replicating in play what they observe in the larger society. And again play may be seen as metacommunication.

The participants in any one tag game are usually cousins. (And let me add parenthetically that cousinship among Mescalero is reckoned well beyond the fourth degree.) Relatives play together much more often than non-relatives. Frequently teams of relatives will join each other for a game, though. During a person's lifetime the family of orientation will join together on important occasions; this family is of vital importance to an individual. When a girl has her puberty feast, for instance, her mother, mother's sisters, mother's sisters' daughters, mother's mother, and mother's mother's sisters will all be helping with the food. When a child needs a babysitter, the sitter will probably be an aunt, uncle, cousin, or grandparent. When a man kills an animal, he divides the meat among his family of procreation as well as among his sisters' families and the household of his parents. Relatives are the ones to turn to in time of need or celebration. And you play tag with your relatives first and others second, if you are a Mescalero Apache child.

By now I assume I've convinced you that this game of tag is indeed metacommunication. Let's look at it as a miniature communication system. Four areas of interest are immediately apparent:

1. Relatives play together;
2. Verbal interaction is minimal with teaching and correction by example and learning by observation;
3. Physical closeness is desirable;
4. Circularity is important while linearity is merely tolerated.

If space allowed, I'd like to relate each of these four items to cultural values as expressed in mythology, the politeness-decorum system, dance, social organization, etc. However, instead I'll be extremely practical and relate these items to an on-the-ground problem: the failures of communication between non-Indian teachers and Mescalero Apache children.

The implications of these four areas for non-Indian teachers working with bicultural Mescalero Apache children are enormous. Relatives do work and play together. In the classroom I have seen two little girls constantly chatter to each other even when they have been placed as far apart as is physically possible. Their teacher is at a loss "to get them to be quiet and work independently". These girls are cousins and are trying to help one another as they've seen their mothers do and as they will be expected to do throughout their lives. This work and play dependence upon relatives should be taken into consideration by non-Indian teachers. It is blatant in play as well as in the larger society.

Minimal verbal interaction characterizes both play and the larger society. When a child causes a fuss in public, the child is ignored or removed from the scene, as I've already mentioned. Children play and arbitrate disputes nonverbally just as they are nonverbally taught rules of behavior in public. When a child attempts to circle counter-clockwise, the game usually disintegrates. Teachers would be more effective if they, too, relied less on verbal instruction and instead tried to find ways of teaching by example so the children could learn by observation as they are used to doing. Discipline would be more meaningful if teachers would correct privately and remove the offending child from the group. As it is, teachers lose face by public correction and they lose the respect of the children as well.

Physical closeness has a positive value for Mescalero Apache people. Closeness implies security and serves to identify co-participants in events, thus serving a phatic end much as some of our verbal chatter, like, "you know", does. Perhaps the Mescalero Apache children should be allowed to practically sit on each other's laps, if they so choose, since to a Mescalero person closeness is security whether in a game, church, pow-wow, pick-up truck, or the home. Closeness could be security in school too. Utilization of the phatic channel differs for Mescalero and Anglo-Americans; non-Indian teachers should be made aware of this.

The Mescalero Apache world-view structures reality into circles and circular patterns whether in meetings, housing, dance, or cosmology. Mescalero Apache children prefer round patterned games. Teachers could easily allow children to sit in circles or clusters rather than in lines and rows. Thus the classroom could more closely conform to the Mescalero view of reality, rather than to the Anglo-American one predicated on lines and grids.

The implications for anthropologists and folklorists are numerous. I've combined theoretical constructs from anthropology and linguistics and applied them to a folkloristic form. I've done this in order to facilitate inter-ethnic communication in an area where such communication is most desirable and least achieved, that is, between Anglo-American teachers, (or those teachers trained on the Anglo-American model) and bicultural children. My model of play as metacommunication obviously is indebted to linguistic theory and particularly to the work of Bateson (1972) and Jakobson (1960).. The statements made during play about culture-specific communication patterns reflect both deep and surface structures apparent in everyday Mescalero Apache verbal interactions. The model also relies upon anthropological theory, especially kinesics and proxemics (Hall, 1959, 1966). Just as friends stand close to one another when they are co-participants in a communicative event, so children place themselves close to each other in play. Movement was seen to follow dance movement; further, children exhibit in play the same stereotyped body movements evident in ritual dancing.

We are also in a position to benefit from the new liaison and working partnership between ourselves and our informants. For instance, I *know* what I've just told you is true as concerns Mescalero values and their evidence in play. I can justify my statements on an etic level. But also I am convinced my statements are valid on an emic level, since my work is open to the people I'm studying and they, in turn, keep me from making data errors. The problems of bicultural education are of interest not only to professional anthorpologists, sociologists, linguists, and educators but also are of vital importance and interest to the parents of the bicultural child. An open, exchanging relationship works to the benefit of us, those we study, and, more importantly, to the children.

I had a social anthropology professor who used to repeat this bit of doggerel:

> Tell me where is structure found:
> In the head or on the ground? (Selby, 1971)

Of course, the answer is both. And the play of young children is one of the easier ways of moving from one level of organization to the other. By making that move, much more than structure is elucidated.

REFERENCES

Bateson, Gregory, *Steps to an Ecology of Mind*, New York: Ballantine Books, Inc., 1972, esp. p. 9-26 and 177-193.

Jakobson, Roman, "Closing Statement: Linguistics and Poetics" in Thomas A. Sebeok, ed., *Style in Language*, Cambridge, Massachusetts: MIT Press, 1960, p. 350-377.

Hall, Edward T., *The Silent Language*, New York: Doubleday and Co., Inc., 1959.

Hall, Edward T., *The Hidden Dimension*, New York: Doubleday and Co., Inc., 1966.

Selby, Henry A., Fall, 1971, graduate seminar entitled "Introduction to Social Anthropology", University of Texas, Austin.

CHAPTER III

Linguistic and Ethnosematic Analyses of Playforms

Introduction

We must be indebted to Bateson (1972) for underscoring the importance of the "this is play" message. The contributors in Chapter I have wrestled in various ways with differentiating play and not-play on an etic level for purposes of furthering play research and theory. Bateson calls our attention to the emic side of this differentiation: How do members of a species signal that their gestures and actions denote play? This question arises because so many of the items which might be included in a play set (in the mathematical sense) are also included in other sets such as an aggression set, a work set, a ritual set, and so on. Bateson uses the term frame as a convenient metaphor to describe the necessary process whereby individuals in interaction define and delimit play.

Discovering the features of these play-frames is the aim of the authors whose papers appear in this chapter. Blanchard, von Glascoe, and Boyd each use different applications of a "new" discipline in the social sciences which has been called ethnoscience by anthropologists and ethnomethodology by sociologists. Despite the considerable controversy that surrounds this new method, it does offer some very inviting techniques for locating "this is play" messages. Particularly with humans, neither observation, nor conventional interviewing is liable to turn up these messages because they are meta-communicative, a commentary on language rather than language itself.

Blanchard offers a clear exposition of the uses of ethnoscience in discovering native definitions of sports behaviors. His very interesting results show that for Anglos the union of the aggression and sports sets is quite large, whereas for Choctaws it is considerably smaller. At the etic level basketball is the same game for Anglos and Choctaws. However, connotatively, features of the game mean very different things to these two groups. In a similar vein, Manning's (Chapter IV) work shows a large union of the play and religion sets for Pentecostal as contrasted with other Protestant denominations.

Von Glascoe takes ethnoscience several steps further in using the exhaustive and complex technique for similarity judgments pioneered by Stefflre (1972). She found that within a single, homogenous society there is considerable variation in the "meaning" of games, preference for them and involvement in playing them. The native taxonomy of games changes developmentally; new game-classes are added with advancing age and others are dropped entirely. This taxonomy and the techniques employed in obtaining it are similar to Lancy's (Chapter II) work on the Kpelle play domain. For the Kpelle, there is no game category per se, but, rather, what we would recognize as games are scattered among several other subcategories of play.

In poker-playing, the "framing" process looms large in importance. Poker is a game and, in Western society, at least, games are play. Yet poker is a gambling game with the attendant possibilities of loss of money, status, etc., for players. This consequence of great loss is antithetical to many other defining attributes of play. The problem for poker-players then is to frame their activity in such a way that consistent damage to some player's morale and esteem doesn't turn the game into "not play." Boyd illustrates how three different poker-playing groups handle this framing problem. Losing players cover their losses by bravado and showmanship gaining status for "Bull-Power" to offset the loss in dollars. "Bulling the game" involves using various communication devices to deceive and confuse other players about one's hand. The messages and not the cards become the medium of play.

While the first three papers deal with delimiting the play frame and describing its contents, linguistic-play, which Greenwald discusses, arises from subtle alterations in non-play frames. To the extent that all actions and emotions are framed, slight changes in these frames may evoke a humorous response. In Greenwald's original presentation, he distributed some comic strips for illustrative purposes. To avoid copyright infringements these had to be removed for publication which is unfortunate. The comic strip uses framing in a very direct manner. Several successive frames establish a premise which is then grossly (and hopefully humorously) violated in the last frame. Greenwald's discussion also illustrates that jokes, perhaps more than any other playform, are culture-bound inasmuch as the linguistic competence necessary to understand them is usually possessed only by a native speaker. Even across subcultures "one man's joke may be another's insult" (LaFave and Mannell, Chapter VI).

REFERENCES

Bateson, Gregory. *Steps to an Ecology of Mind.* New York, Ballantine Books, 1972, pp. 177-193.

Stefflre, Volney. Some applications of multidimensional scaling to social science problems. In Romney, Shepard and Nerlove (eds.) *Multi-dimensional Scaling: Theory and Applications in the Behavioral Sciences*, Volume II, New York, Seminar Press, 1972.

TEAM SPORTS AND VIOLENCE:
AN ANTHROPOLOGICAL PERSPECTIVE

Kendall Blanchard
Middle Tennessee State University

Ethnoscience, despite its waning popularity among certain segments of the anthropological community (e.g., Keesing, 1972; Colby, 1975), provides a unique perspective for the analysis of the relationship between team sports and violence, a problem rarely addressed by ethnologists beyond simple observation

(Mead, 1955: xxv-xxvi; Murdock, 1949:90; Tiger, 1969:152).

In this article I use the techniques of ethnoscience to explore the function of team sports (e.g., basketball, baseball, football, stickball) relative to the broader realities of general conflict, aggression and violence, in specific cultural situations. It is suggested that the structure of sport behavior, including its conflict dimensions, is simply an extension of the cultural environment in which it occurs. These activities neither reduce nor increase the incidence of violence in areas beyond their own immediate domains, but rather provide an artificial context for acting out the several levels of conflict need characteristic of a particular group.

Definitions

When I use the term "sport" I am referring to an artificial form of competitive conflict that involves physical exertion, organization, and an explicit set of rules. "Conflict" I define as any form of disagreement at either individual or group levels (see Table 1). It is understood also as an essential dimension of social process, all human groups having both implicit and explicit conflict needs (Coser, 1956:151-157; Simmel, 1955). By "aggression" I mean a specialized form of conflict involving intended, if not actual, physical contact (Levels IV and V in Table 1) (Cratty, 1973;146).[1] "Violence" is viewed as unstructured aggression, a form of physical disagreement which violates the norms of conflict behavior in a given cultural situation.

Problem

The literature on athletics and violence generally suggests one of two things; that sports either lower violence levels in society at large by providing a significant cathartic experience for both participants and spectators (Ardrey, 1966; Roberts, 1972; Ryan, 1970; Scott, 1968; Wood, 1971) or conversely, that they increase the incidence of such unstructured aggression (Beisser, 1967; Berkowitz, 1962:307; Goldstein and Arms, 1971:89; Hammond and Goldman, 1961; Layman, 1968; Ogilvie and Tukko, 1971; Smith, 1972; Yablonsky, 1963). In some cases, researchers report a neutral effect of sports on violence levels (Turner, 1968; Kingsmore, 1968). Unfortunately, nothing conclusive has come out of these attempts, so that the problem remains unresolved.[2]

---

[1] At this point I limit myself to physical forms of conflict and for this reason cannot use the terms "aggression" and "hostility" interchangibly, as in the case of Berkowitz (1962:1).

[2] In a recent attempt to measure levels of hostility and anxiety as they are effected by basketball participation, I employed the "Today" form of the Multiple Affect Adjective Check List (MAACL) in several situations involving the same persons both in and out of the sport context. Results here were inconclusive, underscoring the difficulty of measuring emotional correlates of team sport involvement, either as participant or spectator.

It is my contention that the sport phenomenon, in its various expressions, functions both to resolve existing conflict in some cases and generate new conflict issues in others, but always within the limitations imposed by broader cultural regularities. This ultimately suggests that the problem is more culturological than psychological. In other words, whether or not the sporting event has cathartic results at individual levels is not the issue. The more functional question is simply how particular societies deal with conflict needs in the sport setting.

Analysis

Anthropologist Richard Sipes (1973) has analyzed the relationship between the frequency of warfare and the existence of physically combative sports

TABLE 1

Conflict (Defined componentially in levels of intensity)

Level	Dimension ➡	Individual	Individual (n)	Group	Group (n)
V	Physical: Lethal intent:	Mechanized / Non-mechanized			
IV	Physical: sublethal intent:	Mechanized / Non-mechanized			
III	Expressed: strained communication	Verbal / Non-verbal			
II	Expressed: normal communication	Verbal / Non-verbal			
I	Unexpressed				

General direction of intensity:

Anglo: ⟶

Choctaw: – – ⟶

in a sample of societies around the world and concludes that sports do *not*

act as alternative channels for the discharge of accumulable aggressive tensions. Rather than being functional alternatives, war and
combative sports activities in a society appear to be components of a
broader cultural pattern (1973:80).

Team sport behavior, as a part of that "broader cultural pattern," provides
a specialized, artificial context for the expression of learned aggression needs
through competitive forms of conflict (Scott, 1968:15). This behavior can be defined more explicitly as it is observed in any particular cultural setting by anal-
yzing its extra-structural, anti-structural, and structural components. These are
illustrated in Table 2 with data from the Ramah Navajo situation.

The extra-structural elements are those patterns that are foreign to the cultural setting in which the team sport is actually manifested, but are essential to
the particular game involved (i.e., rules, equipment). Anti-structure refers to
those forms of behavior that although they violate usual norms are permitted on
certain occasions (cf., Turner's [1969:197] concept of "liminality"). The anti-
structual component is illustrated in the typical Ramah Navajo basketball game
which usually becomes the context for the occurrence of behaviors that are not
only novel, but in fact directly contrary to normative tradition (Blanchard,
1974:11).

It is the structural component that is most important in this discussion.
These are the patterns that are consistent with tradition. Again, in the case of
the Ramah Navajos, there are many elements in the game of basketball as they
play it that are uniquely Navajo; style, purpose, strategy (Blanchard, 1974:9-10).
It is also significant that the cultural rules governing conflict behavior and the
propriety of aggression are expressed through the structural component of sport
behavior. The conflict that characterizes the team sport encounter is defined ultimately by the rules that circumscribe conflict in society at large. These rules
can be isolated using the techniques of ethnoscience and sociolinguistics. For
example, a comparison of English and Mississippi Choctaw conflict domains reveals several significant differences and suggest some distinctive characteristics of
Choctaw conflict rules (see Tables 3 and 4):

1. Choctaw has no equivalent for the English "conflict." In
most cases, the term *itibbi* ("fighting") is used, but this really only
refers to the physical levels of conflict. The phrase *itinkana keho*
(literally, "not peace") is one of several special constructions used to
translate the more generic "conflict," but a direct translation is un-
available.

2. Choctaw appears to have a less elaborate and specialized
conflict vocabulary than does English (see Tables 2 and 3). In other
words, there are fewer lexemes that refer to particular forms of disagreement. Traditionally, this distinction may not have been as

TABLE 2
Conflict defined componentially in English
(levels IV and V)

Killing	murder	stabbing beating shooting poison hanging	
	suicide		
	destruction	bombing gassing shooting	
Fighting	brawling	barroom street	
	rioting	political non-political	
	beating	thrashing clubbing chaining maiming	
	warring		
	feuding		
Contest	sport	contact non-contact	football hockey basketball baseball

TABLE 3

Conflict (iti^{n}kana keho) defined componentially in Choctaw
(levels IV and V)

abi (kill)	illichi (kill)		
	hatak abi (murder)	bali (stab) bali (beat) hu^{n}ssa (shoot)	a^{n}ya (arrows) nali (guns)
	abi (suicide)		
itibbi (fight)	tanampi (war)	itibbi (individuals) et aba ishi (groups)	
	achowa (riot)		
	itiboli (beating)		
	itibbi (contest)	laualli (play)	towa (stickball)

TABLE 4

English conflict categories as weighted by basketball players
relative to participation

Coefficient groupings:

1.0 − .6	.59 − .4	.39 − .2	.19 − .01	0

CHOCTAW

Aggressive

Rough

Angry
Furious
Mad
Agitated
Hostile

Cruel
Enraged
Mean
Outraged
Stormy
Cross

Annoyed
Bitter
Contrary
Incensed
Irritated
Unsociable
Vexed

ANGLO

Aggressive

Rough
Mean

Angry
Hostile
Furious
Mad
Cruel

Agitated
Enraged
Outraged
Annoyed

Bitter
Contrary
Cross
Incensed
Irritated
Stormy
Unsociable
Vexed

evident, but these componential definitions are based on actual informant responses rather than on dictionary entries. Many of the older Choctaw lexographies (e.g., Byington, 1871; Watkins, 1892) contain extensive conflict items, but most of these are foreign to my informants. It is likely that many of these terms have simply been forgotten. I am also suspicious that since the early dictionaries were compiled by missionaries in conjunction with their efforts to translate the Bible, much of the violence of the Old Testament may have been forcibly imposed on the new medium.

3. The distinction between killing another human being and killing an animal is made clearer in Choctaw than in English.

4. The notion of competitive sports is seen by the Choctaw as simply another form of fighting, the term for "contest" directly translatable as *itibbi*.

5. Choctaw speakers make a much clearer distinction between physical and non-physical conflict than do English speakers. This is illustrated in their greater abhorrence and avoidance of violence (see Table 1).

The difference between Choctaw and Anglo conflict meanings can be illuminated by an analysis of the ways in which both groups use conflict language in the sport context.

One of the interesting characteristics of the modern team sport phenomenon among the Choctaw today is the latter's tendency to borrow and employ English conflict terminology within the context of the new games' settings. In these situations it is legitimate for spectators and participants alike to shout threateningly to members of the other team, their own, or to the officials. For example, at a recreation league basketball game it is not uncommon to hear such expressions as "Tear off his head!" "Bust his ass!" "Kill him!" "You dumbass!" "Throw him out of here!" On the other hand, similar-meaning Choctaw expressions are not used in these same situations.

In general, it appears that the English conflict language associated with Western sports events has been borrowed by the Choctaw as a convenient complement to the basic rules and equipment of newly acquired games such as basketball (Blanchard, 1975:8-9).

In light of this observation, I developed a questionnaire in which I attemped to isolate any semantic differentials that might be involved in the way that Choctaw and Anglo basketball players viewed English conflict language relative to their participation in the game itself. I used the 132 descriptive words from the Multiple Affect Adjective Check List (MAACL) and administered the schedule to 13 Choctaw and 12 Anglo males between the ages of 17 and 21 who were actively involved in formal basketball programs as players (Blanchard, 1975:7-9). I asked each respondent to weight the items as he considered them to be prerequisite feelings to doing well in the sport. If a particular adjective were considered completely irrelevant it was left blank. If it were judged significant it was checked and scored from one to three, dependent on the degree of importance the player deemed appropriate. I then grouped the results into Choctaw and Anglo categories and scored the totals for each adjective in terms of a coefficient which reflected both the number of persons checking the word and the degree of assigned importance.

After a preliminary comparison, I removed all conflict and conciliatory terms from the general list and compared these across cultural lines. The results were instructive (see Tables 5 and 6). On the one hand, the Choctaw basketball players thought that feelings like "aggressive," "rough," and "mean," were important to the basketball experience. At this point, they varied only slightly from the expression of the Anglo players. However, when the weights assigned to the almost antynomous conciliatory adjectives were considered, the results were markedly different. Almost predictably, the Anglo athletes assigned very little importance to feelings like "cheerful," "friendly," or "loving," whereas the Choctaw saw no inherent contradiction between the two sets of terms and consistently reiterated the significance of conciliatory moods in basketball competition (see Table 6). It is quite obvious that in the basketball game situation, when Choctaw players use certain English expressions (i.e., "Let's get mean!") they do not intend the same thing as their Anglo counterparts. They are dealing with a different set of conflict needs and rules.

This tendency for the Choctaw to take greater pains to avoid more intense forms of conflict has also been isolated through the recent administration of a non-standardized projective plate test. Thirty-four Choctaw Central High School students and 29 Anglo students from Riverdale High School in Murfreesboro, Tennessee, were shown five sketches roughly depicting conflict events associated with football games. The response of the two groups were dramatically different. Where the violence was evident, the Choctaws expressed strong disagreement; the Anglos generally voiced approval. Again, where the reality of violence was not clear, the Choctaws interpreted the event as having only competitive overtones; the Anglos tended to develop these same intimations of aggression in the other more violent direction (Blanchard, 1975: 9-13).

On the basis of these observations, it is safe to suggest that upon viewing the identical conflict event (e.g., a legal tackle in the course of a football game) the Choctaw spectator sees less intensity of aggression in the contact than does the Anglo in the same situation. At similar physical contact levels the latter is going to see more implicit hostility than the former. This is illustrated in Figure 1.

The horizontal line in Figure 1 represents an increasing amount of physically harmful intent in a conflict situation and is the variable. On the other hand, the vertical line represents the several levels of actual physical encounter that can occur between human beings; from slightest to most complex; from hand

TABLE 5

English conciliatory categories as weighted by basketball players
relative to participation

Coefficient groupings:

1.0 — .6	.59 — .4	.39 — .2	.19 — .01	0

CHOCTAW

1.0 — .6	.59 — .4	.39 — .2	.19 — .01	0
Cheerful				
	Friendly			
	Understanding			
	Polite			
	Good-natured			
	Agreeable			
		Gentle		
		Peaceful		
		Loving		
		Warm		
			Kindly	
			Affectionate	
				Amiable
				Obliging

ANGLO

1.0 — .6	.59 — .4	.39 — .2	.19 — .01	0
		Understanding		
		Cheerful		
		Friendly		
		Polite		
		Warm		
			Agreeable	
			Good-natured	
				Affectionate
				Amiable
				Gentle
				Kindly
				Loving
				Obliging
				Peaceful

FIGURE 1

Ranges of permissible (structural) sub-violent aggressive behavior at the several levels of actual physical contact: Choctaw versus Anglo

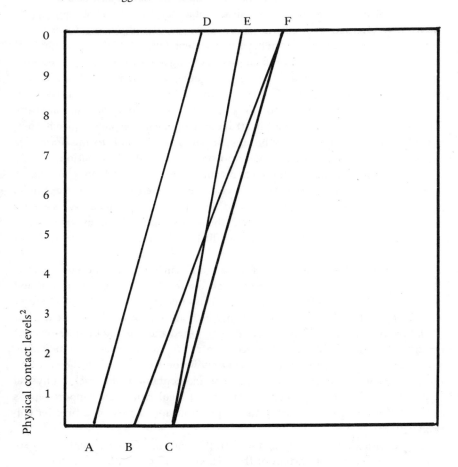

<hr />

[1]These are defined in terms of the amount of intent, explicit or implicit, presupposed in the aggressive act. This is a culturally defined variable.

[2]These are structured in terms of actual, measurable amounts of physical contact. This is an objectively determined constant cross-cutting cultural lines.

shake to full-scale warfare.

The area defined by points ACDE represents the range of permissible aggression in Choctaw society, while BCF is the normative range for Anglos in Murfreesboro, Tennessee. Lines CE and CF are the limits of aggressive intent among the Choctaw and Anglo groups, respectively, so that any expression of physical conflict falling to the right of these lines is perceived as violence.

Within this framework the Choctaw exhibit a greater range of permissible aggressive behavior at the several physical contact levels. For this reason, despite the broader alternatives available to them for the definition of violence, the Choctaws are not as likely to behave in a violent fashion at the same physical contact level as the Anglos. For example, if, during a basketball game, the Choctaw player is violated by an over-aggressive opponent, he will be less likely to react violently because of the flexibility provided by the more extensive repertoire of options open to him short of violence. The Anglo in the same situation will be more likely to opt for an unstructured aggressive response since his perceived conflict situation already borders so precariously close to the normative extreme. Violence is thus a more likely possibility in the Anglo situation.

It is significant that at the higher contact levels (6-0 in Figure 1) what is acceptable aggression for the Anglo is violence for the Choctaw. For example, certain aspects of modern warfare would be defined as legitimate aggression by the former, while the latter would see them as structurally unjustifiable. This may be a critical difference between so-called "civil" and "tribal" forms of warfare.

In general, this model of conflict is consistent with the way in which the Choctaws view themselves in aggressive encounters of all types, both past and present. Not only in athletic behavior, but also in other conflict situations (e.g., war, criminal prosecution) the extent to which aggression is allowed varies, but the normative rule (i.e., the line between structured and unstructured aggression) remains constant relative to the degree of perceived intent implicit in individual aggressive acts (see Figure 1). These acts only become violent when they are perceived to manifest a degree of hostile intent unacceptable at the level of physical contact in which it occurs. Observed structural regularities here support Sipes's (1973:80) contention that combative sport behavior is part of a broader cultural pattern.

The basic factor underlying the definition of aggression restraint in any society is the structure and extent of that group's conflict needs. These in turn are ultimately determined by ecological pressures and economic patterns. I would suggest, then, that conflict rules are initially established with reference to the range of permissible aggression at the higher levels of physical contact. In other words, the degree to which I am limited in my intent to do harm to my opponent in war will determine the way in which I am supposed to shake your hand or slap your back, as well as play games.

The variation of conflict needs from one society to another is well illus-

116

trated in the ethnographic literature. Compare, for example, the case of the eighteenth-century Cheyenne and that of the prehistoric Rio Grande Pueblos. It is obvious in which group one would expect to find more intense conflict needs, and conjunctively, a narrower range of permitted aggression, traits which would probably be manifested in their respective game behaviors.

Team sports function as means of acting out societal conflict needs. This may be either explicit or implicit in the nature of the particular sporting event. For example, among the traditional Choctaw, stickball games were arranged when open hostilities between two communities appeared imminent, specifically to avert unnecessary violence. Among the Creeks, similar contests were staged to determine community statuses as either Red (i.e., war) or White (i.e., peace) towns (Hass, 1940:479). At other times and in other places the conflict resolving function of team sport events have been less overtly evident but still effective (Blanchard, 1975a: 7-8).

On the other hand, team sport contests can become the scene of violence. This is not to say, however, that these competitive sports *cause* that violence. In all cases the aggression becomes violence only when the rules are violated. In this sense there is no "Good Clean Violence" (Kaye, 1973). By definition, violence is abnormal. When it does occur in the sport context it is not because of a failure that can be attributed to the athletic event itself, but rather to a breakdown of the broader cultural rules governing aggressive behavior. Generally, the narrower the range of permissible aggressive behavior, the more likely the restraining mechanisms to fail. Paradoxically, more violence tends to occur in those societies which constrict the manner in which aggression needs can be expressed than in those which increase options here by lowering the level of expected hostile intent in conflict situations.

Conclusion

Sport conflict is culture-specific and structurally defined. It is controlled by rules which can only be explained by reference to the broader conflict needs of society. The violence that occurs in the athletic experience is only incidentally related to the sport itself. It is more directly a product of a weakness in the regulatory controls of the cultural setting in which it happens.

Team sports function to express societal conflict needs and provide a unique setting—an explicitly competitive one—in which it is only *possible* for violence to occur.

REFERENCES

Ardrey, Robert
   1966   *The Territorial Imperative*. New York: Dell.
Beisser, A. R.
   1967   *The Madness in Sports*. New York: Appleton-Century-Crofts.

Berkowitz, L.
    1962 *Aggression: A Social-psychological Analysis.* New York: McGraw-Hill.
    1973 Simple view of aggression. In, Montagu (ed.) *Man and Aggression.* London: Oxford, pp. 39-52.
Blanchard, Kendall A.
    1974 Basketball and the culture-change process: the Rimrock Navajo case. Council on Anthropology and Education Quarterly, V(4):8-13.
    1974a Team sports and conflict resolution among the Mississippi Choctaw. Unpublished paper presented at the annual meetings of the American Anthropological Association, Mexico City (November).
    1975 An ethnoscientific analysis of athletics and conflict resolution. Unpublished report submitted to the faculty research committee, Middle Tennessee State University, Murfreesboro (January).
    1975a Choctaw conflict language and team sports: a problem in language borrowing. Unpublished paper presented at the Southeastern Conference on Linguistics, Nashville, Tennessee (March).
Byington, C.
    1871 A dictionary of the Choctaw language. Proceedings of the American Philosophical Society, Vol. 11:317-367.
Coser, Lewis A.
    1956 *The Functions of Social Conflict.* New York: Free Press.
Cratty, B. J.
    1973 *Psychology in Contemporary Sport.* Englewood Cliffs, N.J.: Prentice Hall.
Edwards, Harry
    1973 *Sociology of Sport.* Homewood, Ill.: Dorsey.
Goldstein, J. H. and R. Arms
    1971 Effects of observing athletic contests on hostility. Sociometry, 34:83-90.
Haas, M. R.
    1940 Creek inter-town relations. American Anthropologist, 42:479-490.
Hammond, L. K. and M. Goldman
    1961 Competition and noncompetition and its relationship to individual and group productivity. Sociometry, 24:46-60.
Kaye, I. N.
    1973 *Good Clean Violence: A History of College Football.* Philadelphia: Lippincott.
Kingsmore, J. M.
    1968 The effect of a professional basketball context upon the aggressive tendencies of male spectators. Unpublished Ph.D. dissertation in physical education, University of Maryland, College Park.
Layman, E. M.
    1968 Aggression in relation to play and sports. Proceedings, Second International Congress of Sport Psychology, 25-34.
McTeer, W. G.
    1972 The criminal athlete: a case study. Unpublished M.A. thesis in physical education, University of Montana, Missoula.
Mead, Margaret
    1955 *Male and Female.* New York: New American Library of World Literature.
Murdock, George P.
    1949 *Social Structure.* New York: Macmillan.
Roberts, John W.
    1972 The effects of degree of involvement upon the level of aggression of spectators before and after a university basketball game. Unpublished M.A. thesis in physical education, Mankato State, Mankato, Minnesota.

Ryan, E. D.
    1970   The cathartic effect of vigorous motor activity on aggressive behavior. Research Quarterly, 41:542-51.

Scott, J. P.
    1968   Sport and aggression. Proceedings, Second International Congress of Sport Psychology, 11-24.

Sevier, V. A.
    1973   A comparative study of aggression and related personality characteristics. Journal of Physical Education, 71:38-40; 50-51 (Nov.-Dec.).

Simmel, George
    1955   *Conflict*. Trans. K. H. Wolff. Glencoe, Ill.: The Free Press.

Sipes, Richard
    1973   War, sports and aggression: an empirical test of two rival theories. American Anthropologist, 75: 64-86.

Smith, M. D.
    1972   Assaultive behavior of young hockey players as a function of socioeconomic status and significant others' influence. Unpublished Ph.D. dissertation in physical education, University of Wisconsin, Madison.

Swanton, John R.
    1931   Source material for the social and ceremonial life of the Choctaw Indians. Bulletin, BAE, 53. Washington.

Tiger, Lionel
    1969   *Men in Groups*. New York: Random House.

Turner, E. T.
    1968   The effects of viewing college football, basketball, and wrestling on the elicited aggressive responses of male spectators. Ph.D. dissertation in physical education, University of Maryland, College Park.

Turner, Victor
    1969   *The Ritual Process*. Chicago: Aldine.

Watkins, B.
    1892   *Choctaw Definer*. Van Buren, Arkansas: Baldwin.

Woods, D. T.
    1971   A comparison of aggression between athletes and nonathletes. Unpublished M.A. thesis in physical education, University of California, Santa Barbara.

Yablonsky, L.
    1963   The new criminal. The Saturday Review (February 2): 54-56.

THE PATTERNING OF GAME PREFERENCES IN THE YUCATAN

Christine A. Von Glascoe
University of California, Irvine

Introduction

This paper describes the differential distribution of urban Yucatec females' interests in the domain of games.[1] Their involvement in the game domain is compared with their understanding of this domain. The principal findings are that:

1) attitudinal measures of involvement ('liking') are more closely correspondent with *overall amount* of game participation rather than with the *recency* of game participation; 2) children play games they do not like, while adults like games they do not play; 3) females' interests in particular games change as they pass from childhood to adolescence to adulthood; 4) of the games they like most, some are those they currently play and some are those they used to play, but in both cases there is an almost one-to-one correspondence between similarity class and recency of game playing; 5) for all females the most-liked games are members of larger rather than smaller judged similarity classes; 6) some games are judged to be members of different similarity classes for adolescents than for girls, and for women than for adolescents or girls.

Such findings as the above contribute evidence to the general thesis that games are multiply interpreted by members, regarding both interest and understanding. Scientific statements about the manner in which members play games or use game knowledge as grounds for inference and action in non-play situations will profit from such a detailed ethnographic appraisal of cognitive and affective dimensions as revealed in members' verbal and behavioral repertoires.

Since Culin's (1907) enormous description and classification of American Indian games, anthropologists by and large have assumed that games could be conceptualized and classified as completely unambiguous collections of rules and well defined playing strategies from all members' points of view. The basic underlying assumption of game taxonomists has been: one game, one interpretation.[2] Furthermore, the scientific interpretation of games, as for example in the case of Roberts et al.'s work,[3] has been predicated on Western European abstract conceptions such as probability theory and the maximization of expected value. Not only is it believed that members relate to games as clear cultural objects, but that they do so under Western European interpretations.

My experience with game players in several Yucatec communities suggests that not only are there multiple conceptualizations of games depending on members' interest and experience, but that players do not necessarily reason probabilistically or make a strategic assessment of playing alternatives in the same way as does the Western European 'rational man.'

Another simplifying assumption made by anthropological game theorists is that not only can games be unambiguously classified, but also that behavioral observations of game playing can serve as a basis for estimating members' game involvement. Eifermann, for example, assumes that one can infer involvement from the behavioral sampling of games played by Israeli children (1971). As will be shown, the (reported) incidence of play need not correlate directly with members' (reported) involvement in particular games.

Measuring the Game Knowledge and
Involvement of Merida 'Middle Class' Females

Two separate game surveys were carried out amongst the females in Merida.

In the first survey (identified as GS-1), members were asked to remember all the games they knew, and of these, whether they liked or played each individual game.[4] Such lists were produced by 15 females in each of three age sets, namely children, adolescents and adults.[5] The union of all the game lists for females produced 169 games, of which 77 of the most frequently reported games were used in the second survey.

The second survey (to be known as GS-2), involved the thirty-some-odd games that I chose as representative of each group's knowledge about, and interest in, gaming.[6] Females partitioned the game set into subsets of games that they conceived as being similar to each other.[7] They then were asked to describe the bases on which their judgments were made. Upon the completion of this task each member rank-ordered the games from most preferred to least preferred, identifying the boundaries of four preference classes within the rank order: those games they 1) liked most; 2) liked somewhat; 3) disliked somewhat; and 4) disliked most. They subsequently re-grouped the games according to those they had played 1) most; 2) somewhat less; 3) not much; 4) never. This measure will be referred to as the overall involvement score. Finally, they were asked to state how long it had been since they had played each game. This measure will be referred to as the recency score.

Measuring the Attitudinal and Behavioral Dimensions of Members' Game Involvement

In GS-1 an attempt was made to establish a stable relationship between an attitudinal measure of game interest (that is, people's feelings of liking or not liking a game) and a behavioral measure of game interest (that is, whether or not a person plays a game). The assumption was that there would be a strong positive correlation between the two judgments. As a matter of fact, the relationship between attitude and behavior was not nearly this straight-forward, as the following discussion shows.

Figure 1 shows the Venn diagrammatic representation of the proportions of each age set's game sphere that are liked and/or played. For example, it can be seen that of all the games that children report that they play, 29% of them are not liked, whereas of all the games they report that they like, only 3% of them are not played. Of all the games that children know, only 5% of them are neither played nor liked. For adolescents, 13% of the games they play are not liked, and 21% of the games that they like are not played. Of all the games known by adolescents, 53% are neither liked nor played. In the case of adults, 12% of the games they play are not liked, while 40% of the games they like are not played. Of all the games known by adults, 40% are neither liked nor played. The data thus show an age-related decrease in the number of games that females play, as well as a decrease in the correlation between the games that they play and the games that they like. Furthermore, as one grows older, the game domain moves from play-dominated to preference-dominated, as seen in the fact that the

121

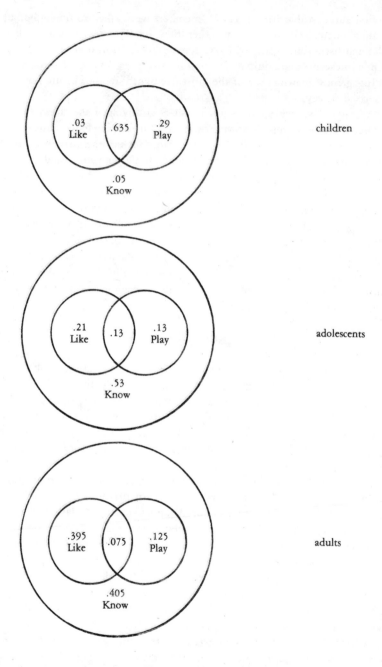

Figure 1:   Venn Diagramatic Representations of the Proportions of Each Age
Set's Game Sphere that are 'Liked' and/or 'Played'

attitudinal dimension of interest (as measured by reported preferences), while declining with the behavioral report of play, does so at a slower rate.

In·the search for a behavior measure of game interest that is more closely associated with the attitudinal measure of game interest, I distinguished between recency of involvement and overall life involvement. Spearman rank-order correlations among the three measures of interest ('like,' 'recency of play' and 'overall amount of play') show the behavioral measure to be better represented by members' reports about how much rather than how recently they have played a game. Specifically, the preference and overall involvement measures correlate at the .01 level for all age groups. The preference and recency measures, while correlated at the .01 level for adolescents, are only directionally correlated for the adults, and totally non-correlated for the children. The measures of recency and overall involvement correlate at the .01 level for adolescents, the .05 level for adults, and are non-correlated for children.

The above findings suggest that relatively high levels of interest can be maintained in the absence of actual participation. This corresponds with findings reported in the next section that adults prefer games that they currently play as well as games with which they have not been actively involved since their childhood.

The Relation Between Members'
Game Interest and Understanding

Two specific relationships are established between members' interest and understanding of games. The first is the relationship between the behavioral measure of interest called 'recency of play,' and one of the principal characterizations of understanding, namely the members' appraisal of the similarity relations existing among the several games of their respective game sets. The basic finding is that, for the two older groups, games that fall in the same recency of play categories map onto particular similarity classes, rather than being divided among them.

The second relationship shows that the most highly preferred games tend to be embedded in similarity classes that contain a greater number of games than do the similarity classes whose members are not highly preferred.

Figures 2-4 show how the highly preferred games of each respective age set, grouped on the basis of how recently they were played, map onto the similarity structure of the games. Figure 2 shows that the majority of the games preferred by women fall into two similarity clusters and into two distinct 'recency' groupings. Furthermore, the two are correlated. That is, games that are cognitively similar to each other and are highly preferred receive similar scores on the 'recency of involvement' measure. Figure 3 shows that the same holds for adolescents. The children's mapping (Figure 4) shows some overlap between classes, such that the 'recency' scores of the preferred games from any particular similarity cluster are not concordant.

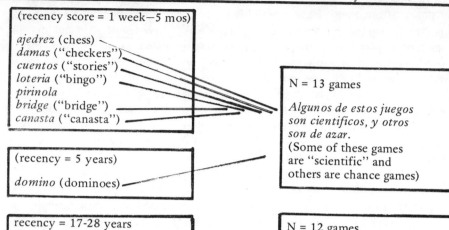

Games from the top third of
the adults' preference rank-
order, grouped by mean
recency of involvement

Mapping of highly
preferred games onto
the similarity structure

(recency score = 1 week–5 mos)

ajedrez (chess)
damas ("checkers")
cuentos ("stories")
loteria ("bingo")
pirinola
bridge ("bridge")
canasta ("canasta")

N = 13 games

*Algunos de estos juegos
son cientificos, y otros
son de azar.*
(Some of these games
are "scientific" and
others are chance games)

(recency = 5 years)

domino (dominoes)

(recency = 17-28 years)

a la rueda de San Miguel
las estatuas de marfil
la huerfanita
el lobo
Maria Blanca
la botella ("spin the bottle")
la pajara pinta

N = 12 games

*En estos juegos se forman
un circulo y dan vueltas,
tomados de las manos, y
cantando.* (In these
games the players form
a circle that rotates while
they sing and hold hands).

N = 9 games

*Son juegos en cuales se
enfilan.* (These are games
in which the players form
lines).

N = 2 games

Son juegos de buscar.
(These are 'searching'
games).

Figure 2:   The Relation Between the
Recency of Play and the
Cognitive Similarity of
Games Preferred by Adults

N = 2 games

*Son juegos que requieren
mucha imaginacion.*
(These games require much
imagination).

Games from the top third of
the adolescents' preference
rank-order, grouped by mean
recency of involvement

Mapping of highly
preferred games onto
the similarity structure

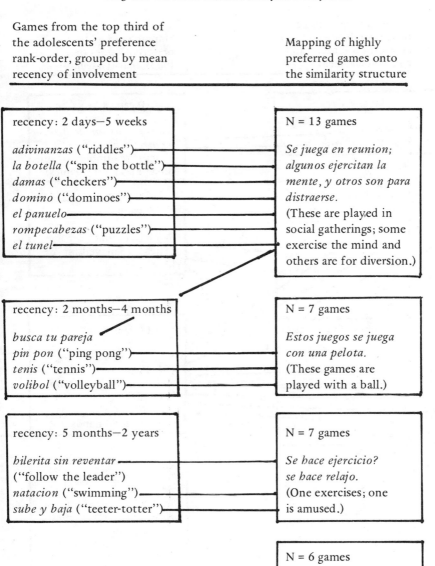

recency: 2 days—5 weeks

adivinanzas ("riddles")
la botella ("spin the bottle")
damas ("checkers")
domino ("dominoes")
el panuelo
rompecabezas ("puzzles")
el tunel

N = 13 games

Se juega en reunion;
algunos ejercitan la
mente, y otros son para
distraerse.
(These are played in
social gatherings; some
exercise the mind and
others are for diversion.)

recency: 2 months—4 months

busca tu pareja
pin pon ("ping pong")
tenis ("tennis")
volibol ("volleyball")

N = 7 games

Estos juegos se juega
con una pelota.
(These games are
played with a ball.)

recency: 5 months—2 years

hilerita sin reventar
("follow the leader")
natacion ("swimming")
sube y baja ("teeter-totter")

N = 7 games

Se hace ejercicio?
se hace relajo.
(One exercises; one
is amused.)

N = 6 games

Estos juegos son
de correr.
(These are running
games.)

Figure 3: The Relation Between the Recency of Play and the Cognitive Similarity of Games Preferred by Adolescents

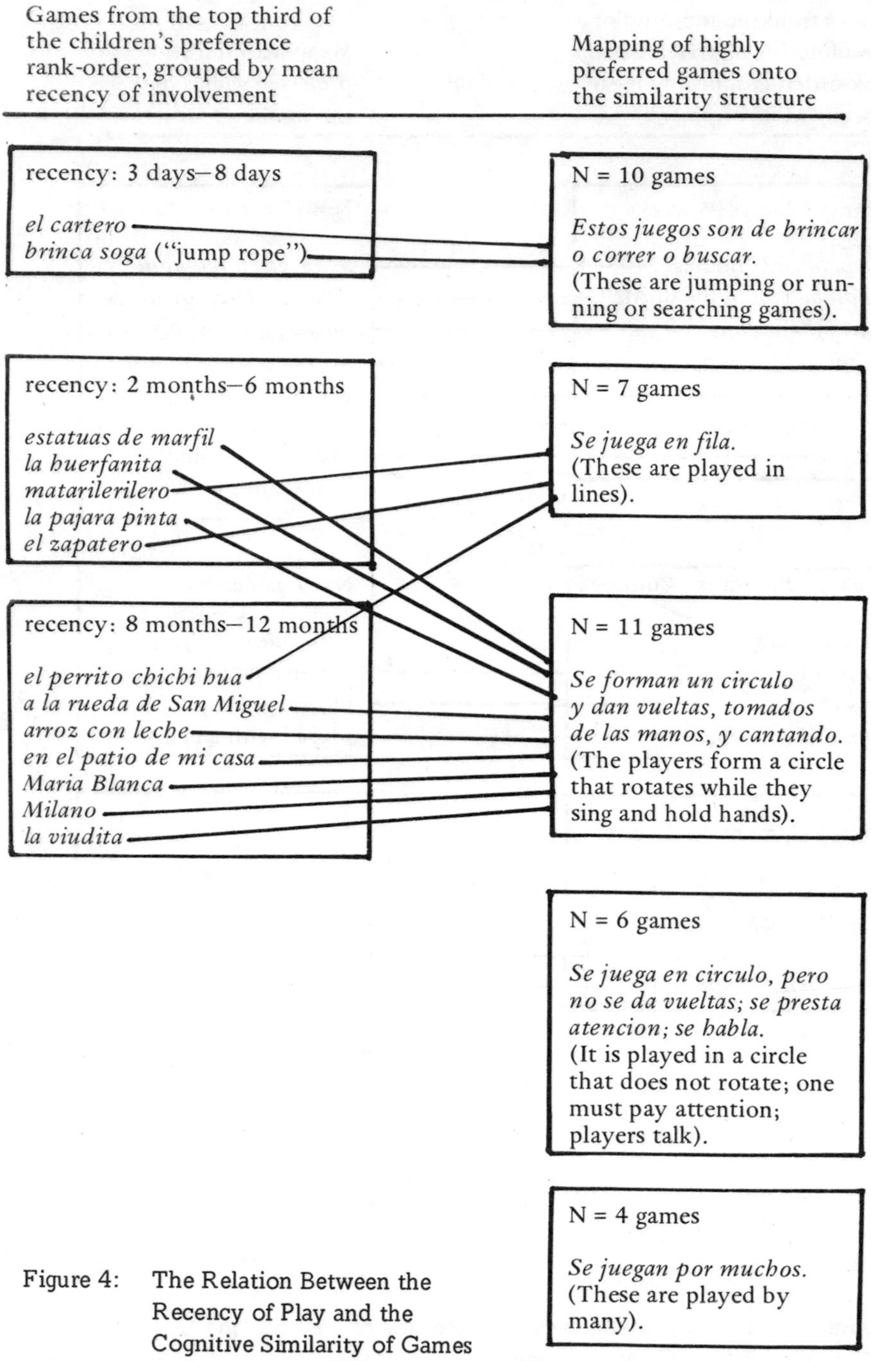

Games from the top third of
the children's preference
rank-order, grouped by mean
recency of involvement

Mapping of highly
preferred games onto
the similarity structure

recency: 3 days—8 days

el cartero
brinca soga ("jump rope")

N = 10 games

*Estos juegos son de brincar
o correr o buscar.*
(These are jumping or running or searching games).

recency: 2 months—6 months

estatuas de marfil
la huerfanita
matarilerilero
la pajara pinta
el zapatero

N = 7 games

Se juega en fila.
(These are played in
lines).

recency: 8 months—12 months

el perrito chichi hua
a la rueda de San Miguel
arroz con leche
en el patio de mi casa
Maria Blanca
Milano
la viudita

N = 11 games

*Se forman un circulo
y dan vueltas, tomados
de las manos, y cantando.*
(The players form a circle
that rotates while they
sing and hold hands).

N = 6 games

*Se juega en circulo, pero
no se da vueltas; se presta
atencion; se habla.*
(It is played in a circle
that does not rotate; one
must pay attention;
players talk).

N = 4 games

Se juegan por muchos.
(These are played by
many).

Figure 4: The Relation Between the
Recency of Play and the
Cognitive Similarity of Games
Preferred by Children

An old ethnoscientific assumption is that a domain's categories only exist as long as members maintain interest in them. That is to say that members' categories must be embedded in the cognitive processes of reasoning and reflection, and in the behavioral process of goal-directed action. Furthermore, it has been assumed that classificatory elaboration takes place in the cognitive areas of central interest. If this is true, then it should be the largest similarity clusters that contain the greatest number of preferred games. To test this hypothesis I rank-ordered the similarity clusters from largest to smallest and computed the proportions of above-median and below-median groups whose members were highly preferred. For all three age groups the hypothesis is confirmed. That is, similarity clusters that are above the median in size contain an average of 51% preferred games, while similarity clusters that are below the median in size contain only 18% preferred games. I cite this as evidence that low interest is commensurate with the region of the domain that has relatively sparsely populated similarity clusters.

The Evolution of Game Interest Through Age Groups

Intergroup comparison of the game inventories and the similarity structures in which they are embedded shows that differences in game interest and understanding change with age. Changes occur both in interest (as expressed by the preference rankings), and in cognitive understanding (as expressed by changes in both the membership of similarity clusters and the existence of whole clusters). In terms of cognitive understanding, the following kinds of changes are seen: 1) games are both added to and deleted from similarity clusters whose intensional definition remains constant (this occurs between non-adjacent as well as adjacent age sets); 2) games are added to or deleted from similarity clusters whose intensional definition changes concomitantly; 3) not only does the membership of similarity clusters change, but whole classes of games appear and disappear (sometimes to reappear later). In terms of attitudinal changes, games move from one level of interest/preference to another. Examples of the above-named kinds of changes are to follow.

An example of the case where games are added to and deleted from similarity clusters whose intensional definition remains constant is seen between the children and the adults vis-a-vis "running" games. The children's inventory includes *pesca pesca* ("tag"), *pesca china* "stoop tag"), *pelota* ("ball") and *la abuelita*, while the adults' inventory of "running" games is composed of *pesca pesca*, *pelota* and *encantados* (another form of "tag"). Both groups agree that the primary feature of these games is that running takes place, and additions or deletions have no effect on this conception.

Condition (2), where a change in the composition of a similarity cluster is accompanied by a change in the intensional definition of that cluster, occurs between the adolescents and the adults vis-a-vis the set of games that are played in "social gatherings" (refer to Figure 5). For the adolescents, this group of

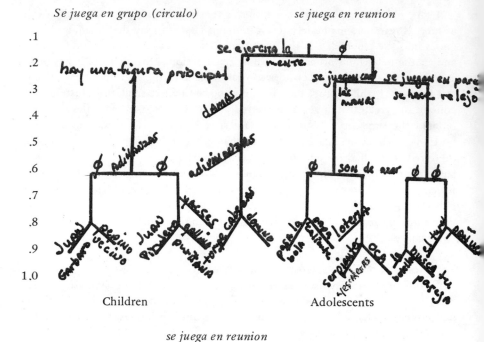

Figure 5: Classificatory Change as Seen in Comparable Similarity Clusters of the Three Age Groups of Merida Females (game names written diagonally, features written horizontally)

games contains three major subsets, one of which contains three games of "chance." For them, the primary distinction is that if a game does not "exercise the mind" it is either "played with the hands" or played in "couples." The adults' set of games that are played in "social gatherings," however, is composed half of "scientific games" and half of "chance games." For them, "scientific games" are either played on a "checker board" or in a "group of people." Similarly their "chance games" are either played with "dice" or in "groups of people."

Another example of condition (2) can be seen in the simultaneous development of a game cluster and the movement of the game *adivinanzas* (riddles) into it. Figure 5 shows that *adivinanzas* is classified by children as being one of the "circle" games that involve "central figures." For the adolescents *adivinanzas* is part of the large class of games that are played in "social gatherings," and is seen primarily as a game which "exercises the mind." Adults recognize that the game not only helps to "develop the mind," but that it is "scientific." That is to say that the adults recognize the possibility that there is an available heuristic that allows the game to be played in a calculated way, and that this is a feature of the game rather than of the game playing process. The differential composition and conceptualization of this game class can thus be seen as part of an evolutionary chain of development, wherein there is an age-related elaboration of game classes. The classificatory shift can be seen in Table 1, which shows the number of members from each age group, who used each feature in describing the ways in which *adivinanzas* is similar to the other games. In summary, it can be seen that the description of *adivinanzas* across the three age groups moves from a description of the roles and social nature of the game to a characterization of the difficulty of being able to puzzle out a solution, and finally to the location of the game among the other games that must be played "scientifically." It is important to notice that there are no other "scientific" games in the children's game set. While the adolescents' game set includes games that will be called "scientific" by the adults, they are seen by the adolescents as games that require thinking, but not of a specifiable kind.

The third condition of game evolution is where whole classificatory sets appear or disappear. For example, Figure 6 shows *pelota* ("ball") to exist in the child's similarity structure as a "running" game. In their whole game set *pelota* is the only game that is played with a ball (with the exception of *yacses* ("jacks")), which is clearly conceptualized differently (see Figure 5)). The adolescents, on the other hand, elaborate a whole class of ball games, some of which are distinguished by the use of "rackets." Adults, however, are apparently no longer interested in such games. For them, *pelota* recedes to the status of a "running" game and is, as in the case of the children, the only game in the whole adult inventory that uses a ball.

Another case of the appearance and disappearance of a whole classificatory set is shown in Figure 5. This is a game set which neither exists in content

TABLE 1

The Differential Use of Features With Which Members Described
the Similarity Between *Adivinanzas* and Other Games

Descriptive Feature	Children	Adolescents	Adults
requiere imaginacion (it requires imagination)	2		
hay una figure principal (there is a central figure)	3		
se juega en circulo (grupo) (it is played in a group)	6	2	6
se pone atencion (one must pay attention)		2	7
se anima (one becomes excited)		3	
se juega en reunion (it is played in social gatherings)		4	2
ejercita la mente (one exercises the mind)		11	3
sirve para desarrollar (rapidez de) la mente (it serves to develop mental acuity)			4
es un juego cientifico (it is a scientific game)			6

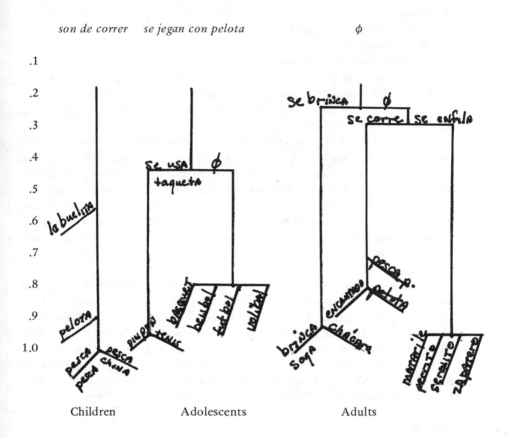

Figure 6:   The Evolution and Devolution of a Game Class as Shown by the
Antecedent (children's), Fully Elaborated (adolescents') and Vesti-
gal (adults') Environments of *Pelota* (game names written diagonally,
descriptive features written horizontally).

nor in descriptive features among the children. For the adolescents they are games that are played in social gatherings, and in which the players amuse and divert themselves. The overwhelming characteristic that is recognized by these girls is that the games are played in "couples." The women's game inventory includes only one of these games (la botella), and for them it is embedded in a group of games that are played in "groups" and which "require attention" on the part of the players.

A final example of condition (3) is the case where a game or a set of games is preferred by persons of non-adjacent age classes. For example, the set of games that are highly preferred by the children, and includes such games as la huerfanita and Maria Blanca is unimportant to the adolescents, but reappears as highly preferred by the adults.

The assessment of preferential differences is problematic in the sense that the 'same' game is conceived, and therefore implicitly played, differently. For example, the game adivinanzas ("riddles") is favored by only three children but by 14 adolescents. However, the fact that the skill that is required to perform well at adivinanzas differs in the conception of each group suggests that it may be played as a different game by each of them. Since I have no data that speak to the question of why people prefer particular games, preference can only make sense in relation to a changing definition of what constitutes cognitive awareness.

The movement of particular games along the preference axis shows that in about half of the cases differential preferences are associated with differential classification/description. This suggests that as a game moves in the similarity structure (that is, as the players' conceptions of the game change) the possibilities of re-evaluation increase. Thus, for example, as a child's conception of adivinanzas changes, so can their dislike of it change. Going in the opposite direction, the conceptual changes that take place vis-a-vis la botella between adolescence and adulthood correspond to a decrease in people's preference for it.

Discussion

My findings that games are differentially identified, classified and evaluated by the several members of a community, can be confirmed by anyone who examines game involvement in detail using members' reports of their attitudes about and their interest in games, as well as behavioral observations. The primary evidential thrust in this paper has been with regard to members' interest in games, and the way these interests articulate with the cognitive organization of the game space. Specifically, the findings are: 1) the attitudinal (preference) measure of play is most closely associated with the summary behavioral measure of total time played; 2) generally speaking the ratio of prefer to play increases as a function of age; 3) the classes of the similarity structure correspond with classes of preferred games defined in terms of recency of play for adolescents and adults; 4) by and large the preferred games are embedded in larger, rather than smaller similarity classes; 5) age-related changes occur in both the cognitive and preferential structuring of the domain.

I know of no thorough discussion of the relation between classificatory structures and evaluative structures. To generalize from the foregoing data, I suggest that people's interest and involvement in particular games waxes and wanes. The cognitive attitudes develop along with interest. As interest sharpens the person carries out a more and more explicit rational inquiry into the possibilities for identifying and classifying the states of affairs (games). One of the results is the ability to classify a larger number of just noticeably different concepts.[8]

The larger intention of this paper has been to support the idea that the classification of games must, with the now available procedures, be carried out in terms of members' conceptions of category systems.

NOTES

[1]The data discussed in this paper represent a portion of a larger study carried out by the author in two Spanish speaking communities of the Yucatan (von Glascoe 1975).

[2]For a discussion of this issue see von Glascoe, 1974 and 1975.

[3]A notable exception is the detailed study of tick-tac-toe as carried out by Sutton-Smith and Roberts (1967).

[4]For a complete description and rationale of the procedure see von Glascoe 1975, pp. 24-25.

[5]The rationale for this approach grew out of my previous studies where age and sex were cited by respondents as being major dimensions in terms of which the game domain is cognitively organized. Its efficacy was later verified by the fact that indices of game knowledge, preference and involvement plotted across individuals partitioned the overall population into groups which fairly correspond with the demographic variables of age and sex (von Glascoe, 1974).

[6]Criteria for this judgment are fully explained in von Glascoe, 1975.

[7]Judgments were made on the basis of each member's subjective interpretation of the word 'similarity.' No cues were given by the investigator concerning the possible criteria for such judgments. The groups could be of any number and any size.

[8]I have elsewhere demonstrated the relationship between cognitive understanding and larger, rather than smaller groupings in the game classification task ('similarity sort') (1975).

REFERENCES

Culin, Stewart
    1907 *Games of the North American Indians.* 24th Annual Report of the Bureau of American Ethnology to the Secretary of the Smithsonian Institution, 1902-1903, by W. H. Holmes, Chief. Washington, D.C.: U.S. Government Printing Office. pp. 3-846.
Eifermann, Rivka R.
    1971 *Determinants of Children's Game Styles.* Jerusalem: The Israeli Academy of Sciences and Humanities.

Roberts, John M., Malcolm Arth and Robert Bush
    1959   *Games in Culture*. American Anthropologist 61:597-605.
Sutton-Smith, Brian and John M. Roberts
    1967   *Studies of an Elementary Game of Strategy*. Genetic Psychology Monographs. 75:3-42.
von Glascoe, Christine
    1974   *Evidence for Multiple Cognitive Realities in Yucatec Game Cognition*. Paper presented at the 1974 Annual Meeting of the American Anthropological Association (to be published in the International Journal of the Sociology of Language).
von Glascoe, Christine
    1975   *The Case for Multiple Game Cognitions in the Yucatan* (unpublished doctoral dissertation). University of California, Irvine.

POKER PLAYING AS A DRAMATURGICAL EVENT: BULL POWER, THE MEANING AND COMMITMENT FOR EFFICACIOUS GAMESMANSHIP

Susan H. Boyd
University of Montana

My paper concerns symbolic interactions of poker players who frequent three different commercial gaming establishments in Missoula, Montana. I chose a game situation bounded by a distinct physical setting and a micro-environment in which the behavior of the participants was governed by game etiquette, rules of procedure and game meanings. Inspiration for this field research was stimulated by Manning's analysis of club environments in Bermuda (Manning 1973) and Geertz's interpretive analysis of deep play in the Balinese cockfight (Geertz 1973). Deep play, being in over one's head with more to lose than gain during a game, prompted another mode of analysis of the poker games: Goffman's approach to social interaction as a dramaturgical event (Goffman 1961 and 1967). Rather than describe functional mechanics of the poker game, I explore its social semantics as webs of significance spun by the *dramatis personae* who also participate in the symbolic framework of wider society.

I explore the three games in relation to value constellations with these possibilities:

1)   What goes on at these establishments bears no relation to the lives and thoughts of patrons in their everyday existence;

2)   Poker games and "real" life are somehow related but patrons of the three bars come from different social milieu and generational groups; consequently they think, act and play differently; and

3) Despite differences in patrons' ages and social milieu, there is something that makes their play activity distinctly alike, i.e., there is a common symbol system for all participants of the gaming encounters.

My task is to identify referents and contents of play symbolism and to discover key themes and meanings of the gaming experience as well as commitment to the competitive nature of the poker game. As a dramaturgical event, poker games are analyzed as innovative, symbolic context for social interaction and role formation; i.e., the explication and manipulation of sanctioned or stigmatized statuses of players. Play is instrumental for the creation of interpretive insights, heightened moods and actions in the assimilation and experience of socially relevant themes and symbols. Poker games become dramatic foci that behave more like prisms than mirrors; i.e., in the play environment, there is a refraction of social dialogues, choruses and monologues.

As my fieldwork progressed, I discovered bundled constellations of meaning and action which centered around a general presentation of American life—financial success as a key prestige factor for individual status within the American community. The participants frequently mentioned, enacted or alluded to thematic contents of the games; making or losing money, how to intimidate players and not be intimidated yourself, manipulation by deceit and sexual identity of males and females.

Within the gaming environment, I discovered symbols and action fields that provided a framework and explanation of statuses and male identity (Turner 1967). The symbols and action fields are represented by the semantic domain of Bull Power and the game action strategy of *bulling the game*. Bulling strategy and player typologies associated with action categories (playing tight or loose) and status categories (winner versus loser) are recognized by only two of the three gaming groups.

1) The players at the Oxford Bar, aged 55-82, represent occupational groups who are skilled and unskilled blue-collar workers, civil service employees and retirees.

2) The Oxfordians are contrasted with the players of the Stockman Bar. Most of the Stockmen, aged 27-58, are businessmen and professionals with some college experience or advanced vocational training.

The third game, at the Top Hat Bar, involved participants who had fragmented educational and occupational experiences. Top Hatters, aged 20-25, did not enact social drama or symbolic contents of the semantic domain of Bull Power.

Bull Power contains a polemic and distinctive feature of game strategy and meanings as explicated by the players. A dichotomy of actors is represented by *Tight Ass* players versus *Loose Ass* players. A *Tightie* refers to a player who is a defensive strategist, since he waits for *the nuts* (a *cinch* or *pat hand*) and *checks* (passes) rather than raising the bid. Tighties do not rely on luck for game "strategy." A Loosey is an offensive strategist who attempts to build *the nuts*, *bets* and *raises* heavily and relies on luck to make his *cinch hand*. Both Tighties and Looseys believe in the efficacy of their respective philosophies of game management; Tighties play a game of statistical probabilities, whereas Looseys build action with luck in mind.

A group of descriptive terms relates to Bull Power and the statuses and strategy relationships of the players: *bull shitting*, the deception of players; *bulls*, high-status personae,[1] and *bulling the game*, shoving in a large raise in bid to force opponents out of *the action*. Bulling is the most frequently enacted action strategy used to intimidate opponents and to conceal the contents of one's hand. The strategy is used to increase the probability that a Tightie will fold when not holding the nuts and that a Loosey will be hard pressed to outdraw or outwit the player who is bulling.

Superficially, two criteria are essential for bulling the game: a sizable number of chips and the ability to initiate and perpetuate aggressive strategy, even while holding mediocre or bad hands. If one bumps opponents with a formidable raise and scares them, he literally buys the pot. If you are a *high roller* who manipulates a large stack of chips, you can psychologically and finally break opponents while holding poor hands. It becomes a question of effective competition by sham and aggression. On the surface, Bull Power is overtly aggressive gamesmanship which dazzles and confuses players with less guts and money. However, competition in poker games is complicated by covert means to bull the game. For example, a player who is virtually unsystematic in play is the enigmatic screwball, a Loosey who plays everything in sight, or a clever Tightie who takes well-timed risks. Bulling the game can mean that a tight player is *running scared*; he reverses the imputed threat, opting for an offensive strategy of a Loosey, by plowing in with a large raise and *flashing* (exposing) his power cards to opponents. Deceptive strategies, such as *talking loose* while playing tight, misrepresent a player's intentions.

A Loose Ass who bulls the game views statistical probabilities as a positive factor during his performance (the odds are in his favor) whereas a Tightie defensively appraises odds to determine who might be statistically capable of beating his hand. House owners and managers, high-status friends of the house or buffoon entertainers may enter the game and bull with house money to build action, excitement and most certainly the house rake-off. Some bulls rely on house backing, while others rely on sheer aggressive output or mental prowess.

To arrive at player explanations and descriptions of constituents for winners and losers, I asked players to arrange index cards with action strategies into categories of Tight versus Loose players, and later to arrange cards in categories of winners versus losers.[2] I intended to discover:

1) game action strategies used by Tighties versus Looseys;
2) effective strategies versus ineffectual strategies in categories of

136

winners versus losers; and

3) whether there was a mediatory class of players who borrowed strategies from both Tighties and Looseys.

I found that a Tightie is more prone to break even, whereas a Loosey wins and loses the larger amounts of money. A conservative player who takes well-timed risks not only mediates action strategies but also statuses. The conservative risk-taker successfully combines criteria of both Tighties and Looseys and consistently wins Big Money. Nonetheless, the Loosey's derring-do is prized by some because of its overt displays of courage and aggressive gamesmanship. Tighties partake of common sense and patiently weigh the frequency of pat hands.

The most graphic illustration of the difference between Tighties and Looseys was verbalized by a kibbitzer at the Oxford, and provides a prime example of the games kibbitzers play as spectator-interactionists. During one evening a player won consistently. When asked by the kibbitzer how he managed to do so, the player replied, "Brains? Hell! Give me luck. It's just luck." These statements contradict the player's operational philosophy, since he assesses game strategy based on statistical odds. The kibbitzer piped up with the following analysis of winning in a poker game:

> That's right. It's luck, you betcha. Ya don't need brains. Give me luck anytime. Brains are for shit. Brains is shit.

The kibbitzer is bull shitting, of course, and happens to be one of the "all time great Tighties" in Missoulian poker circles. However, by reaffirming the Loosey's philosophy of winning, the myth is retained and given credence. Tighties and conservatives milk the players who rely on luck, "lay of the cards," or who are emotionally jacked on the excitement of winning easy money. Analytically speaking, the Looseys are exegetically mythologized as the stereotyped gambler, whereas Tighties are mental bulls who are operationally defined as the "Statistics Man" (Turner 1967). The winningest bull combines a bit of gumption and experience in risk taking with brains; he is the mediatory class of players.

Highly manipulative players code-switch[3] between Tighties and Looseys as the situation demands to manipulate the philosophical rift, i.e., to maximize opponent's beliefs. Manipulative players will choose participation to act out certain roles or statuses for the audience. They actuate the most efficacious posture for winning, and most nearly epitomize the fellow who loves smart dealing while playing a ruthless game of quick decision-making, i.e., when to deceive and when to *pull in his horns*. The most successful player, in terms of winning money without cancelling his victories, bulls the game mentally and sometimes physically to control the rhythm of play and emotional expectations of his opponents. He uses stratifications and alienations of Tighties and Looseys to cajole and soothe the opponents.

The stigmatic status of being a loser, a fool who is easily duped, is rationalized by Looseys as "brains is shit" versus a belief of Tighties that "luck is shit." This is most poignantly expressed in social terms of the bovine metaphor of "Oxen and Stockmen," who is the possessor of a successful social self and who is possessed. In the play environment, thematic foci of money, sex, intimidation and lying are defended from polar stances. Manhood is defined as mental skills versus emotionally charged physical skills. Skills are tested in deceptive. strategies; who is deceiving whom with ritual distinctions between those who believe in luck as opposed to those who do not, and player analyses of the natural world, couched in terms of a "scientific" approach to gamesmanship, rather than the "super natural" world of Lady Luck.

Within the status hierarchy of the Oxford house, shills, friendship personae and managers or owners have different styles of play based on well-demarcated statuses. Shills are usually thought of as losers and are required to play tight. Since shills do not have money to make money, they are emasculated by controls of the house; shills represent steers. Owners and managers, like bulls of the stock market, pump up the action and increase the cash volume in the games, while shills initiate and sometimes hold a game together by a stable and less flashy style of play. High-status friends of the house and buffoon entertainers use house money to build action. It is not unusual for house personae to manipulate cash flow to the extent that they "rob from the rich and give to the poor."

The constant patter of sexual imagery in the bovine metaphor counterbalances and explicates womanhood in categories and symbols of powerlessness. Sexual imagery in the poker games is a symbolic affirmation of powerful social and political competition for statuses and roles; bulls can have lots of cash or bulls are mentally alert and clever. Cognitive maps of Bull Power envelop discrepancies and the nature of the social gaming world; and failure of gaming expertise is translated into the imagery of being sexually deprived of the nuts. To put a lock on someone's nuts is a social and economic besting of male friends, neighbors and enemies. Bulls as American males are explicated not only in sexually convincing imagery but also in a hierarchy of moneymakers and smart dealers. Symbols of the semantic domain of Bull Power cluster sensory and obligatory experiences of socialization and gamesmanship of the American man.

Comparative analyses of symbolic interaction and perceptions of institutional structures provide some interesting insights to social dramas played within these poker games. As a dramaturgical event, things and events in play are seen as decisions to act, enact and challenge The Social Order, i.e., each play environment produced a social currency of communicative forms and images of order and disorder (Peacock 1968 and Munn 1973). Legalization of gambling presents the Oxford personae with an adaptive socialization, since the prior illegal game status now becomes a respectable means to pursue the American Dream. Oxfordians are attempting to clothe former stigmatic aura with new garments of moral order and respectability, including new formulations of spatial-behavioral contexts. Formerly, Oxfordians perceived themselves to be pariahs, especially those who chalked up a record with The Law. Now Oxfordian social face is rationalized in lines of law-abiding entrepreneurism. Personae of the Oxford, so long enacting the socio-economic system as fantasy, are now presented with a social reality of means in the play environment. Oxford myths are loaded with a folk level model of "justice prevails," i.e., myths are mini-morality plays stressing the demise of cheaters.

In contrast to the Oxfordians, the youngsters of the Top Hat interact on the basis of their perceptions and strivings for a transvaluation of American society. Top Hatters recite new myths and symbols, which portray alternatives to The System and create new charters for action. According to Top Hatters' perceptions, the System stinks, and Top Hatters enact stigmatic statuses with open disrespect, especially the use of illegal drugs and anti-capitalistic rhetoric. Top Hatters' claims that the poker game is not a moneymaker are reinforced by a pervasive egalitarianism. Whereas the killing of ambition to make money and love of smart dealing is an untenable civic position in the eyes of the Oxfordians, Top Hatters enact social dramas designed to kill the old economic and political order.[4] Top Hatters lack a commitment to compete; gamesmanship centers on socializing within the peer group. Top Hatters were the only poker players who sang during the games.

Although the game rules and etiquette of the Stockman resembles that of the Oxfordians, there are more covert experiential and intellectual parameters of bulling the game. Stockmen are community interactionists who enact multidimensional roles based on wider participation in social and economic networks of Missoula. The games of the Oxford and its setting contain a different commitment to a life style unique to Oxford personae who are involved in ramified gambling interests, like horse racing and sports cars; however, there is no core group of Stockmen nor overwhelming sense of Stockmen identity attached to the play environment.

Symbolic interaction and commitment to deep play can be summarized as follows:

1) Oxfordians' life style is highly aggressive, hierarchically ordered and represented the most sex-linked contents used for taunting and bulling the game. Oxfordians define a traditional set of criteria for manhood, including displays of mock and real physical threat-making. In contrast to Oxfordians, Stockmen rarely used sex-linked topics for taunting. Stockmen chose a gentleman's game with polite and orderly behaviors. Skill and covert means to bull the game are main parameters for Stockman game expertise,and play is more overtly defensive. The Top Hat play world uses sex-linked topics as pun or word play, and conspicuous egalitarianism is valued above competition.

The complex criteria for successful competition and

financial manipulation are most eagerly sought after by the Oxfordians who are earnestly engaged in deep play, most nearly attained by the Stockmen and challenged openly by Top Hatters. Poker games offer a structure and means for enacting emotionally and intellectually convincing experience for a traditional American world view and ethos of Oxfordians and Stockmen. However, Top Hatters use the poker structure to explicate their dissatisfaction with statuses based on competition and financial success.

2) An intriguing feature of the play world are those players who adjust to diverse game and social environments. Transitional personae move from one game and one house to the next with facility by adjusting to appropriate emotions, linguistic-paralinguistic behaviors and philosophies of the gaming encounters. Transitional personae are most adept and perceive themselves as socializing agents with various social postures, faces and lines. Transitionals appear to enjoy a transcendent quality of play; they toy with faces, lines, postures and guises for the pure pleasure of mental and social playwriting. Unlike a majority of Oxford personae, who are earnestly engaged in deep play, transitionals subsume moneymaking as part of the pleasurable experience of pure play. Top Hatters play seriously with faces and lines of social transvaluation, but code-switch less frequently from the security of peer group games. Since there is an emergence and transcendence of the ordinary world, transitional and expert poker players are social artists who synthesize behaviors from sensory, situational and ideational realms of experience.

3) The play world is a great "place" to observe man as symbolizer, actor and acter. An interpretive approach for the ethnography of play may shed some light on "meaningfulness," i.e., constituents with different sensibilities or logics within sensory, situational and ideational experience. Hearing only one authentic voice is simply not enough when faced with multifaceted behavior in play. The approach of interpretive anthropology seeks a pluralism of play forms and contents that resonate in multiple meanings within a dynamic setting of playful social interaction.

NOTES

[1] *Bull cook* refers to the head hash slinger of a restaurant. In personal correspondence, Dr. Edward Norbeck states that a bull cook in a logging camp has a very low status. It is interesting to note the relative or variable status of bull cooks (as perceived internally and

externally) in logging camps, prisons and restaurants.

[2] I used techniques which are fully described in Berlin, Breedlove and Raven (1970); however, action and status typologies did not have a rigid 1:1 fit like material referents of botanical taxonomies.

[3] Code-switching not only refers to alterations from "transactional to personal styles" (Gumperz 1964) but also manipulation of language (Hymes 1974 and Burke 1962); stylistic and paralinguistic variation (Albert 1964 and Ervin-Tripp 1964); and nominal versus verbal stylization by Tighties and Looseys (Wells 1960).

[4] Process and drama are discussed in Peacock's (1968) analysis of *ludruk* symbolism and social change, and Brecht's interpretation of drama as prompting the audience's decisions to act (Peacock 1968).

REFERENCES

Albert, Ethel
  1964 *'Rhetoric,' 'Logic,' and 'Poetics' in Burundi: Culture Patterning of Speech.* American Anthropologist 66.6(2):35-54.
Berlin, Brent, Dennis Breedlove and Peter Raven
  1970 Covert Categories of Folk Taxonomies. In *Man Makes Sense.* Eugene Hammel and William Simmons, Eds. Boston: Little, Brown and Co.
Burke, Kenneth
  1962 *What are the Signs of What?* Anthropological Linguistics 4(6):1-23.
Ervin-Tripp, Susan
  1964 *Interaction of Language, Topic and Listener.* American Anthropologist 66.6 (2):86-102.
Geertz, Clifford
  1973 *The Interpretation of Cultures.* New York: Basic Books.
Goffman, Erving
  1961 *Encounters.* Indianpolis, Indiana: Bobbs-Merrill.
  1967 *Interaction Ritual.* Garden City, New York: Doubleday Anchor Books.
Gumperz, John M.
  1964 *Linguistic and Social Interaction in Two Communities.* American Anthropologist 66.6(2):137-153.
Hymes, Dell
  1974 *Foundations in Sociolinguistics: An Ethnographic Approach.* Philadelphia: University of Pennsylvania Press.
Manning, Frank
  1973 *Black Clubs in Bermuda.* Ithaca, New York: Cornell University Press.
Munn, Nancy
  1973 Symbolism in Ritual Context. In *Handbook of Social and Cultural Anthropology.* John Honigmann, Ed. Chicago: Rand McNally and Co.
Peacock, James
  1968 *Rites of Modernization.* Chicago: University of Chicago Press.
Turner, Victor
  1967 *The Forest of Symbols.* Ithaca, New York: Cornell University Press.
Wells, Rulon
  1960 Nominal and Verbal Styles. In *Style in Language.* Thomas Sebeok, Ed. New York: Wiley.

LANGUAGE IMPOSITIONS ON LINGUISTIC HUMOR

David Greenwald

In my own acquaintance with the studies of play and language, I am disappointed in the limited extent to which either study appreciates their amalgam—linguistic play. On the basis of seniority, this neglect is more onerous to language theorists than to play theorists. Compared to linguists, who comprise a plurality of generations, play theorists are neonates. Symposia and publications devoted solely to play are just now starting to appear on a hoped-for regular basis. By contrast, the 50th Summer Linguistics Institute has passed, and *Language* is publishing its 50th volume.

Although a few modest studies on play are found amongst linguistic publications, play is otherwise an area obscured, avoided, and ignored in linguistic tradition. Instead, linguistics has flourished on ideals of scientific method and formalism, and has thus accredited little interest to play-forms of language, or, for that matter, to language-forms of play.

A primary fact about language, which linguists well know, is that as long as native speakers are alive, it is always changing. Over long time periods this change is markedly noticeable, and surely happens because over short time periods and in the present, speakers produce new language.

Language changes occur both in the creativity of our casual and ordinary language uses, as well as in the creativity of our premeditated efforts for novelty, mimicry, affect, and surprise. In the course of ordinary speaking, language is being composed as part of an ongoing output—part or all of which may never have been put out before—by speakers deploying a system that conventionally behaves according to certain rules and combinatorial arrangements. Grammarians concentrate on the orderly containment of this system that is language. Acknowledging that indeed language varies and changes, they elect to suspend it temporarily so as to be able first to transcribe it, and then offer theories to reflect the information of a language as known to its speakers. Linguists thus have treated grammar as the algorithm for a language system. Creativity fits into such a linguistic theory as the ability of the system, and of idealized native speakers, to generate new (even novel) well-formed output.

Purposeful play with language has been left outside the capacities of linguistics, and the sparse occurrence of works on linguistic play has been one consequence of the decision in linguistic theory that a grammar attempt to be impersonal. It should reflect the knowledge of a linguistic person whose "linguistic competence" allows him always to produce well-formed utterances without either the blunders or the quips nearly every person with normal verbal abilities makes.

Competence, or idealized grammatical knowledge, is a necessary element in recent linguistic modus operandi. To seek commonalities between languages, or to profit from recognizable deviation in any language performance, we must understand the predictability of non-deviance. All linguistic performance is tested on the touchstone of competence, and even Chomsky, the promoter of competence-performance in linguistic lexicon and theory wrote in 1961 that "a well-chosen deviant utterance may be richer and more effective" than an utterance which is well-formed but plain (Fowler 1969: 75). Had Chomsky's professional interests included literary criticism, his concept of creativity might have been more encompassing.

I want to reject the view, perhaps useful for purposes other than mine, that all verbalization is play. Such a view is suggested by Farb, in his work for general readers entitled "Word Play: what happens when people talk". Farb sneaks the phrase "language game" in on the analogy to a game as a business-like interaction: *My game is life insurance*. He then writes further that

> ... the language game shares certain characteristics with all other true games. First of all, it has a minimum of two players (the private, incomprehensible speech of a schizophrenic is no more a true game than is solitaire). Second, a person within speaking distance of any stranger can be forced by social pressure to commit himself to play, in the same way that a bystander in the vicinity of any other game may be asked to play or look on. Third, something must be at stake and both players must strive to win it—whether the reward be a tangible gain ... or an intangible one like the satisfaction of besting someone in an argument. (1974:6)

By his first and third comments, Farb seems to rule out linguistic play in any framework other than social interaction. But solitary play with language is both normal and pleasurable, and there need not always be "something at stake" to occasion linguistic play.

Earlier than Farb, Wittgenstein (1958) used the word *Sprachspiel* ['language-game' in English] as a philosophical metaphor relating play to many aspects of language. Wittgenstein's writings have found a receptive audience. but since I am unqualified to evaluate philosophical motives, I can only make a superficial separation of Sprachspiel from "linguistic play". Both Sprachspiel and Farb's "language game" apply even (and especially) to ordinary, daily language. But by "linguistic play" I wish to convey an image of the spectra of language uses that are extra-ordinary.

I will not attempt definitions of "linguistic play", or of "creativity", "language imposition", "transformation", "duplicity"—partly for reasons of space limitations. I warn the reader that I am using "transformation" in a sense essentially unrelated to its use as a term in generative grammar. Not will I formally define "social horrors", those sensitive areas of social contact and thought. Instead, I will turn to chosen examples to make concepts such as "linguistic humor" meaningful while bypassing exacting definitions.

Example (1), from the Manhattan Yellow Pages telephone directory, appears in a display for an exterminating company. I present this as a "sight gag", humor that is not verbal at all, excepting the words used elsewhere to identify the type of business advertised.

Example (2) uses language directly to portray a ridiculous notion.

(2) "Excuse me, I have to water my lamb-chops."

(2) could be portrayed visually. And (2) translates into to virtually any language without transgressing any grammatical borders. Facts of biology, rather than facts of English, render the idea of watering lambchops humorous.

(1)

(3) Mother: Why sonny, what are you crying about?
Son: Pop just hit his finger with a hammer.
Mother: Why not laugh, I would have.
Son (still crying): I did!

Example (3) depends upon language as the communication channel between son and Mother. The words used in (3), such as the opposites *cry* and *laugh*, are indispensable to the joke, and the mother's reactions are reactions to an utterance. However, the joke uses no structural feature of English. (3) can easily be shifted into other languages, or stated in paraphrases; its form as (3) is powerful because the reader is called on to complete a fragmented punch line and fill in the missing action. The humor of (3) comes from this verbally induced surprise, and from the social discomfort attendant upon the son's punishment.

Similarly, (4) relies on language as the staging ground of the humor, but does not take any special advantage of English.

(4) Professor: "In writing stories for children, my lad, you should write so that even the most ignorant can understand."
Lad: "Yes, sir. What part don't you get?"

The same joke, in translation, would be as funny in any language unable to exempt, grammatically, the speaker from inclusion amongst the referents of the sentence's subject "even the most ignorant." Since in English no grammatical imposition forces the Lad to exclude the Professor, in violation of social harmony he makes an unexpected assumption. The social horror suggested in (4), namely the defamation of the Professor (this example is from a 1925 college humor magazine) is not really part of the verbal message, but is extralinguistic knowledge.

(5) David: "I'm delivering a paper in Detroit."
Claude: "Oh, how much do they pay nowadays for delivering papers?"

The ambiguity of *deliver papers* is a peculiarity of English known to Claude, as a speaker of English. To put the ambiguity to work, he relies in (5) on transformations. He deletes *in Detroit* and pluralizes *paper* to *papers* (still keeping the statement general), with the result that Claude's *papers* and thus David's *paper* are understood to have had alternative interpretations.

The cunning behind such plotted and planned linguistic humor is recognizable: two interpretions, preferably contradictory or controversial, vie for the same linguistic space. The humor-maker's deliberate use of a linguistic device such as repetition or transformation, to germinate twin interpretations is what I call "duplicity". Even without the added impact of a social horror [in (5), menial employ], the duplicity enacted within the language system, within its impositions, is appreciated as humor.

(6) His money's doubly tainted. 'Tain't yours and 'tain't mine.

The author of (6), Mark Twain, expressly warns us, for the joke itself is "doubly tainted". The implied transformation of *taint* into a verb denoting nonownership takes advantage of the imposition of the sound shape [teynt] onto more than one meaning. Beyond the humor of linguistic duplicity in (6), the social theme of monetary want is again exploited.

Neither (5) nor (6) is likely to have a translational equivalent outside of English. Examples (7) and (8) show the impositions of language on humor from the other side.

(7) G a

(8) C'est pas un steak, c'est un oiseau, car il est un peu cuicuit.

Both of these examples are from French, and neither has an English equivalent. (7) is to be read, in French G *grand a petit* 'Big G little a'. There is no duplicity in the English version, but the French is homophonous with *J'ai grand appetit* 'I'm very hungry'. A French child might well feel duped if caught on the wrong end of (7). (8) gives two alternatives *steak* 'steak' and *oiseau* 'bird', both possible interpretations of *cuicuit*. *Cuicuit*, a reduplicated past tense form of *cuir* 'to cook' signifies "overcooked" in a juvenile style, while *cuicuit* is also an onomatopoetic name of a bird.

(9) The fresh clam, from Shiang-River cooking with very special chef's hot spicy rich sauce.

In example (9), a description of an item on the menu in a Chinese restaurant, grammatical impositions in Chinese are expressed in a word-for-word translation into English. Such rearrangements of heads and modifiers in grammatical constructions serve to stimulate our native linguistic imaginations and appeal to our sense of the absurd and ridiculous. (Cf. Example (2)).

(10) Salesman: "I got two orders from Hardnut and Co. today."
Boss: "Good, good."
Salesman: "Yep. One to get out and the other to stay out."

Example (10) turns good news to bad on the duplicity of *orders*. Further humor comes from the misunderstanding between the Salesman and the Boss, and from their mutual failure at business.

(11) —Hobbs, your somach is too fat. You'll have to diet.
—Dye it! My God, what color is it now?

(11) presents a dual synyactic interpretation of the homophonous sound sequence in *diet* and *dye it*. We laugh at the linguistic duplicity, at Hobb's misunderstanding, and at the absurdity of a fat blue or yellow belly.

(12) Arresting Officer to Judge: "We arrested this man while committing a burglary."
Judge to Defendent: "What drove you to such a heinous act?"
Defendent: "My chauffeur."

Example (12) forces a second interpretation of *drove you*. Since the judge asks *What?* the man's response *my chauffeur* violates the linguistic imposition and expectancy of a nonanimate agent. The animate interpretation then results in a situation ludicrous to our normal social order.

(13) Mother: "Would you like to come and rock the baby for a bit, Tommy?"
Tommy: "You bet! But I haven't got a rock."

In example (13), Tommy does a semantic transformation on *rock* 'stone' [an object] to *rock* 'hit with a stone' [an action]. Tommy can do this because of the homophonic coincidence of *rock* as 'stone' and 'sway'. The social horror of (13) is Tommy's mischievous idea, which flaunts his mother's authority and provides an outlet for his jealousy and aggression.

(14) Papa: "Daughter! Isn't that young man gone yet?"
Daughter: "No, father, but I've got him going."

(14) again takes advantage of a transformation: *gone* to *got him going*. [Compare this example ·to (5)]. The language duplicity that results is additionally humorous in broaching the delicate areas of dating and romance (this example also c. 1925).

(15) —She seems to be always sifting evidence.
—That's because she's straining for grounds for divorce.

(16) Professor: "Holmes, your answer is as clear as mud."
Holmes: "Well, doesn't that cover the ground, sir?"

(15) and (16) each deploy several items towards duplicity. In both instances, one of the key words is *ground*, and its range of singular and plural usages is indicative of the linguistic coincidence available within English. Example (15) also depends upon the accompanying duality of *straining*, and it introduces the social horror of divorce. In (16) the phrase *cover the ground* has a dual interpretation,

accompanying *clear as mud*'s literal and figurative interpretations. As in (4), (13), and (14), authority is again the social target of the joke-maker.

(17) Father: "Young man, I understand you've made advances to my daughter."

Young man: "Yes, and since you've mentioned it, I wish you could get her to pay them back."

(18) Movies have been released so many times, they ought to be free.

Example (17) presents a plurality of social themes, as well as a clever parallel duality created by *making advances* and *pay them back*. The sympathetic duality of *released* and *free* in (18) helps make the comment on the everpresent social issue of rising prices.

(19) Husband: "I want to talk to you."

Wife: "All you ever talk about is yourself."

Husband: "I don't think so."

Wife: "All I ever hear from you is 'I this' and 'I that'."

Husband: "I can't agree with you."

Wife: "Every other word you use is 'I'."

Husband: "I do?"

Wife: "Aaarrgh!"

Example (19) shows the husband employing the simplest of devices—repetition—to thoroughly frustrate his wife. The victims in (12) and (19) have been wounded linguistically.

My examples were selected to provide clear instances of playing with the language system, and in so doing the sample is biased towards jokes concocted for the reader who is the privileged observer, and sometimes victim, of a duplicitous set-up [see (7)].

My term "duplicity" is a new term which I find handy, but I am not claiming by it any new discovery. Fowler is aware of it as

. . . . the demand the deviation makes on one's interpretive ingenuity to recognize its own ingeniousness, to hold two structures, or formatives, in mind simultaneously. (1969:77).

A more eloquent statement cognizant of duplicity is Mary Douglas's:

Whatever the joke, however remote its subject, the telling of it is subversive. Since its form consists of a victorious tilting of uncontrol against control, it is an image of the levelling of a hierarchy, the triumph of intimacy over formality, of unofficial values over official ones. (1968:366)

The same author also comments on humor in the expression of social concerns:

To the pleasure of the joke itself, whatever that may be, is added enjoyment of a hidden wit, the congruence of the joke structure with
the social structure. (1968:368)

This is the nature of humorous linguistic play: unofficial, brief, a relief at
the moment just because it is at the moment, often touching a social pressure
point.

Linguistic play is a pervasive play form, easily accessible, and valuable to
those whose interests lie in the behavior of *homo ludens*. Linguistic play reveals
attributes noticed in other kinds of play: uncertainty and surprise; the strange
made familiar and the familiar made strange; set conditions to identify specific
play-forms; imagination and esthetic appeal; arousal fulfillment; means of equal
or greater importance than ends; and, in the absence of movement and contact
in speech alone, competitive power struggles fought on verbal battlefields.

Linguists are familiar with the agon in their own sort of linguistic play.
Now that they realize that they will continue to disagree over grammatical acceptability, they are cashing in on the richness of linguistic deviance. What was
at one time regarded as recreational linguistics [e.g. the multiply-ambiguous *The
chef tossed the salad in the bathtub*] now becomes an issue. Theory has been
stretched to accommodate regional and stylistic variation. Poetry, long the lone
play-form in the linguistic periphery, is being joined by puns, riddles, verbal
gibes, and learning games.

The playfulness of linguists has become increasingly apparent, practiced
most widely in duplicitous title play [e.g. *The Chicago Which Hunt*, a 1969 conference on relativization]. According to Douglas, any such play is "subversive".
The outcome of these acts of subversion remains to be seen. Hopefully they will
serve beyond distress signals, towards an expansion of legitimate linguistic enterprise.

REFERENCES

Douglas, Mary
    1968 The Social Control of Cognition: Some Factors in Joke Recognition, in *Jour-
           nal of the Royal Anthropological Association* 3(3):361-367.
Farb, Peter
    1974 *Word Play: what happens when people talk*. New York: A. Knopf.
Fowler, Roger
    1969 On the Interpretation of "Nonsense Strings" in *Journal of Linguistics* 5:75-83.
Wittgenstein, Ludwig
    1958 *Philosophical Investigations*, Basil Blackwell, trans., London: H. Mott, Ltd.

CHAPTER IV

Expressive Aspects of Play

Introduction

The title òf this section was devised with a different set of papers in mind. Elizabeth Mathias (St. John's University) was to have discussed the expression of values in Sardinian shepherds' poetry; inclement weather prevented her from attending the meetings. Her place was kindly filled at the last minute by Harold Olofson. David Greenwald's paper, "Language Impositions on Linguistic Humor", was shifted to Chapter III and was replaced in this chapter by Frank Manning's contribution, which had been presented at another session in the meetings. But, since it can be argued that nearly all play, with the possible exception of individual fantasy and day-dreaming, is "expressive", I shall let the title stand. And another apology is in order: I am writing this introduction as a stand-in for Frank Salamone, who chaired the session, but who was conducting research in Nigeria when this volume was being prepared.

The papers seem disparate, but common themes can be seen. In his keynote address, Professor Norbeck noted that among Huizinga's attributes of play is that it is "essentially unserious in its goals although often seriously executed". I think these papers show that play can be *very* serious in its goals; indeed, that serious goals can often be most successfully achieved through a play-medium. (Making this statement raises a problem which I shall return to later.) Norbeck subsequently cites another of Huizinga's traits of play, that it "creates order and is order", and with this sentiment all four of these papers agree.

Indeed, this aspect of play is explicitly recognized by both Manning and Salamone. Their papers nicely complement each other. In the characters of Manning's Pentecostal minister in Bermuda, and Salamone's Bori, a "friendly witchdoctor" of the Gungawa of Nigeria, can be seen persons who cannily make use of frivolity as a medium whereby they can drive home a hard "serious" message. It is significant that both authors see a "trickster" element in their central characters; the re-creation of order through disorder is generally recognized by folklorists as a universal function of the Trickster. Manning notes, "by joining together evangelism and entertainment the ritual order thus transmutes the social order, establishing an alternate mode of reality". Furthermore, both authors have amplified a sentiment of Norbeck's as to why play has received so little serious study: its association with "frivolous" by both scholars and theologians. Salamone recognizes that although commonly-assumed analogies place "play" and "profane" on one level, and "religion" and "sacred" on another, both pairs of terms in fact reflect aspects of the same reality; "each is what it is *because* of the presence of the other, not in spite of it" (my emphasis). Indeed, through play profane man may more easily approach the sacred.

Fascination with the apparent juxtaposition of dichotomies in cosmological systems is in vogue today among the social sciences, but this may be a risky prepossession, because it can tend to imply that such apparent dichotomies are polar opposites, and hence mutually exclusive. Both Manning and Salamone have convincingly demonstrated that at least one dichotomous pair, "play" (profane) and "religion" (sacred), are mutually complementary.

Olofson, too, notes the function of play as providing a vehicle for achieving a serious goal. Through the *wasan misisi* drama, Hausa youth of Zaria, Nigeria, act out roles which are "pretend", because the actors know full well that they could never achieve such positions in "real" life. But at the same time, in their play-rivalry they are mirroring—and thus, perhaps, gaining skills in—what is in fact an integral aspect of Hausa social relations. Olofson thus gives further illustration of what is widely recognized as a fundamental aspect of play, that it can be both expressive of *and* instructive in the strategies of social relationships in the "real" world.

We are over-loaded with Nigerianists!—my own brief contribution discusses some of the functions of song-contests among the Bachama. Again, through play and frivolity very serious goals may be sought, and, as among the Eskimo and Tiv, and in other well-documented cases, the institution of the verbal contest can be seen to act as an agent of social and political control.

The reader may have noticed something of an apparent paradox in my initial premise, which forms the basis for the above observations. Huizinga says play is "essentially. unserious in its goals". Play has been seen by some as voluntary activity, detached, free from constraints. If play activity can be said to have serious goals, and furthermore, if the players themselves *recognize* serious goals, then *is it play*? I think it is, but this raises again the problem which we as students of play have constantly, even studiously, avoided: the problem of definition. Professor John Buettner-Janusch, commenting on papers presented at a symposium organized by Professor Norbeck and held during the 1973 meetings of the American Anthropological Association—a symposium described by Norbeck as "the first scholarly conference in the field of anthropology attempting to deal with all aspects of human play" (Norbeck 1974:iii)—stated the problem quite succinctly: *"What in the world are we talking about?"* (Buettner-Janusch 1074:94; emphases original). Professor Norbeck raised the same problem in his keynote address, delivered shortly after members of our association had spent an hour in open seminar talking around the problem. Our Association is young, but the foundations of the topic on which we focus are at least as old as the emergence of the class Mammalia, from which the genus Homo is a very recent offshoot. Tackling the definition problem should receive highest—and immediate—priority.

—*Phillips Stevens, Jr.*

REFERENCES

Buettner-Janusch, John
- 1974 "Commentary". In Edward Norbeck, ed., *The Anthropological Study of Human Play*. Rice University Studies 60, 3, pp. 93-4.
Norbeck, Edward
- 1974 "Foreword". In Norbeck, ed., *The Anthropological Study of Human Play*.

THE REDISCOVERY OF RELIGIOUS PLAY:
A PENTECOSTAL CASE

Frank E. Manning
Memorial University of Newfoundland

The rapid growth of Pentecostalism in recent years has drawn the attention of theologians, social scientists, journalists, and others. Yet a survey of the extensive bibliography compiled by Gerlach and Hine (1970:229-241) indicates that the literature falls into two basic categories: works that are polemical or apologetic, and studies that deal almost exclusively with social or psychological questions. With few exceptions the symbolic aspects of Pentecostalism have been overlooked.

I would like here to explore a symbolic perspective and in particular to view Pentecostalism as a form of play. As space is limited, I will focus on a single theme, illustrated by a single case. The theme is the ludic juxtaposition of sacred and secular elements in ritual symbolism. The case is the religious conversion of a drunken man at a Bermudian church service.[1] I will try to show that this event —like the Balinese cockfight analyzed by Geertz (1972)—can be seen as a "metasocial commentary" on the temper and meaning of cultural experience.

THE DRUNK AND THE DEVIL

The most popular weekly service at the New Testament Church of God in Bermuda is the evangelistic meeting on Sunday night. The service attracts both the active membership of more than two hundred "saints" and an equal number of "unsaved" persons. Some of the latter group are on the verge of contrition and conversion, while others come primarily to enjoy the music, jokes, and comical incidents for which the service is widely known. In addition there is a sizable aggregate of bystanders outside the church, peering through windows or listening to the proceedings through amplifiers placed above the main door. Appropriately, there is often a prayer from the pulpit "that those who come for curiosity will be satisfied."

The first hour of the service takes the form of a hootenanny. Led by the choir and the dozen musicians on stage, the congregation sing, clap, and occasionally dance as familiar hymns are repeated twenty times over. Prayer and scripture reading punctuate the music, as does a special collection which is typically announced with a humorous remark such as "Oh God, please touch their hearts and touch their pocketbooks."

The second hour of the service is broadcast. As it opens with a continuation of the enthusiastic congregational singing, transistor radios are passed around the church so that persons may hear themselves on the air. Following next is the "special singing," a phase in which individuals and groups dedicate hymn selections to church members who are sick.

About halfway through the broadcast hour the pastor steps to the pulpit, addressing his audience in the following vein:

> Greetings to you here in this auditorium, as well as those who are out in radioland. By God, we are really having a ball here this evening. We are really enjoying the blessings of the Lord. Glory be to God. I trust that you have already enjoyed the Lord, and I assure you that it will get better further on.

Remarks of this type are usually followed by topical commentary. On one occasion he joked about his recent conviction in court for a speeding violation by suggesting that a "speeding demon" jumped on his foot and made him exceed the limit before he knew what he was doing. By then he had already gone through a radar trap and was being pursued by a constable.

On another occasion he observed that Bermudian women are wearing their skirts too high and thus giving unnecessary temptation to men. Regrettably, he added, a few women in the New Testament congregation must be included. To satirize them he turned his back to the audience, pulled his cassock up to his thighs, and suggestively wiggled his buttocks. This led to a broad attack on Bermudian hedonism. Instead of coming to church, he claimed, people are going to the Forty Thieves Club (a famous nightclub named after Bermuda's merchant aristocracy of forty white families). "I don't go there," he laughingly moralized, "I'm not a thief."

After several minutes of such commentary the pastor announces that he must get to the "Word of God." His tone grows angry and urgent as he narrows his preaching down to a constant theme: the day of judgment and world destruction is near, as shown by the growth of sin in Bermuda and throughout the world; the devil is doing what he did in antediluvian times; repent of your sins and accept Jesus Christ as your personal saviour; you may not be alive tomorrow. The approval of the congregation is given by their shouts of "Amen," "Preach, pastor, preach," "Carry him through, Jesus," "It's the truth," "All right, now," and so forth.

It was during this time of the service one night that a young man in a drunken stupor staggered into the church. He was assisted to the front by a member of the congregation who subsequently knelt beside him, kept him from falling over, and prayed aloud for his salvation. Joined by other men, the pastor went to the side of the drunk and spoke to the assembly.

> This brother wants to be delivered tonight. This brother wants to be set free. He wants to be loosed from the enemy tonight. He's bound. He's tied . . . . The enemy has got him tonight . . . .
>
> We're going to take a stand tonight against this demon, this devil. Brother, you're going to be delivered tonight . . . . Glory be to God. Thank you, Jesus . . . .

At this point the drunk began to feel sicker, and they sat him down in the front row. Those around him commented that his moaning and shaking were signs of the struggle between Jesus and Satan. As the drunk leaned forward to vomit the pastor held his head and began a frenzied prayer:

The blood of Jesus is against you, demon. Right now in Jesus's name I command you, loose your hold on this man. Come out, come out, come out. (The drunk vomited, and two men went to get saw-dust to cover the floor.)

He's coming out. Glory be to God. Right now the blood of Jesus prevails against you, Satan. Right now in Jesus's name I command you to loose your hold on this man . . . .

The drunk tried to vomit again, but was unable. The pastor stood over him, continuing to pray and trying to induce the vomit. Meanwhile, the congregation, elated over the first regurgitation, broke into a singing, clapping chorus:

By the blood of Jesus,
By the blood of Jesus,
By the blood of Jesus,
He's washed as white as snow.

The chorus had been sung for about ten minutes when the drunk started vomiting again. The pastor signalled the band to stop playing and exclaimed:

This is it, This is it. This is it. Come out, Satan, come out . . . Hallelujah! Hallelujah! Hallelujah! Hallelujah! . . . He's coming out. Glory to God. Thank you, Jesus . . .

The drunk wanted to vomit more, but couldn't; again the congregation responded with a chorus:

There is power, power, wonder-working power,
In the blood of the Lamb,
There is power, power, wonder-working power,
In the precious blood of the Lamb.

The chorus was sung about 15 minutes, during which time the drunk vom-ited twice more and people danced in the aisles, rejoicing in the expulsion of Satan. When he thought the vomiting was over the pastor stopped the band and spoke to the assembly:

We have witnessed a manifestation of the power of God here tonight. Jesus said, "And these signs shall follow them that believe. In my name they shall cast out devils." In the name of the Lord we've been casting out devils here tonight. Glory be to God.
God is confirming his word. Amen. He is helping us in these

last days with signs. Even though in the last days we're told about abominable things ... we're so glad that in the last days devils are also being cast out ....

At least four demons came out of this brother tonight. The last one to come out was a demon of lust. My God, brother, if you'll believe, if you'll accept what happened tonight, you'll move on through this island victorious ...

You've got to realize now, when the devil comes out of you, when this (pointing to the vomit) comes out of you, every desire of the lust of the flesh, my friend, is gone. Right now your body is empty. It's clean.

Remember that when these evil spirits come out, they float around in the air. They're looking for a place to rest. If you ain't careful, they'll get into you. They'll get into somebody else. Demons have got to have a place to live .... When he comes out of you, brother, or anyone else, he seeks rest. He also comes back to the temple he's just come out of. And when he looks in and sees it swept, garnished, and cleaned, you know what he does? He goes and looks for seven other spirits, he goes and gets his friends , and comes back. And anytime you let him or one of his friends get back in, those last days are worse than the first ....

And I ask you to believe, to believe that you're set free from the hand of the enemy. And while the devil has gone out, the spirit of God has come in. God wants to use you. He's brought you here for a purpose. He'll make you what he desires you to be. May God bless you tonight .... (the man began again to vomit).

That's it, come on. There's more there. Thank you, Jesus. In the name of Jesus the blood prevails against you, Satan .... There's more there. Come out, come out, come out ... (the man vomited again, and the band began another chorus) ... Thank you, Jesus, thank you for the blood tonight ... Oh, my God ....

The chorus was played three times, then the pastor raised his hands and spoke to the assembly:

Thank you for delivering this man, tonight, my God, Thank you for setting him free in the name of Jesus .... He feels much better now. We thank you because there's power in the blood, there's deliverance in the blood. Hallelujah! We're so glad because the lion of the tribe of Judah has broken the chains ....

As the drunk slumped over in his seat the pastor seemed satisfied that the spiritual battle had exhausted him beyond the point of giving testimony. He left the drunk and returned to the pulpit, reverting to the humorous style and mood evidenced at the beginning of his sermon. "We really felt a gush of the Holy

Spirit here tonight," he quipped. He joked about the enthusiasm and histrionic behavior of some of the church members, made a few announcements about activities during the week, and finally brought the proceedings to a close with a brief benediction. It was 11:30 p.m., three and a half hours since the service had begun.

After everyone had left the church two members of the congregation carried the drunk out to drive him home. As they approached the car the drunk leaned over to vomit again, although this time it was only the dry heaves. "He must have been to a party before he came here tonight," commented the man holding him up. "But it doesn't matter because this won't happen again."

The drunk then turned and feebly thanked his helper, adding that he didn't recognize him. "It's not important to know me," was the reply. "Just know the man I serve. Know Jesus."

As the owner of the car drove away with the drunk in the back seat, I turned to the other church member and naively asked why the man had vomited so many times. "He had too much to drink," was the simple reply. "He was really very drunk."

COMEDY AND COSMOLOGY

Two conjunctions of sacred and secular symbol systems can be discerned in the drunk's salvation episode. The first, which is rather general and diffuse, is between evangelism and entertainment in the intentionality of the church service. The second, which is more specific and obvious, is between religious knowledge and common sense in the interpretation of the man's symptoms. These conjunctions situate the event in two independent orders of meaning, the condition which Bergson (1956:23) identified as invariably comic.

The church service has two unambiguous aims: to evangelize the gospel of salvation and to serve as a form of entertainment. Ritual symbolism joins edification and enjoyment, hell-fire preaching and mundane joking, holiness and histrionics, solemn piety and profane humor. The duality of purpose is reflected in the standard answer that my informants gave for going to church: "to have a good time in the Lord." In its attempt to encounter God through the dance rather than the dirge or the doctrine, Pentecostal ritual exemplifies the playful and festive spirit that religious sociologists such as Berger (1970) and Cox (1969) have advocated as the solution to Christianity's ills.

Much of the symbolic dualism of Pentecostalism pivots on the Holy Ghost. Like the many trickster deities of the North American Indians (cf. Miller 1973: 30), the Holy Ghost is conceived in terms of both sanctity and buffoonery. He is both the most sacred and the most ludic personage of the Trinity. The unique feature of Pentecostalism, the experience of speaking in unknown tongues, is attributed to the spiritual baptism of the Holy Ghost. Other valued mystical powers such as healing and prophecy are similarly traced to the efficacy of the

Holy Ghost. Furthermore, it was generally believed by my informants that a curse against the Holy Ghost was the one sin that could not be forgiven. Yet within the context of ritual the Holy Ghost is also conceived as a kind of master of ceremonies. It is he who inspires the dramatic behaviors that are the criteria of a "good" service. A memorable illustration of this view occurred at the end of one service when the preacher asked for a round of applause for God the Father. The congregation, anticipating what was to follow, responded with a brief ovation. Next he asked for a hand for God the Son, and there was a similar response. Finally he asked for applause for God the Holy Ghost, and there was a standing, cheering ovation that lasted about fifteen minutes.

The conjunction of evangelism and entertainment in ritual represents an inversion of the social order. As I have shown elsewhere (Manning 1973), there is a polar opposition in Bermuda between the churches, centers of evangelism, and the workmen's clubs, centers of entertainment. Evangelism exemplifies ethical behavior, while entertainment and its accessories (liquor, dancing, sexual arousal) epitomize sin. By joining together evangelism and entertainment the ritual order thus transmutes the social order, establishing an alternate mode of reality.

It is this sense of "otherworldliness" that allows the interpretation of the vomiting seizure as a cosmological struggle between the blood of Jesus and the power of Satan, resolved when the demons are driven out and the man is thereby "saved." (This view was vindicated two nights later when the man returned, sobered and spruced up, to testify that he had indeed accepted Jesus as his personal savior.) But what is of special interest is that the ritual actors are aware not only of the man's spiritual depravity but also of his physical condition; they see the event in terms of both religion and common sense.

During the church service the religious perspective is primary, providing the explicit interpretation of all that happens between the altar rail and the front row. The common sense perspective is implicit, showing through in the actions taken to protect the drunk from injury and to salve the aesthetic sensitivities of those around him by covering his vomit with sawdust. After the service, however, the relationship between the two perspectives shifts. When the man attempts to vomit again the church members taking him home state that he must have been to a party and frankly acknowledge that he is drunk. Yet religious awareness is evidenced in their counsel that it is more important to know Jesus than his human servants.

The alternation of conceptual perspectives is characteristic of play. To borrow Huizinga's (1955:13) classic phrase, play is a "stepping out" from ordinary reality into another realm of symbol and meaning. Unlike the mentally deranged, however, the playful realize that their special reality is not exclusive. They see it alongside other realities to which they must likewise relate. Thus play involves not only a "stepping out" but also a "stepping in"—a return to ordinary, common sense awareness in the manner seen at the end of the Pentecostal service.

The capacity of play to transcend empirical understanding closely associates it with religion. Indeed, as Norbeck (1974:39) points out, play and religion are overlapping entities in pre-industrial cultures. It was the Protestant Reformation that severed the two, stigmatizing play as a sinful waste of time and idealizing ascetic rationality as the model of ethical behavior. An evolutionary logic of the type developed by Bellah (1964) points to the consequences of this theology. Purged of play, Western Christianity has been gradually deprived of a transcendent dimension. The most cryptic and perhaps ultimate expression of this trend was the Death of God movement, a symbolic pronouncement that God was no longer transcendent but instead had become part of the secular world.

Yet there are signs—among them the phenomenal growth of Pentecostalism and its interdenominational spinoffs—that the secularization movement has run its course and that play and transcendence are on the way back. Modern (or perhaps post-modern) man is regaining an appreciation of Huizinga's (1955) insight that we are *homo ludens* as much as *homo sapiens* or *homc faber*, and is becoming more conscious of Mumford's (1967) point that the species made myths and rituals before it made tools. In short, we are learning again not only to play and to believe but to recognize that play and belief have an essential affinity.

The drunk's salvation is a metasocial commentary on this process. It interprets a field of belief not by expounding its precepts but by revealing a glimpse of the experience that is shared by the community of faith. It is a story about what it is like to have unwavering convictions about transcendent reality and yet to take a deeply ludic view of man's place in the cosmos. Such a story is increasingly resonant as religious play is rediscovered.

NOTE

[1] I have elsewhere (Manning n.d.) offered an extended discussion of this incident and an ethnographic portrait of the church.

REFERENCES

Bellah, Robert
    1964 "Religious Evolution," *American Sociological Review*, 29: 358-374.
Berger, Peter
    1970 *A Rumor of Angels*. Garden City, New York: Doubleday Anchor.
Bergson, Henri
    1956 "Laughter," in W. Sypher, ed., *Comedy*. Garden City, N.Y.: Doubleday Anchor.
Cox, Harvey
    1969 *The Feast of Fools*. Cambridge, Mass.: Harvard University Press.
Geertz, Clifford
    1972 "Deep Play: Notes on the Balinese Cockfight," *Daedalus*, 101: 1-37.
Gerlack, Luther P., and Virginia H. Hine
    1970 *People, Power, Change*. New York: Bobbs-Merrill Company, Inc.

Huizinga, Johan
    1955 *Homo Ludens*. Boston: Beacon Press. (First published in Holland in 1938.)
Manning, Frank
    1973 *Black Clubs in Bermuda*. Ithaca, N.Y.: Cornell University Press.
    n.d.   *The Salvation of a Drunk*. Unpublished manuscript.
Miller, Stephen
    1973 "The Playful, the Crazy, and the Nature of Pretense," Paper delivered at the
        Annual Meeting of the American Anthropological Association.
Mumford, Lewis
    1967 *The Myth of the Machine*. New York: Harcourt, Brace.
Norbeck, Edward
    1975 *Religion in Human Life*. New York: Holt, Rinehart, and Winston.

RELIGION AS PLAY—BORI, A FRIENDLY "WITCHDOCTOR"

Frank Salamone
St. John's University

On play we may move below the level of the serious, as the child
does; but we can also move above it—in the realm of the beautiful
and the sacred (Huizinga 1955: 19)

Introduction

Huizinga (1955:20) found it surprising that anthropologists had paid little
attention to the interrelationship between play and religion. With very few exceptions that neglect seems to have persisted into the present. Analysis of reasons for that neglect would require a separate paper.[1] However, the existence of
that neglect is a fact that has retarded the development of a more complete qualitative understanding of the religious experience.

By insisting on the serious nature of religion while treating "play" as synonymous with "frivolous", scholars have failed to focus on an important aspect
of the sacred, namely, its playful nature. The sacred, as Huizinga (1955:19-20),
following Plato, states is supremely playful. Indeed, Levi-Strauss' (1955) identification of anomalous categories with the sacred is a case in point. Play soars beyond ordinary boundaries and creates a world in which extraordinary things are
possible, where the unthinkable is thought and the forbidden is performed as a
commonplace. In other words, Levi-Strauss' anomalous categories are categories
of play.

Perhaps, the difficulty inherent in treating the sacred and play as com-
patible categories lies in a basic misunderstanding of the nature of play. According to Huizinga (1955:17) the major characteristics of play are "order, tension,
movement, change, solemnity, rhythm, rapture." These are the very characteristics of ritual play and, I would add, of religious belief as well. In a very real

sense, religion is a game with clearly defined rules, a goal or objective, a "playing field", and a means for procedure. It does indeed take people outside themselves. In short, it is play.

In the following passage Huizinga (1955:26) summed up the point for what he termed "primitive" or "archaic" ritual and then immediately broadened to include all religious ritual.

> Primitive, or let us say, archaic ritual is thus sacred play, indispensable for the well-being of the community, fecund of cosmic insight and social development but always play in the sense Plato gave to it—an action accomplishing itself outside and above the necessities and seriousness of everyday life.

This paper attempts to apply Huizinga's insights to one case, that of the Gungawa of Yauri and Borgu Divisions in Nigeria's North-Western and Kwara States, and by applying them to suggest extensions fruitful for cross-cultural investigations. The goal of the proposed suggested extensions is to present a hypothesis explaining at least part of the connection between play and religion —the sacred and the profane are really two aspects of the same reality. It is not merely that they alternate with each other. That games, for example, may be held on the sacred field after rituals are performed. Rather, it is the inextricable union of the two in the same event that emphasizes the inseparability of the concepts. Whatever is sacred is also profane, and conversely, whatever is profane is also sacred. More strongly, each is what it is because of the presence of the other, not in spite of it. It is this paradox that is at root the cause of the play element so profoundly present in religion. It is play that allows one to approach the sacred while at the same time signalling its sacredness—its apartness, for as Douglas (1973:111) points out, "Whenever in the social situation, dominance is liable to be subverted, the joke is the natural and necessary expression, since the structure of the joke parallels the structure of the situation."

This play quality of the sacred, exemplified in ritual, may also be used by religious practitioners to communicate their approachability. This may be especially necessary in the case of part-time specialists who also engage in secular occupations, as is the case among the Gungawa.

The Gungawa (Reshe)

Elsewhere (Salamone 1974, and 1975) I have described the Gungawa at length. Suffice it here to provide a brief summary. Until the completion of Kainji Dam in the late 1960's forced their resettlement, the Gungawa (island-dwellers) were a riverine people who practiced exploitative alternation of resources, shifting from onions to millet, guinea corn and rice as the season and occasion warranted.[2] Fishing supplemented their income and complex and friendly arrangements with the Serkawa (professional fishermen) preserved fishing boundaries.

Today the Gungawa find themselves on extremely poor farm land, land especially ill-suited for onion and rice cultivation. In addition, their movement from riverine positions and the other ecological changes consequent on the building of Kainji Dam have abrogated their agreements with the Serkawa, and Serkawa have taken over the dried fish export trade once dominated by the Gungawa.

Faced with no real alternatives, Gungawa increasingly used a long-established pattern of ethnic identity change and became Hausa. The procedure for doing so is well-known in Yauri. They became Muslims, spoke only Hausa in public, swore off the consumption of indigenous alcoholic beverages, dressed in a Hausa manner and called themselves Hausa. Such behavior gained them tangible and immediate benefits and was in keeping with a traditional function of the Gungawa identiy, an identity that has served to incorporate new groups into Yauri and Borgu societies while supplying members to the ruling Hausa group.

One of the major characteristics of the Gungawa has been their "pragmatism". They have quite openly borrowed cultural practices from other groups in order to maximize their opportunities. This has gained them a consistent reputation of hard-working industrious people, an evaluation shared by the British, Dukawa, Hausa, Kamberi and members of other groups who have come into contact with them. This pragmatism has been quite adaptive in the multi-ethnic setting of Yauri and Borgu. It has facilitated Gungawa interaction with each of the other groups in the area.

One of the major mechanisms for facilitating ethnic interaction has been the transethnic importance of Gungawa religious practioners, particularly that of the man whose title is Bori.

The Gungawa Ideal Religious Leader

Among Gungawa, real power is cloaked in modesty, for the naked display of power is culturally condemned. As Harris (1930:299) pointed out the truly powerful official in a Gungawa village, the retired Balkari, takes a "semi-humorous" title such as "Had Enough", "Resting", "Can Feed Myself". It is this man's contention that he is through with the exercise of power and only occasionally will stoop to use it when his people prove too foolish to handle their own affairs. For example, during an especially severe riot between two villages resulting from a wrestling match, the former Balkari appeared and asked why an old man ready to die had to be called from his rest to settle the affairs of children. His presence was sufficient to quel the riot immediately, and he quickly returned to his rest.

Those who possess power among the Gungawa are those who least appear to and who most deny their influence. They tend to make the least display of their power, to dress more simply than others and to live more modestly than those who may appear to exercise power. Furthermore, there is a palpably benign quality to those with real as opposed to apparent political power among the Gungawa. What is true of political leadership is a *fortiori* applicable regarding religious leadership.

Each village has a priest (Wahunu), described in the following passage (Harris 1930:299).

> An important personage in the village life is the Wahunu, who, for want of a better description, may be termed the village priest. To Wahunu is entrusted the making of prayers and supplications at the communal shrine or shrines of the village. He does not, however, interfere in any way with the individual shrines of each household which have been inherited and are in the care of individual families. To Wahunu is entrusted the care of all the property sacred to the village shrine, and he himself may be distinguished by his staff of office with its rings of iron . . . Wahunu, although an important person in the village life, is, as befits the village priest, a benign personage, and his main interest is centered in the good health and people of the village.

The village priest (Wahunu) is primarily concerned with the spiritual life of people of one village. Harris (1930:300) implies quite correctly that the *Ubwa* (doctor) may be concerned with the needs of people of more than one village. Furthermore, he is a doctor, a healer, who works through visible things to cure diseases which are frequently "spiritual" as well as physical and no clear-cut distinction is made between religious and secular practioners. In fact, the Gungawa and others in the area generally regard the *ubwa* as more powerful than any other practioner because he deals with both spiritual and physical cures. Among these *ubwa* is one who is not only more powerful and famous than any other *ubwa* but is, as I shall argue later, the chief priest of all Gungawa. Harris' (1930: 300) description of the position and status of the *ubwa* in general is an important one.

> Boka (Hausa) or Ubwa is the village doctor, skilled in the use of herbs, and sometimes skilled as a fortune-teller. Not all the islands have an Ubwa, and consequently those who are practiced in the art of herbs sometimes travel far afield and have a considerable income.

> The Boka, at the Island of Hella (whose title is Bori) is far-famed throughout Nigeria, and it is no unusual sight to see, in the cosmopolitan crowd in the market at Yelwa, natives of Abeokuta, Warri and the Southern Provinces, all of whom have come up for treatment by this Boka and his famous speaking tree. This tree, which is a baobab, is sacred to the Bori spirit Doguwa (Inna), and is said to give answers to the questions put to it by Bori.

Further evidence of the repute of Gungawa doctors is given in Gunn and Conant (1960:14-15, 19 footnote 6, 46 footnote 8). After summarizing their description, I will describe the role[3] of the man who was the Bori in 1972 and try to amend their description and Harris' where appropriate, for they fail to present an adequate description of the role of the Bori. Nor have they set that role in its proper theoretical perspective.

Summary

Medicine and its practitioners are held in high repute among Gungawa. People come great distances to receive care from their doctors. In addition to being famous for medical skill, Gungawa are considered especially skillful *bori* practioners.[4] In fact, as Harris (1930:300) suggests the most famous of these practitioners are doctors. The fact that the most famous of these doctors occupies the inherited position named "Bori" underlines the relationship.

There is some confusion among non-Gungawa, especially Hausa and European ethnographers, of the religion (*maigiro*) and magic (*tsaffi*). Both in religion and magic *bori* (spirits) are used which are often termed *aljani* to fit them into an Islamic framework.[5] In fact, the use of the term *bori* leads some people to confuse the work of the doctor (*ubwa*) with that of Hausa spirit possession specialists. Gungawa doctors do not cause spirits to possess anyone. They do talk to the bori on behalf of their clients and convey their responses. It is also important to note that they are not possessed by spirits and that the spirits do not speak through them. The client can hear the spirits as well as the doctor, although perhaps more faintly. The spirits do tend to speak in an oracular fashion, demanding interpretation.

The spirit most associated with Hella is *Doguwa* (Inna). In addition, the Bori of Hella has hereditary ties with the keeper of a very famous and important shrine to *Ubangba* (the strong) in the neighboring village of Mnhuh. That shrine is currently under the care of the Bori's patrilateral uncle.[6] The Bori, thus, draws on the importance of his association with what is essentially a fertility shrine and his famous talking familiar spirit. The significance of this alliance or union of magic and religion in one person will be discussed below.

The Bori of Hella

Hella is part of Yabo village (a governmental administrative village unit) in Gungu District, Yauri Division, North-Western State. In 1966 it had 104 adult males of Yabo's 380 adult males (ca. 1,520 people), while all of Gungu District had 2,691 adult males (ca. 10,764 people). Niger Dams Resettlement figures differed slightly from those of the various District Heads. For example, their figure for Gungu District was 2,691 adult males as opposed to the 3,109 counted by District Heads. However, both agreed on the figure of 104 adult males for Hella. The allied village of Mnhuh also within Yabo had either 39 or 56 adult males, depending on whose figures are correct. In appearance, size and every other aspect, Hella is typically Gungawa. In short, it is not the largest nor the smallest of Gungawa villages. Its uniqueness lies in the fact that its *Ubwa* (doctor) is the Bori, or chief priest of all Gungawa, a fact not really recognized by Harris or Gunn and Conant.

Physically, the current Bori is not impressive, and he does all in his power to emphasize those aspects of his physique that remind his fellow Gungawa of a benign trickster. He is about fifty years old, short, and slightly overweight, a characteristic he does all in his power to exagerate through the manner in which he wears his clothes. These he wears carelessly draped over his body, so that his gown opens at his stomach. Whenever Bori notices that anyone is looking, he protrudes his belly to draw an inevitable and predictable laugh. In reality, Bori still possesses a fine athletic build, a legacy from his youth when he was the champion wrestler of the Gungawa. His wrestling scars, the result of a badly healed shoulder break, are displayed as badges of honor.

In sum, Bori's manner is benign, and he enjoys playing the buffoon. For example, at an intravillage wrestling match at Mnhuh, he came shouting and laughing from Hella to greet me. Failing to pull me away to his own village, he left and then returned with a calabash of guinea corn beer (*giya*). He then began a mock wrestling match with another elder which quickly became a contest to see who could pull enough of the other's gown to expose the most rump. None of the wrestlers showed any pique at having their scene so easily stolen by Bori.

Among resettled Gungawa, Bori is one of the few who still follow old occupations. He still goes on the river to fish. In addition, he weaves fishing traps and sells these to the Serkawa. Bori is saddened by the Islamization of the Gungawa and of his own village. In his village, for example, only four people are not Muslim—he, two of his ten sons, and one brother. However, he bears the Muslims no malice, for they did what they had to do.

He demonstrates that lack of malice in a very direct manner. In times of trouble all men, he says, come to Bori and he refuses no one—Christian, traditionalist, or Muslim. As he quite accurately observes, his fame extends from Sokoto to Ibadan and people of all ethnic groups (*kabila*) and religions (*addini*) come to him. If they have no money, he still cares for their needs. If they have no shelter, he provides it. If they are hungry, he feeds them. In fact, Bori is willing to share his fee with other practioners as he demonstrated when he sent chickens to the Catholic mission station with the message, "We are both in the same business. You cure men's outsides. I cure their insides."

Bori's tolerance extends to issues of faith as well as those of practice. On a visit to the Catholic mission station he was impressed with the sanctuary lamp and began to talk to it, believing that Jesus must live there since his own spirit, Inna, lived in a tree near his home on old Hella. Bori reasons that Christians pray to Jesus because he is nearer to them than God. As he says, "I believe in Allah. But I do not pray to him. He is too far away, too distant. My spirits are close to me. They understand my needs." If Jesus lives at the mission station, Bori is willing to consult him for advice as well.

As mentioned above, his favorite spirit, Inna or Doguwa, still lives in the

163

sacred baobab tree at old Hella, on the flooded island. He is bitter that the tree was not replanted at new Hella. However, Doguwa still comes to see him. Interestingly, all the other spirits visit him only on Sundays, for they have abandoned the old tree and moved elsewhere. Bori can summon these spirits whenever he so desires, for unlike the otiose god they are near him. Even if they are in America, he said, "They will come at my call in the twinkling of an eye."

Bori can summon his spirits at any time. His preferred place of communion with them is a two room hut (daki). In the first room there is a miniature statue of a Kamberi spirit with a bow and arrow and two hoes. It is similar to a number of statues found in traditional Gungawa villages. The second room is divided from the first by a curtain and has the famous talking pots. A Fulani spirit occupies the second room and signifies his presence through rattling the pots in response to Bori's summoning shaking of rattles and verbal calls. Before calling the spirits Bori prepares himself by draping a sacred cloth over his shoulders and kneeling forward.

People who are present at the ceremony hear the spirits answer him. A good deal of playful banter takes place in which the spirit questions the motives of those who have come to Bori. Invariably Bori assures the spirit that the client is a good person who means him no harm. He begs the spirit not to harm the supplicant and to be kindly disposed toward him. Finally, the spirit renders his decision. There is an air of playfulness in the proceedings which demonstrate his closeness to the spirits.

As Bori is close to the spirits, so, too are the people close to him. There is no fear of him despite his clear possession of great powers, and even though he can curse as well as bless. For example, he has an altar on which he sacrifices chickens. These chickens can be sacrificed to kill Fulani cows that trample the farms of Gungawa farmers. Thus, the sacrifices that cure illness can also kill. Despite this tremendous power, there is no fear evident that he will misuse it. His playfulness is used to communicate helpfulness, approachability, and benigness in order to allay fears of misuse of power among Gungawa. It is behavior grammatically consistent with the transmission of his intended message, "I help them all. I am more powerful than them all." His gentleness, then, is not weakness any more than the humorous appearance of the bori (spirits) signifies their weakness. Their large heads on small bodies bring smiles to the faces of children, but they also signify the intelligence and wit of the bori, who are very much like many of the other trickster gods of Nigeria. Furthermore, they are reminders of the importance of "using one's head" in problem solving.

It is also important to add that the Bori's playfullness is not shallowness, for through his playfullness he is able to express basic Gungawa values, and he is fully aware of that fact. He is also aware that he is left alone to practice his religion because Christians, Muslims, and traditionalists from many ethnic groups throughout Nigeria come to seek his help.

As he says, "Those who prefer to talk with god (Allah) have become Muslims." Perceptively, he adds that what they really wish to do is to become like Hausa so that the government will leave them alone. The government of Yauri had been noted for its religious tolerance. However, under the late Northern Premier, Ahmadu Bello, conversion pressure became almost unbearable. It was then that waves of *mallamai* (Islamic teachers) were sent from village to village to seek conversions (Cf. Salamone, in press).

He has nothing to gain from becoming a Muslim and nothing to lose by refusing to convert. In fact, his conversion would cost him great loss of status (rights and duties) and would also be dysfunctional for Yauri society. In other words, it is to everyone's benefit to preserve the position of the Bori.

In order to understand the significance of this fact it is necessary to go beyond Gunn and Conant's (1960) and Harris' (1930) accounts and realize that the Bori is not just an important doctor. He is also a priest. In face, he is the hereditary chief priest of the Gungawa who presides at their annual religious harvest festival, the only festival at which representatives from all Gungawa villages attend, signifying the ethnic unity of the group while reinforcing it. His position is further strengthened in that he is assisted at this festival, held at the end of the rainy season, by the keeper of the sacred shrine at Mnhuh, the shrine of Ubangba (the powerful one, Gunganci) or *Mutamin bisa* (the man upstairs, Hausa).

In sum, the especially powerful position of the Bori is emphasized by his use of spiritual (non-material) and physical (material) items. The Bori occupies an anomalous position, a sacred one. Unlike others he performs medical and priestly functions, bridging two worlds and uniting them in his person.

Conclusions

This brief case study of the Gungawa Bori suggests that cross-cultural investigation of the interrelatedness of the nature of play and that of the sacred will be rewarding. Both assert the existence of new possibilities, of a new order of things. They suggest the existence of a reality behind visible or existential reality. The arbitrariness of the world is also exemplified in sacred play. Furthermore, the playful aspects of the sacred while not detracting from its grandeur do make it more approachable.

There is deep significance in Bori's statement that he never talks to Allah because he is too far away. He says he believes in him, but he is too distant to care for the everyday problems of people. Therefore, belief in an otiose god is relatively emotionless, bloodless, and rather abstract. Certainly it is not original to note that even in highly monotheistic systems people create intermediaries who are more real to them than a distant god. Innumerable examples abound in the literature regarding these "minor spirits", ranging from turning their statues to the wall to warning Jesus that if he does not grant a favor the applicant will tell his mother on him.

Whatever else they are, these intermediaries are playful creatures who aid people to approach the sacred through providing them with a sense of greater control over it. Thus, play removes enough of the fear of the unknown to make the sacred work for society. Bori is an example of one who is highly skilled in the grammar of playfullness as befits a societal intermediary with the sacred. In fact, Bori is himself a sacred person because he occupies (or perhaps, better, signified by his occupation of ?) an anomalous category. His playfulness brings the sacred close to the Gungawa, something quite in keeping with their pragmatic ways.

Finally, both play and the sacred suggest the game-like quality of sociocultural life. It is this intimation of the reality behind reality, pointing to the arbitrariness of any given social structure and its generative culture that reinforces the feeling that life itself is play, following rules in a set-apart arena for action. This perception lends power to the lived-in reality of a given sociocultural system. Play and sacred ritual suggest the possibility of change, for this very reason, that is that all existing arrangements of sociocultural variables are arbitrary and not really eternal. New games can be played with different rules. In addition, both lend themselves to reinterpretation, for both are made-up and ambiguous. It is this constant perception of their double-meaning that gives them so powerful a role in life, for it provides an opportunity for the possibility of change under the guise of persistence. In this, games and play are kin to the joke, for it is in the nature of the joke to be ambiguous, or, better, to see the dual nature of reality and to comment on it. It is, in fact, the double-meaning inherent in the combination of the sacred/profane (this world/other world) dichotomy that gives the sacred its power and the combination is itself play.

It was this that Plato (quoted in Huizinga 1955:19) refers to in the passage which most succinctly recapitulates this paper's theme: "Life must be lived as play, playing certain games, making sacrifices, singing and dancing, and then a man will be able to propiate the gods, and defend himself against his enemies, and win in the contest."

NOTES

[1] Among these reasons would be the false dichotomy between play and the sacred. Huizinga (1955: 19-26) took great pains to demonstrate the compatibility of these concepts. However, to most people, unfortunately, including scholars, they have remained antithetical concepts. Furthermore, religion is supposed to be a serious thing. The Reformation is not quite dead in the United States, and its condemnation of the "frivolous" in religious life still seems to have great weight among religious scholars.

[2] About 50,000 Gungawa were resettled. Very few settlements of Gungawa remain in riverine areas. Shabanda, which I have mentioned in writings cited above, is one such area.

[3] I am using the term in Goodenough's (1969) sense.

[4] "True *bori*", as opposed to the Hausa version, refers to spirit consultation.

[5] According to Gunn and Conant (1960:46 footnote 8), the name comes from the Hausa "gero". They do not explain why all non-Hausa in Yauri and Borgu use a Hausa term for their religion. Furthermore, the inevitable Hausa association of *bori* with the possession

cult is not found among Gungawa. In other words, while there are possessed Gungawa, not all activities or practitioners dealing with the *bori* are concerned with possession, only a very small percentage are related to such activities. To the Gungawa, the *bori* are an integrated aspect of their religion. To the Hausa they are a survival of pre-Islamic religion, used for areas Islam does not deal with.

[6]Significantly, Mnhuh has resisted Islam, and its resistance is in large measure attributable to the strength of its elders. The presence of this famous shrine has no doubt aided their resistance to Hausafication.

REFERENCES

Douglas, Mary
    1973 *Natural Symbols*. New York: Pantheon Books.
Goodenough, Ward H.
    1969 Rethinking Status and Role: Toward a General Model of the Cultural Organization of Social Relationships. In Stephen H. Tyler, ed. *Cognitive Anthropology*. New York: Holt, Rinehart and Winston, Inc.
Gunn, Harold and Francis Conant
    1960 *Peoples of the Middle Niger Region, Northern Nigeria*. Bedford: Sidney Press Ltd.
Harris, P. G.
    1930 Notes on Yauri (Sokoto Province), Nigeria, *Journal of the Royal Anthropological Institute* 60: 283-334.
Huizinga, Johan
    1955 *Homo ludens*. Boston: Beacon Press.
Levi-Strauss, Claude
    1955 The Structural Study of Myth. *Journal of American Folklore* 67:428-444.
Niger Dams Resettlement (NDR) Archival Material at Yauri, North-Western State, Nigeria
Salamone, Frank A.
    1974 *Gods and Goods in Africa*. HRA Flex, New Haven: 2 volumes.
    1975 *Becoming Hausa*, Africa 45.
    In press Competitive conversion in a Small Emirate in A. Baharati, ed., *Ritual Man*. The Hague: Mouton.

PLAYING A KINGDOM:
A HAUSA META-SOCIETY IN THE
WALLED CITY OF ZARIA, NIGERIA

Harold Olofson

Introduction

In his classic *Man, Play, and Games*, Roger Caillois analyzed four elements of play, claiming that two of them, rivalry and mimicry, are not often found together, and when they are, their co-occurrence is accidental. His only explanation for this was that there is little in either of them that promotes their working together, although they are not incompatible, as is evidenced in the case of spectators identifying themselves with performers in a competition (Caillois 1961:

72). I present here a case where they are found together and where they are not only not incompatible, but can be interpreted as achieving a very meaningful message of socialization which is carried in their symbolic combination.

Rivalry between Hausa male youth is discussed in a previous article by Ames, Gregersen, and Neugebauer (1971). They describe the boastful drum-message (*take*) epithets, each of which is publicly known to be associated with a particular youth. These play an important role in courtship. At girls' dances, Hausa praise-singers (on behalf of themselves and the musicians) cleverly play off suitors against each other by stimulating them to drain their pockets to have their epithets drummed in girls' names (Ames *et al* 1971:16). This situation is repeated among males later in life for the favors of courtesans and is called by the Hausa *gaba* (rivalry). The situation of rivalry presented here is the dry-season youth festival, previously only mentioned in passing for the Hausa of Nigeria by M. G. Smith (1965:144-145)[1] and Ames *et al* (1971:22-23). I give here a more complete description, different in some details from their data, which I received from a young Zaria informant who had himself participated in three of the festivals in his late teens. This description comes primarily from his memories of the last festival in which he played.

The participants, from the ward of Zagezegi within the walls of Birnin Zazzau (Zaria City), called their play *wasan misisi*, or "play of the misses," with a borrowing from the English. The term *misisi* referred to the uniforms bought by the males to be worn by their girl-friends in the play. This was a renaming of the institution; the older term, still used in the villages and in other towns, is *kalankuwa*. Bargery's dictionary (1934:538) has many entries for it, none of which relate to the play directly, but some of which are obviously relevant to an understanding of the meaning of the word in the play context:

(1) "A large gathering of farm-workers on a big farm of an . . . important official." Note that the play usually takes place at harvest, when many of the trappings can be paid for with money from cash crops; also, that at the center of the play is the reigning "king" of the youths.

(2) "A coil of stalks, grass or small sticks placed on a wall . . ." In terms of the play this meaning could refer to the fenced-off nature of the play-ground.

(3) "Gossiping with or looking on at one who is at work, without offering to assist." Here one is reminded of the spectators who come to watch, some being invited guests of the participants, and seated inside the arena.

(4) "Circumlocution; evasive talk." The play is an imitation of some aspects of adult life, and insofar as it is, Hausa adults can only look upon it as a childish activity. It is a brief respite for youth from the "serious" world.

Description

My informant's plays were organized by an adult who took an interest in the activities of youth. This is common in many areas of Hausaland. The individual is usually given the honorary title of *Sarkin Samari*, "Chief of the Youths," by the townsmen. The organizer of the *wasan misisi* received rather the title of *shugaban wasa*, "play-leader," from the youth of the informant's ward. "He just seemed to take charge," and brought about expressive innovations in their plays which made them a caricature of the modern world, and thereby superior, in the eyes of the participants, to the plays given by other wards.

Those to play in the important "title roles" were selected by the vote of the boys in a General Meeting called by the leader sometime before the play. The Governor (*Gwamna*) was selected with the approval of the leader on the basis of his Fulani qualities—the lightness of his skin and slimness of his build. (In more traditional versions he would be called *Sarki*, "Chief" or "Emit.") The Queen (*Sarauniya*) was chosen by the boys through a vote "on the advice of the girls." Also selected were the Governor's Orderly (*Odilan Gwamna*), Prison-Warden (*Yari*), policemen ('*Yandoka*), Treasurer (*Ma'aji*), Judge (*Alk'ali*), Secretary (*Magatakarda*), doctors (*Mallaman Dafta*), and nurses (*Duba Gari*, literally, "inspect the town.") The last two roles wore white uniforms. The young boys who had been circumcised and who thus "had sense" were to act as messengers (*masinjoji*) between all of the participants, and they learned the mechanics of the play by early meaningful participation, while performing a duty common to children in everyday life. Praise-singers and drummers would also be present and active.

On the day of the play, a suitably sized field (*sarari*) was fenced off with barbed wire and arranged with electric lights. Seats, a record player, records, and enough soft drinks to last the night were brought. The Governor's "throne" was designed by the leader in the form of a carpeted table with two cushions, one for the Governor and one for his "wife," the Queen. (In previous years the Queen had to remain with the other girls during the play.) Painted steps led up to the throne, and the leader fashioned a bomb, made of wood and painted green, to be placed in front of the Governor as a symbol of his office. Youthful "police" were to be stationed at either side of this bomb at stiff attention, wearing caps and holding play guns also designed by the leader, while two others were to march back and forth between them for long periods of the play. These youths all had uniforms made for them by Zaria tailors.

When the young men and women assembled, in the evening, the play started off with great pomp. The Governor and Queen approached in an open car protected by four real "highway patrol" police, two in front and two in back. The girls shouted *Gyara gari, ga Gwamna ya zo!* "Prepare the town, there is the Governor coming!" and the popguns were shot off. The youth police opened the car doors and the Governor appeared in a white uniform designed by the leader, with a striking hat which was a foot tall with paper attachments and brim turned up back and front, to replace the cowboy hat (*bodila*) of previous years. (This was probably an imitation of the "colonial service dress uniform complete with a plumed pith helmet" mentioned by Ames *et al* (1971:23)). The Governor was escorted to the throne but on the way he walked around to see his people. Upon reaching his position he made a speech into a microphone, thanking the people for coming and hoping that the play would be successfully concluded without fighting. Quarrelling among the participants, say over females, would intrude on both the play-frame and the Hausa ideal of smooth social interaction based on a state of harmony (*jituwa*). As the entertainment began by listening to music and watching the dancing of the girls, real policemen prevented the males and females from crossing to each others' sides, while youth police went outside the enclosure to ask for donations from uninvited spectators. Special guests, usually friends of the leader, would arrive and were seated inside at their own tables. Fighting among the players or crossing the field without the permission of the Governor would lead to the offender being taken by a policeman before the Judge and fined.

Music, dance, and conversation continued until one in the morning, when, amidst the drumming of *take* and the shouting of praise-singers attempting to get rivalries going, girls sent food brought from their homes to their boy-friends. This included chicken or other meat, rice, tea, and cigarettes. The "doctors" and "nurses" inspected the food and bowls to see whether they were clean. If a girl's food did not come up to modern standards, she could be taken to the Judge and fined or imprisoned under the Warden. But this apparently happened very rarely, as the girl would be greatly saddened and embarrassed, however, she would be prevented from giving her food to anyone. Some boys might get food from many different girls, but each boy would place a gift of money on the empty plate to be returned by a messenger to his favorite, knowing that the money to be given later for her *kwanta*, "untying," would go to others rather than to her.

Kwanta took place at two o'clock in the morning. The girls sat on a table and each could not move until a boy-friend "untied" her by giving her a gift of money. One girl could be untied by many boys, and a boy could untie a girl from which he did not receive food. This money would actually go to the Secretary, who wrote down the amounts, the names of the donors, and the girls in whose names the money was given. It was then passed on to the Treasurer, and from him eventually to the praise-singers, drummers, and real policemen. Some of it would also be used for taking a photograph of the participants in the morning.

When the *wasan misisi* was finished (and the ending of performances in Hausa culture is not strongly marked, being usually a gradual dissipation of the group), the girls went to their boyfriends in the night for *tad'i*, "chatting," frequently an euphemism for sex-play. A gift of money would be given to the girls at this time. My informant suggested that parents did not object to this because they strongly suspected that marriage would take place between a girl and the boy who had bought her uniform. But in no case could marriage between the courters be a certainty as a result of *wasan misisi.*

Thus youthful rivalry is an important feature of this play-world, involving competition for sexual favors and possible spouses. Disappointments were possible. A girl could make a liaison with some boy who untied her other than the one who bought her uniform. Or she could send food to someone in addition to her boy-friend and receiving money back arrange a meeting with him instead. In these cases, the original suitor could reclaim the cost of the uniform from her.

Another rivalry existed, that between the players and the youth from other wards. The real purpose of the presence of the local police at the play was first and foremost to prevent the latter from spoiling the festival. They might have interfered otherwise with the approach of the rulers to the play-ground, or threatened to tear down the barbed wire or "crash" the proceedings, or throw stones. It is obvious that the play, with all of its innovations, was put on also for the admiration or jealousy of these cross-town rivals. It was important to the actors that their play be superior to those of all the other wards in the town, plays which they would have a chance to witness. Thus the youth of the ward of Zagezegi readily accepted the ideas of their leader. My informant and those who had taken roles in these productions soon stopped participating in the belief that they had staged the best *misisi* in town and should leave their successes for the emulation of the youth coming up after them. But the informant, as an adult, could only judge the performances of these later editions as but poor imitations of the one's he and his age-mates had enacted. It is also likely that he had grown out of the enjoyment of *misisi.*

Interpretation

Though I was unable to witness a *wasan misisi* personally while in the field, I offer here a few points of interpretation which a general knowledge of Hausa culture helps support, in the hope that further research can be done to confirm or modify them.

1. It is clear that the play is a simplified and miniaturized duplication, a caricature in fact, of the population, hierarchy and administration of a Hausa emirate. It is simplified in the sense that some traditional components are left out, such as priest (*liman*), District Head, and courtesan. The emphasis has shifted to a parody of a "modern" state; the players want to be seen as modern youth and it is this that is designed to impress spectators from rivalrous wards. Thus the "King" has become the "Governor" with his power symbolized by a bomb, and he is a person who likes to listen to records and drink soda-pop. The Queen moves onto the throne with him. The girls are made to conform to modern standards of sanitation and their modern apparel gives the festival a new name, while the policemen wear modern uniforms and carry modern (toy-) weapons.

2. This form of play is popular in an adolescent period that follows a childhood in which rough play and vertigo were prominent.[2] This reconfirms Caillois's transition from *paidia*, the turbulence of childhood play, to *ludus*, with a refinement of rules and intellect and no emphasis on vertigo. Caillois saw *ludus* as having a "civilizing quality" (1961:27), that is, symbolizing a transition from nature to culture. The youth are beginning to identify with the wider structure of their, in this case changing, society, an identification which is reinforced in the aim to put on a clever, up-to-date mime.

3. The elements of mimicry and rivalry that go to make up the play are in a particular relationship. The mimicry, the acting-out of a play-kingdom, provides a *frame* for the activities and rivalries of the play-populace, just as a real state structure provides a frame within which are played out the daily activities and rivalries of workaday life. Out there may be another subtle comparison that can be made between the two frames. In the play, it is no doubt the case that everyone sees the role of Governor, of Queen, and so on as "pretend," or, as the Hausa would say, as "play" (*wasa*), but the rivalries *within* the frame of mimicry are real. Here the play takes on the appearance of a masquerade party among our own courting youth. Sexual liaisons are made, disappointments may be felt, and potential real-life consequences in the form of marriage could result. True, in some ways the preparation of food by the girls for the boys, the gifts of money given to them by their suitors, and the ultimate "chatting" looks like a parody of marriage. But one suggests that the participants would have seen this as being *more* "real" than playing one of the roles in the play. To put it another way, the rivalrous behavior within the frame is analogous to and even connected with rivalry in real life, and, just as the play-kingdom frame is identified as "pretend," so might it be an "unserious" consideration on the part of people in everyday life that they themselves could hope to achieve the real-life roles of king, queen, judge, even nurse or policeman.

4. Thus the possibility arises that the play-kingdom is a *meta-society*, "a society about society," and the elements in it so combined as to provide subtle teaching on the wider context, messages which bathe and socialize the actors in ways that may be more or less out-of-awareness.

Caillois described *identification* as follows:

". . . a degraded and diluted form of *mimicry*, the only one that can survive in a world dominated by the combination of merit and chance. The majority fail in competition or are ineligible to compete, having no chance to enter or succeed. . . . Chance, like merit, selects only a favored few. The majority remain frustrated. Everyone wants to be first. . . . however, each knows or suspects that he will not be . . ." (1961:120)

In *wasan misisi* we see identification and mimicry, but at the crux is a meta-society which leads people to awareness at some level of *ascribed* status which prefigures life chances. First of all, the Fulani rulership is a matter of ascribed status which the young people playing the more prestigious roles will have no chance to achieve. Rather, there is the expectation, with social pressure, that boys should take up the occupation of their fathers. Secondly, achieved status, like those of judge, doctor, nurse, or policeman may be defined as unlikely because of limits imposed by individual economic resources and the strong competitiveness involved in entering institutions of training. My Zaria informant himself had failed to reach secondary school, despite a strong primary school performance, because his father had refused to engage in bribery. Thirdly, rivalry in commerce, the most Hausa of pursuits, may lead to great riches. But these can never in turn mean a rise of occupational status into rulership. The wealthy trader instead engages in conspicuous consumption, in the acquisition of wives, courtesans, lorries, compounds, and clients. Merit is gathered through alms-giving and repeated journeys to Mecca, while the trader proliferates more and more lines of work to pointlessly increase his wealth.

The play may teach its participants to maintain public poise in the face of frustrating defeat, both in life generally, and in the play specifically in terms of sexual rivalry when the defeated wooer ought not show his disappointment by quarrelling. But what answer does the play provide to the frustrations of ascribed status and the limitations of achievement? I suggest that the answer is merely *rivalry*,[3] in the pursuit of occupations and activities which are inherited or learned from within a realistically, reachable realm of life. The actors in the play meta-society may know that this is as close as they may ever come to the roles they play.[4,5]

NOTES

[1] I refer the reader to this source for an excellent ethnographic background on the Hausa.

[2] I do not mean to imply here that all Hausa youths of Zaria or elsewhere engage annually in *kalankuwa*. Some never may. For example, many females who are married off at an early age cannot engage in it (except perhaps as messengers), and a boy may be sent away to a Koranic school at the time when age-mates at home perform the play. In many towns some years can doubtless go by without any performance at all.

[3] Rivalry, in fact, is a major characteristic of Hausa social relations. To give only a few prime examples, it is evident in trade, in competition within a craft, in getting marriage partners, between co-wives, between brothers, between clients sharing the same patron, among the rulership for office in title, among practitioners of the *bori* cult, between courte-

sans, and so on. Hence a widespread belief in sorcery.

[4]My informant did not see "guinea-corn townships" established in the bush as mentioned by Smith (1965:145). But this is only to stress that we are dealing with something that reflects the world, which changes as the world changes, and which varies from town to town. This may have been an old-fashioned style of setting up the site for the play. Let us glance briefly at some other variations.

Jerome Barkow has graciously supplied me with field notes taken on a *kalankuwa* held in the village of Wurinsalla in northwest Zazzau. His data suggests that it may also be performed just after the planting of the crops. The celebration was attended by hundreds of people from neighboring villages, including Maguzawa and pastoral Fulani, as well as praise-singers, drummers, courtesans, a snake-charmer and a hoe-thrower. Maguzawa girls performed dances for Maguzawa males at one end of the village, while the *kalankuwa* occurred at the other, with little cross-spectatorship. The acting out of titled roles was not greatly evident. Three elements stood out, however. One was gambling (*caca*), usually banned on religious grounds but for this holiday allowed by the Wurinsalla Village Head. Fifteen circles of gambling youths were counted, ignoring traditional Hausa gambling games and playing European cards. Second, there was the "untying" of girl friends. Each girl sat in a chair and when untied a praise-singer would announce the names of the courters and the amount given for the girl. A village tax-collector then took up the money, which eventually found its way to the Village Head. Third, in the late hours couples drifted off to engage in sex-play (*tsarance*).

My incomplete notes for Funtua in southern Katsina indicate a system of youth titles held by people who are no longer young. *Sardin Samari* was an honorary post over the youth of the entire town. The actual task of organizing a *kalankuwa* fell to the *Magajin Garin Samari*, "Mayor of the Town of Youths," who got the participants together for meetings. If a festival is desired, money is collected to build a big hut and buy soft drinks. A main activity appears to be the dancing of the girls for the pleasure of the boys. A Queen is selected by the girls as the most beautiful among them; it is her duty to select the best dancer in the *kalankuwa*; a gift is then taken to her at the direction of *Sarkin Samari* through his "orderly." There is a treasurer who pays praise-singers and drummers out of a collection coming from on-lookers, in part, who are charged sixpence for tickets. Policemen stop quarrelling in the hut, and a Judge fines those brought to him by a policeman. By the time I arrived, the youth of the town had shown little interest in holding a *kalankuwa* for two years, although some did go to watch it performed in neighboring hamlets. It seemed that the present "officials" were long overdue to be replaced by younger and more enthusiastic cadres.

Claude Raynaut (1972:121-135) has an excellent discussion of the organization of youth in the rural Hausa village of Soumarana in Niger, which I did not see before writing on *wasan misisi*. The youth there have a wide range of titles many of which reflect historical changes. Here, too, the King has become a Governor, and the positions of commandant, engineer, customs-official, and the like, have appeared. The festival is called *wasak kara*, "the millet-stalk play," and is celebrated with the appearance of that grain, leading Raynaut to claim that it is a survival of ancient rites of fecundity. The village of Soumarana is divided into two moieties, the youth of which have traditionally enjoyed a lively rivalry. Each side has its own *wasak kara* and separate hierarchy and, when performing a *wasa*, invites those of the opposing side. Over a period of three years, pairs of rivals exchange the roles of guest-host with each other and exchange gifts ostentatiously in a manner which Raynaut describes as a potlatch. He sees these exchanges as a symbolic expression of the unity of the two moieties' dissymmetry as well as their complementarity. His discussion of the functions of the youth organization are similar to portions of my interpretation for *wasan misisi*. In his view the play helps participants to absorb the values of struggle and competition which motivate

Hausa society, and the hierarchical structure of the youth organization helps to familiarize them with the organization of the wider society. Moreover, some of the roles help them to realize a social discipline which individuals must adhere to in social life (Raynaut 1972: 125).

[5] I would finally like to thank William Bezdek for a critical reading of an earlier version of this paper. All remaining shortcomings, however, are mine.

REFERENCES

Ames, David, Edgar Gregersen, and Thomas L. Neugebauer
    1971 *Taaken Samaarii: A Drum Language of Hausa Youth*. Africa 41, 1:12-31.
Bargery, Rev. G. P.
    1934 *A Hausa-English Dictionary and English-Hausa Vocabulary*. Oxford University Press.
Caillois, Roger
    1961 *Man, Play, and Games*. Free Press of Glencoe.
Raynaut, Claude
    1972 *Structures normatives et relations electives*. Mouton.
Smith, M. G.
    1965 The Hausa of Northern Nigeria. In *Peoples of Africa*. James L. Gibbs, ed. New York: Holt, Rinehart, and Winston. Pp. 119-155.

SOCIAL AND JUDICIAL FUNCTIONS
OF BACHAMA SONG-CONTESTS

Phillips Stevens, Jr.
State University of New York, Buffalo

Johan Huizinga (1950:66ff.) has shown that variations on the "slanging-match" in various cultures, conducted principally for the maintenance or increase of honor and prestige and serving various other social functions, can degenerate into open conflict—or can change in function from a *"joute de jactance"* (lit. "boasting-match") to a jural proceeding. He notes (pp. 84ff.) that three play-forms can be distinguished in jural proceedings in "archaic" societies: the game of chance, the contest, and the verbal battle. Speaking of the latter, parallels to which he sees between lawyers in modern legal suits, he notes, "here it is not the most meticulously deliberated juristic argument that tips the balance, but the most withering and excoriating invective" (1950:84). He notes further that "the transition from the *joute de jactance* proper to the reviling-match as a legal proceeding is, however, not very clear." In spite of his discussion of Eskimo drumming-matches, the transition remains unclear—probably because among the Eskimo societies he discusses, drumming-matches serve social and legal functions simultaneously, there being no other form of jurisdiction.

The "legal" nature of Eskimo song-contests has been queried by Gluckman (1965:190ff.) in response to Hoebel's (1954:51ff.) application of the term. In regard to ·a similar practice, that of "drumming the scandal" among the Tiv of central Nigeria (Bohannan 1957:142ff.), Gluckman points out that the nature of the relationship between the litigants should be more closely investigated. Bohannan's and Gluckman's terminology for and classification of non-Western legal systems has formed the bases for a still-unresolved debate (cf. Gluckman 1969, Bohannan 1969, Pospisil 1972).

This paper discusses the nature and functions of formal song-contests and insult-bouts among the Bachama,[1] a chiefdom in Adamawa, northeastern Nigeria. It offers no resolutions to issues in the Bohannan-Gluckman debate, although I am forewarned by their discussion of the nature of "legal", "judicial", etc., as terms applied to non-Western institutions. The data provided herein are simply intended to amplify Huizinga's discussions of the functions of verbal contests with social and judicial implications, and to provide, along with the Tiv institution of "drumming the scandal", additional West African data. Because of space limitations I have opted for ethnographic description; detailed analysis will be postponed.

Composers and Singers

When asked to rank professions according to degree of esteem and popularity, Bachama most often placed "composers" (*waniye, wanito*, s.) very high, often behind only hunters and warriors. Skilled composers are not common. Many villages have none, few have more than one. A successful composer is one who is well-known and respected in many villages; to be successful, one must demonstrate a variety of talents. A *wanito* is a singer and leader of a chorus, as well as a composer of lyrics and melodies; hence the Bachama word will be used hereinafter.

A wanito must have a good voice, clear, strong, and versatile. As leader of a permanent "chorus", he must be possessed of a certain degree of innate charisma; he must be able to keep his following. He must have those talents characteristic of successful composers elsewhere: originality and the ability to convey a message of current social relevance. And finally, his profession demands a great deal of tact, for the situations in which he performs are very often of high social and political sensitivity.

Waniye and their followers are called upon to perform on many social occasions, notably funerals and weddings, social dances, and hunting and religious festivals. On all occasions the *wanito* is spokesman for a distinct group. And so he is in almost constant demand, and his repertory must be vast indeed. Moreover, the supply of songs at his command must be constantly up-dated and restocked. Undue repetition and stagnation is a sure road to the demise of any *wanito*. So he spends many hours with his "chorus", relatives and others from his own compound or ward, reviewing and revising old songs, and rehearsing new ones. When a festival time is approaching, the *wanito* spends all of his time at this, and those young men who are among his company of singers perform his other chores for him. These rehearsals are crucial to the *wanito*'s success, and in certain situations they are often done in secrecy so that the gist of any new song might not leak out to a rival *wanito*.

Such situations are verbal contests and "battles" between rival *waniye* groups, or, in less common instances, any social groups who enter into a dispute and are ordered by the Chief to settle their quarrel with a song-contest. It is such contests that are significant here. As a means of settling disputes they assume jural importance, and they clearly exhibit one of the "social functions of humor". It is in such situations that the *wanito*'s mettle receives its severest test. I shall briefly consider three such instances: rivalry between *waniye*, specially-adjudicated song- and abuse-contests which may result from such rivalry, and the ongoing and highly humorous verbal battling between two broad ecologically-determined groups, the "people of the banks" and the "people of the bush".

Wanito "Battles"

Experienced, seasoned *waniye* assume with impunity extraordinary license. Having become skilled in the use and application of proverbs, veiled language, and double *entendre*, and taking full advantage of the contexts in which they perform, the composer-singers find occasion to vent grievances, make sarcastic personal asides regarding personages or current events, praise themselves and abuse other *waniye*. A *wanito* of only mediocre talent will use caution in attempting such forays in sensitive areas.

It is known, even expected, that a wanito will use any occasion to achieve whatever ulterior ends he has set for himself. If he is clever in manipulating the situation, so that he at once fulfills his immediate function and can get in some jabs at whatever target he has sighted upon, he will succeed in increasing his esteem. But he must carefully weigh the situation, and appraise his own abilities so that he will know just how far he can go without leaving himself too precarious and vulnerable.

A *wanito* in any context occupies a privileged position, because during his performance he is invulnerable; he cannot be silenced. He knows that retaliation, if any is forthcoming, must await another time. But he knows that his would-be competitors will be listening, usually by proxy, to his words, and that they will hone their verbal barbs very keenly for a possible return match. And he also knows that popular opinion will provide a check on his propriety; according to the Bachama saying, "*Lomo hase a we pomo*—an unpleasant matter does not decay", he might have to be wary of the possibility of a degree of social ostracism, as well as the possibility that he may have begun a *wanito* battle which he can not finish.

One famous (better, "infamous") *wanito* "war" which is still referred to from time to time, began during World War II, toward the end of the reign of Chief Mbi (1921-1941), and continued under his successor, Ngbale (1942-1968). It is difficult to determine how the contest started. It involved originally two well-known *waniye*, called Ngakto ("Fishhook")[2] and Sondo.

For overstepping his office and becoming intolerably abusive, Ngakto was jailed by Mbi. When he was released he was exiled. When Mbi died, Ngakto returned, rallied his forces, and the war was renewed. It came to involve all the inhabitants of the wards of both *waniye*. With Ngakto and Sondo as their "captains", one ward became *"Jamani"* and the other, *"Ingilan"*. And thus, World War II was kept alive in Bachamaland. The "battles" were fought in the traditional contexts of funerals, weddings, festivals, etc. Tensions ran high, tempers flared, and in some instances, actual fighting broke out. Finally, in 1952, Ngbale lost his patience. The case was brought to court, and each wanito was fined £5 (a harsh penalty for that was a time of drought) and was ordered to desist. The "war" was declared a stalemate.

This type of prolonged verbal combat is called *nya hodye*, "fighting at home". As a result of this particular case, relations between the two groups were seriously weakened, and even today they are strained. This was an extraordinary case. Normally the Chief could exercise another option, that of calling a formal song-contest over which he himself would be the judge. Probably the reason why Ngbale took the case to the local court instead was that the affair had begun under Mbi who had himself imposed punishment on one offender. Mbi was a powerful and extremely popular Chief, and Ngbale acted prudently by deferring to government-sanctioned authority.

Formal Song-Contests

In the case discussed above, Ngbale might have resorted to a chiefly prerogative: summoning both sides in the dispute to the Palace, allowing each to exhaust its stock of abusive songs, and then declaring the "winner" and the end of the dispute. No such formally-adjudicated song-contest took place during my time in Bachamaland (September 1969–March 1971), and from what I was able to gather the last such occasion was one called by Mbi in the late 1930's and is poorly remembered. The following discussion is therefore largely hypothetical.

Any minor dispute, usually one involving a misfortune arising out of negligence or carelessness, can be settled through a song-contest (*kawatu dimse*, "song battle"). Most often such an affair has already been taken up by the *waniye*, and by the time the Chief intervenes it has mushroomed far beyond its original implications and has begun to threaten domestic peace. Using traditional situations, such as funerals, *waniye* enlarge on the affair, until actual names may be used and personal or family references made, and the songs become personally abusive. Adherents to either side may grow in number, until the dispute comes to involve an entire ward, even a whole village.

When it has reached this point, the Chief may intervene. He will set a certain evening for the disputants to assemble at the Palace. By this time, news of the on-going quarrel has spread far and wide, and this occasion may draw hundreds ofspectators. People come from distant villages with their own *waniye*, singing their own songs, dancing their own dances. Much beer is brewed and it becomes a great festive occasion. In the evening after supper the Chief assembles the two parties. Each group sits on the ground behind its own *wanito*, facing its opponents. The Chief takes a place to the side, to sit in judgment of the competition. Several of the finest *waniye* of other villages have assembled as advisors to the Chief; if a singer falters, or begins to repeat himself, they will point out such lapses. And so the competition goes on, sometimes far into the night, the *waniye* and their choruses alternately singing their songs of abuse at the other side.

Many criteria seem to be involved in the Chief's judgment. One is the number of songs in one group's repertory; the group that can outlast the other without repeating itself is most likely to be declared the winner. But also, the content of the songs, the originality of their lyrics and melodies, the cleverness of the *waniye* in manipulating the language, are taken into consideration; I was told that the Chief might retire with his *wanito*-counselors to ask their views on such factors before pronouncing judgment.

But the affair is not so easily ended. Even with one group declared the winner, both are shown to be losers in the final analysis. The Chief delivers a speech to them all in which he chastises them severely for having allowed this business to get so far out of hand, and for having caused so many innocent people to suffer. They have done a very bad thing, he concludes, and he will see them all at the palace in the morning. Let them go and sleep on it.[3]

All know that there will be punishment meted out to both sides. Dancing and merry-making continue until dawn, when the people go off for their breakfast. After breakfast the offending parties are called by the Chief; the spectators, not wishing to stay for this sad moment, have departed for their own villages. The two *waniye*, accompanied by most, if not all, of their following, report before the Chief for the sentence. In earlier times, I was told, punishment was severe; the *waniye* might be locked up in "prison" (*gborowe*-shackles) for some weeks, then brought out and publicly flogged; in more recent times fines of money were levied, from five to ten pounds each.

A formal song-and-abuse-contest with less drastic implications takes place on the third day of the great *Pato* festival jointly held by the riverine villages of Numan and Imburu. This festival takes place early in the dry season, usually in November, and is the time of preparation for the annual cooperative hippo hunts. The festival occupies six days, each named, each devoted to a particular activity.

The third day is the one with which we are concerned. People of the original three wards of Imburu gather at the festival-ground. Any person, man or woman, who has a complaint to make against any other can vent his feelings at this time. One by one such plaintiffs come forward and call out their charges. Any problem that has developed over the past year, if a debt is owed, if a personal wrong of any nature has been committed, the offender is singled out and loudly told about it. Complaints against persons can range from the uttering of abusive remarks to charges of adultery. When the accuser has finished, the accused steps forward and defends himself. There are no face-to-face confrontations, and the whole process is reasonably orderly—albeit noisy. Plaintiff and defendant can call witnesses, who will either agree to the charge or refuse to testify by walking away. The whole argument is judged by the crowd, by its signs of approval or disapproval. And the crowd is a harsh judge; unless one has a good defense, he will be socially stigmatized until he makes satisfactory recompense.

This is not categorized as *nya bodye*, nor does it involve very much that is humorous. Nothing is sacred; one's family and whatever **bar**-sinisters lurk in one's genealogy can be resurrected. Accusations of witchcraft or adultery, cases of homicide and suicide which are even two or three generations in the past, might be mentioned in support of the credibility of the alleged recent transgression.

The "People of the Banks" and the "People of the Bush"

Dependent solely upon their places of residence, all Bachama belong to one or the other of two rather nebulous divisions; people resident in riverine villages, or along marshes or inland ponds, are *Ji-Zange* ("people of the banks"), while those living away from the river are *Ji-Bawe* ("people of the bush". *Bawe* refers to either the savanna or woodlands.) A kind of permanent joking relationship exists between the two groups. This form of relationship is evident on many occasions, whenever a social gathering brings members of the two groups together. It is openly manifested almost exclusively during song-fests, in the same contexts as those discussed for the *wanito* "battles". On these occasions the *wanito* exercises his proudest role, that of spokesman for his group in its constant friendly feud with the other.

The rules of the game are similar to those discussed above. With a few exceptions, only one side enjoys the offensive on any given occasion. Exceptions are social dances, or any spontaneously organized song-fest, when opposing *waniye* may face each other. Most commonly, the *waniye* of the host area enjoy the prerogative. If, for example, visitors from *zange* or *bawe* villages have come to the other area for a funeral, marriage, or religious festival, they are a captive audience. For that time they are the butt of the others' taunting songs, and they must endure their role. They cannot retaliate on the spot, but they know they will have their chance for revenge later.

The content of jokes between *Ji-Bawe* and *Ji-Zange* is most often concerned with the subject of *muroune* (the attributes of manhood and manliness; from *mura*, a Man). *Muroune* is best measured in terms of success in hunting or warfare; success in the former is measured in terms of the ferocity of the animals one has slain. Among the *Ji-Zange* the most esteemed animal is the hippopotamus; among the *Ji-Bawe* it is the lion, or the buffalo. *Muroune* also refers to courage in the face of danger; a *mura* (*morye*, pl.) is one who stands and fights no matter what the odds. The opposite is *vauto* (*vauye*, pl.), coward; one who runs away, or one who cries from pain, or one who prefers to stay at home with the women. Indeed, it is far more honorable for a warrior or hunter to die in the bush than at home. *Muroune* entails other virtues, as well; honesty, fairness, and providing for one's family, are among them. In the songs, each group belittles the other's claim to *muroune*. To the *Ji-Bawe* the hippo is a "frog"; to the *Ji-Zange* the lion or buffalo are merely a "dog" or a "deer".

Proximity to the river is also a subject of the songs. The *Ji-Zange* boast of their fishing prowess, and their constant supply of fresh fish; the *Ji-Bawe* must wander and seek for their food in the bush. The *Ji-Zange*, moreover, have an ample water supply and they bathe at least once daily, whereas the *Ji-Bawe* do not bathe, and are constantly dirty. The *Ji-Bawe* counter by saying that the *Ji-Zange* catch *da-vakye* ("seeds of the fish"; minnows and other tiny fish), because they are afraid to go after anything bigger. Moreover, the *Ji-Zange* are "under water" (referring to the annual flooding of the Benue) so that they become water-logged, limp, and useless, and "their truth floats down the river with their shit (*kalato*)".[4] And so it goes.

And it is all mainly in fun. The song-contests between the two groups provide much merriment, and afford the *waniye* the opportunity to be particularly clever in their search for new ways in which to shame and abuse the other group. But, if function is sought, it can be found. The members of one group know that their activities, and particularly their failures, will be constantly observed by members of the other; and that any failures will probably be incorporated into the songs they will hear sung at their next meeting. And this awareness accompanies the people during their cooperative activities, and, I was told, it serves to strengthen their *muroune*. Thus, if the *Ji-Bawe* find a lion particularly difficult to kill—say it has been wounded and hidden itself in a thicket—they will say to each other, "If we cannot kill this animal, what will the *Ji-Zange* say of us?" And similar sentiments will be expressed among the *Ji-Zange* on a particularly frustrating hippo hunt. By this example, of course, a function of joking relationships in general is suggested; it forces individuals and groups to mind their obligations and their social behavior, for lapses could be used publicly against them.

NOTES

[1] Fieldword in Adamawa was conducted from September 1969 through March 1971 and was supported by a Field Grant and Fellowship from the Cultural Anthropology section of the NIMH, and by assistance from the Program of African Studies, Northwestern University.

The Bachama are a chiefdom of farmers, fishers and hunters occupying approximately 1200 square miles of the lowlands along both sides of the Benue River. Their presently-recognized territory extends roughly 45 miles downstream from the confluence of the Gongola River with the Benue, and from three to 16 miles inland from the river on either side. Their language belongs to the Chadic branch of the Afro-Asiatic family. I have discussed further aspects of their socio-political organization elsewhere (Stevens 1973).

[2] A *wanito* takes a nickname (*kwaku wanune*) by which he becomes properly known. Ngakto's full nickname is Ngaktu Kombo: ngakto—fishhook, Kombo—a village known for a marsh containing many crocodiles. But the implication is more than a hook that catches crocodiles; it is also a playful waning: be careful of how you deal with me, if I "hook" you, you will not easily shake me off.

[3] This is the traditional means whereby a Chief passes judgment on any offender. Sentencing is never immediate, for it might be regarded as having been levied out of anger. The Chief should have some time to "cool down" (*bo yedi*, literally, to "settle his stomach".)

[4] *Kalato* refers to both the intestines and the feces. The English vulgarism is deduced from the context in which the word is here used.

REFERENCES

Bohannan, P. J.
  1957 *Justice and Judgment among the Tiv*. London: Oxford University Press.
  1969 "Ethnography and Comparison in Legal Anthropology". In Laura Nader, ed., *Law in Culture and Society*. Chicago: Aldine.
Gluckman, Max
  1965 *Politics, Law and Ritual in Tribal Society*. Chicago: Aldine.
  1969 "Concepts in the Comparative Study of Tribal Law". In Laura Nader, ed., *Law in Culture and Society*. Chicago: Aldine.
Hoebel, E. A.
  1954 *The Law of Primitive Man*. Cambridge: Harvard University Press.
Huizinga, Johan
  1950 *Homo Ludens: A Study of the Play Element in Culture*. Boston: Beacon Press.
Pospisil, Leopold
  1972 *The Ethnology of Law*. Reading, Mass.: Addison-Wesley Modular Publications.
Stevens, Phillips, Jr.
  1973 The Bachama and their Neighbors: Non-Kin Joking Relationships in Adamawa, Northeastern Nigeria. Ph.D. Dissertation, Northwestern University. Ann Arbor: Xerox-University Microfilms.

CHAPTER V

Observational Study of Play in Primates and and Young Children

Introduction

One of the great advantages that students of primate behavior have enjoyed is that (discounting Washoe and Sarah) they can't converse with their informants. They have been forced, therefore, to carefully and painstakingly observe the behavior of the animals they study. The techniques of behavioral observation and description have been slowly refined by ethologists and primatologists to the point where art and artifice serve scientific ends.

Detailed observation has been critically missing in anthropological studies of children's play. In the literature, children are perceived as wards of parents and caretakers; their behavior a response to some manner of "rearing." Therefore, much information on play behavior is obtained by interviewing and/or observing the caretakers. It is undoubtably this focus on child rearing that has led some investigators to claim that in the society they studied, children don't play. In the papers in this chapter, play is rigorously defined, the methods for studying it clearly specified, and the results justify the investigators' efforts.

Oakley's paper is an introduction to the methodology of primate play research for a non-primatologist and is very welcome. If the study of play is to become a serious science, research must aim at establishing generalizable results. Anthropologists pursuing questions on human play might well find opportunities to address these questions through research on colony animals. One broad question which Oakley and Reynolds deal with is the "need" for play. Knowing whether primates, in general, need to play is fundamental to our understanding of play. If there is indeed such a need, deprivation effects should be demonstrable and Oakley and Reynolds succeed in showing these for at least one species of monkey.

Oakley also stresses the need for scrupulous definition; a problem repeatedly addressed in the papers in Chapter I. She mentions the need to habituate the population under study to the presence of the researcher. This issue may be critical in studies of children's behavior as well. Finally, she points up the various meanings attached to the word "observation." Observation is not a single, straightforward technique, but, in the work of ethologists takes on all the complexities of a multi-cell experiment.

Doyle applies an ecological/ethological framework to the study of preschool children at play. Here again the definition problem arises and Doyle reviews the literature pertaining to this area. His single-multiple niche model offers greater promise of theoretical utility than earlier definitions which employed fairly arbitrary criteria in dividing up children's play. Play in institutionalized settings such as schools, camps, playgrounds, etc., has received very little attention from anthropologists, but, like the primate colonies only more so, these settings are quite numerous and accessible and provide low cost opportunities for advancing play research and theory.

Schwartzman follows up her literature review paper (Chapter I) by showing how adherents of several theoretical persuasions might analyze a make-believe play sequence in a preschool. Her own alternative is to view children as actively manipulating the play to reinforce their own roles and statuses in the peer group. What's clear from her work is that this "sideways" perspective is only possible if one is thoroughly familiar with the character and personalities of one's subjects and their patterns of interaction in play and other situations. Needless to say, previous investigators of children's play have not always done this and this may partly explain why theories have evolved in which play is abstracted from the daily lives and behavior of children. As I mentioned in the introduction to Chapter II, there may be a shift in emphasis underway from a focus on children's games to a focus on childhood. It is with this latter focus that a "sideways" perspective on play is achieved.

METHODOLOGICAL CONSIDERATIONS FOR
STUDIES OF PLAY IN PRIMATES

Fredericka B. Oakley
Yale University

This discussion is based on the author's experience in studying primate behavior, especially that of infants and juveniles, over a number of years in several laboratory and colony situations, and on her attempts, successful and otherwise, to record, analyze and manipulate play behavior experimentally with the goal of understanding and elucidating the social and neurological substrata of play in primates.

First I would like to offer a definition of play which applies well to mammals in general, and to primates in particular. The definition of play has been a particular problem for ethologists. In observing primates other than man we are fortunate in that much play behavior is accompanied by a specific facial expression restricted to the play context and widely known as the "play face." This is a facial expression in which the mouth is loosely open, the teeth covered by the lips, and the corners of the mouth retracted slightly. The eyebrows may be slightly raised (Altmann, 1967. An illustration [10.6] appears in Hinde, 1974.). The existence of this element alone could be taken as a baseline for defining play, but, in addition, the following elements may be observed:

(1) A reordering of ordinary behavioral sequences
(2) Exaggeration of movements

(3) Repetition of movements or behavioral sequences

(4) Incomplete behavioral sequences, and

(5) Increased tempo in movements.

In addition, it has been noted that sequences of behavior that would be otherwise labeled as aggression, for instance, are recognized as play because they are silent. Other definitions of primate play may be found in Dolhinow and Bishop (1970), Loizos (1966) and Reynolds (1972).

It will be noted that the foregoing is a structural definition of play, and not a motivational one. The question of *why* animals play is one that we hope to answer through our research.

I am not prepared to offer here a theory regarding the relationship of monkey play to play in humans. I have been impressed in these proceedings with how little I know of the play of humans. Rather, I would like to offer suggestions on ways that students of human behavior might study monkey play. I offer these suggestions for a number of reasons. Of the first order is the fact that there exist, throughout North America, many colonies of primates available for study. Many of these colonies are seriously under-utilized. It is a difficult and expensive undertaking to establish a colony of nonhuman primates, and those that exist should be exploited as much as possible. I have myself found easy access to monkeys at two universities, two medical schools, and a Veteran's Administration hospital. The fact that some of these monkeys were being manipulated for other research necessitated some creativity of approach, but by no means precluded research. Another reason to encourage the study of captive animals is that few students who have as their main concern studies of human behavior will ever have the time or resources to conduct adequate field research on feral populations. I believe that it is a grave mistake to too seriously undervalue the worth of laboratory and colony researchers. In the field of primate ethology, in particular, we are in serious need of the fresh insights and divergent points of view that could be offered by students whose formal training does not overlap with ours; students, for example, of sociology and physical education. A final reason to recruit new primate watchers is to help you to look with a critical eye at the work of primatologists when you encounter it. Even the slightest first-hand experience has a profoundly demystifying effect.

Before attempting to offer suggestions for how newcomers might study primates, I would like to direct attention to the contribution of Prof. Carlton to this volume. I believe that he has addressed a problem of particular concern to behavioral scientists in an especially straight-forward way. That is the problem of working from a firm philosophical-theoretical basis when one embarks upon behavioral research. In particular, the problem of scrupulous definition is worthy of consideration. I would like to add to Prof. Carlton's discussion one additional caution, and that is to resist what Michael Scriven (1966) has called, "the perennial temptation of logicians—make the portrait neat and perhaps the sitter will become neat." This temptation is by no means peculiar to logicians. We are all given to it at some turning. My point here is to remind you that it is easy to improve the appearance of what we have done after the fact, but that it is deceptive to do so. It is necessary to be scrupulously cautious in the design of research; no amount of subsequent cosmetology can ever improve the damaged child of our labors. To continue in this vein briefly, Abraham Kaplan in his *The Conduct of Inquiry* has exhaustively treated many of the philosophical and theoretical problems of designing and conducting research. It is rewarding to turn to his volume when complacency threatens.

I will now turn to specific suggestions for the study of social behavior, in particular play, among primates.

The first consideration in any study should be to understand the subjects and their place in nature. With regard to nonhuman subjects, this is an especially important problem. When the animals studied are living in a feral state, this preliminary assay must include consideration of the ecology in general, and any special stresses such as seasonal variation in weather and food resources. One special problem is a geographically unnatural habitat, as in the case of some manufactured communities such as Cayo Santiago Island near Puerto Rico, where rhesus monkeys indigenous to the Indian Peninsula have been introduced and allowed to range freely (Altman, 1962). Another special problem is that of rapidly changing habitats as was the case at Chobi, on the banks of the Nile River in East Africa where a rapidly deteriorating habitat and overpopulation had a serious impact on the social structure of monkey groups. (Gartland and Brain, 1968). When subjects are living in captivity, this assay effort must be based upon a synthesis of research from the available literature describing the animals in their natural habitat, and the student's best efforts to judge the functionally important deviations from that condition, as well as consideration of factors of population density and makeup. In order to utilize successfully the convenience of the colony situation, the student must maximize the significant similarities between the ecology of captive animals and that of their feral conspecifics. Thus in a colony or laboratory situation, efforts must be made to "normalize" the age-sex ratio of the subjects to be studied and to provide an environment of sufficient richness by providing for climbing, hiding and sleeping places and objects for manipulation, play, and attention. It is also desirable to allow for natural biological periodicities in lighting arrangements, and to provide a feeding situation that is appropriate with regard both to nutrition and to the distribution of foodstuffs. These particular problems in setting up a colony are really not difficult to solve once the experimentor accepts the importance of doing so. Gartland and Brain (1968) have commented on the importance of understanding the limitations of colony situations, and Jay (1968) has offered suggestions for the structuring and study of monkey colonies.

Once the student has made satisfactory efforts to normalize the population and assayed the inevitable skew from normal that remains, he must be satisfied that he has established a workable baseline, or else he must continue to manipulate the ecology until he has done so. He must be prepared to describe and rationalize this baseline.

When it is impossible to materially improve a situation, as when one is sharing an established colony with other experimenters, the baseline may necessarily be at great variance with what one would desire. When this is the case, the student must ask what he can reasonably hope to achieve in the given situation. This is a time to be on guard against the "perennial temptation."

This brings us to the next step in experimental design, that of establishing reasonable goals. When the subject of study is one as complex as play behavior, we must necessarily be circumspect in what we can hope to achieve. The goal of a lifetime may be to understand the structure and function of play, but the goal of any given study may not be. Moreover, the more unnatural the study situation, the more circumspect we must be. The place for leaps of faith must be in our own cogitations when entertaining hypotheses; we must not demand too many of our colleagues when we share our results. Some years ago, Frank Beach offered an amusing overview of such problems in an address to the American Psychological Association called "The Snark was a Bojum" (Beach, 1950).

A mundane but important further step in beginning studies is to habituate the study population both to its environment and to the observer. Here, only time works. In my own studies I have used as an index of animal-to-observer habituation the willingness of mothers with small infants to approach to within five feet of the cage or fence front. It is important in this regard that the observer dress and deport himself in a consistent fashion, and that this fashion be different from that of persons who encounter the animals for other purposes. Veterenarians, for instance, have a tendancy to wear white coats, and since they generally make disruptive intrusions into animal colonies, I always try to look as little like The Doctor as possible.

Next, one must establish a system for recording behavior. I always compile a "lexicon of social behaviors" for a group. This is culled from the literature on the species and from my own observations. In recent years I have coded these lexica for computer input so that, whatever I ultimately do with the data, they are in a handy form for programming. The compilation of this lexicon is a place for a degree of intuition, since it is desirable to establish behavioral units of reasonably equivalent weights.

There have been numerous systems of description used in primate studies, these range from the enormous time-sampling check sheets used by some experimental psychologists for instance, to the rather poetic discursions of some early field workers.

My own preference is to confine myself to an established behavioral lexicon, and to make time continuous recordings verbally onto tape. (This makes it imperative to habituate the animals to my voice, as well as visage, incidentally). Codification is done from these tapes. For nonmanipulative, naturalistic studies of infant and juvenile behavior, including play, I have written several analytical computer programs, both based on linguistic models (Oakley, in prep). This is in accordance with my structuralist approach. My point here is not to suggest that this is an especially fruitful methodology (although I believe that it is), but to show that given a well understood theoretical framework, or even a good stolen model, techniques of observation can be developed which are particularly useful for achieving well understood goals. I stress this because the great bulk of what has been written about monkey play has been either fallout from more general field studies, or impressionistic treatises on the incidental effects of experimentation which affected play as one variable. The reports generally lead to the same conclusions 1) "Pity the monkeys (and children) who are not allowed to play" and 2) Play is necessary for good health and practice for adult life (Suomi and Harlow, 1971; Dolhinow and Bishop, 1970). Such is the state of the art.

Finally, as a physical anthropologist, I would like to make a plea for the importance of understanding our closest phylogenetic relatives (and indeed the animal kingdom in general) for developing a generative understanding of ourselves and our place in nature. In this regard, I direct your attention to the studies of Eibl-Eibesfeldt (1972) and N. G. Blurton-Jones (1972) both of whom have attempted comparative studies among and between animals, including man, and have stressed the importance of ethological studies of social behavior in man. I do not claim that this is even remotely a panacea for man's ills, or that we are only naked apes after all, but I do remind you that it is "a small planet."

I would like to conclude with the words of Robert Hinde, an ethologist who has contributed, perhaps more than any other individual, to our understanding of behavior. In the preface to his book, *Biological Bases of Human Social Behaviour*, he opened with these words:

> Understanding human behaviour involves problems infinitely more difficult than landing a man on the moon or unravelling the structure of complex molecules. The problems are also more important and more urgent. If we are to tackle them, we must use every source of evidence available to us. Studies of animals are one such source. Sometimes such studies are useful to the extent that animals resemble man, and sometimes they help just because animals are different and permit the study of issues in a simplified, isolated, or exaggerated form. They may assist us in understanding the behaviour of man not only through factual comparison between animal and man, but also by helping us to refine the categories and concepts used in the description and explanation of behaviour and social structure. But the use of animals involves dangers: it is so easy to make rash generalizations, to slip from firm fact to flight of fancy, to select examples to fit preconceptions. Studies of animals must therefore be used circumspectly, and the limitations of their usefulness specified.

REFERENCES

Altmann, Stuart A.
    1962 *A field study of the sociobiology of rhesus monkeys, Macaca mulatta*. Ann. N.Y. Acad. Sci. 102: 338-435.
    1967 The structure of primate social communication. In *Social communication among primates*. Stuart A. Altmann, ed. Chicago: The University of Chicago Press.

Beach, Frank A.
    1950 *The Snark was a Bojum*. American Psychol. 5(4):115-125.

Blurton-Jones, N. G. (Ed.)
    1972 *Ethological studies of child behavior*. New York and London: Cambridge University Press.

Carlton, Richard
    1975 *Sport as art: Some reflections on definitional problems in the sociology of sport*. Address to the first annual meeting of The Association for the Anthropological Study of Play, Detroit, Michigan.

Dolhinow, Phyllis J. and Naomi Bishop
    1970 *Development of motor skills and social relations among primates through play*. Minnesota Symp. in Child Psych. 4:141-198. John P. Hill (ed.) Minneapolis: University of Minnesota Press.

Eibl-Eibesfeldt, Iraneus
    1972 Similarities and differences between cultures in expressive movements. In *Non-verbal communication*, Robert A. Hinde, ed. New York and London: Cambridge University Press.

Gartlan, J. S. and C. K. Brain
    1968 Ecology and social variability in *Cercopithecus aethiops* and *C. mitis*. In *Primates: studies in adaptation and variability*, Phyllis C. Jay, ed. New York: Holt, Rinehart and Winston, Inc.

Hinde, Robert A.
    1973 *Biological bases of human social behaviour*. New York: McGraw-Hill Book Company.

Jay, Phyllis C.
    1968 Analysis of behavior: Remarks. In *Primates: Studies in adaptation and variability*, Phyllis C. Jay, ed. New York: Holt, Rinehart and Winson, Inc.

Kaplan, Abraham
    1964 *The Conduct of Inquiry*. San Francisco: Chandler Publ.

Loizos, Carolyn
    1966 *Introduction, Play in mammals*. Symp. Zool. Soc. London 18:1-9.

Oakley, Fredericka B.
    In Prep. A linguistic model for the description and analysis of social behavior in primates: The nature of play and the ontogeny of social behavior. Ph.D. dissertation, Yale University, New Haven, Ct.

Reynolds, Peter C.
    1972 Play and the evolution of language. Ph.D. dissertation, Yale University, New Haven, Ct.

Scriven, Michael
    1966 *Primary philosophy*. New York: McGraw-Hill Book Company.

Suomi, Stephen J. and Harry F. Harlow
    1971 *Monkeys at play*. Natural History Magazine, December.

DIFFERING RESPONSES TO SOCIAL PLAY
DEPRIVATION IN TWO SPECIES OF MACAQUE[1]

Fredericka B. Oakley   Peter C. Reynolds
Yale University   Australian National University

Introduction

There is good evidence that play is a legitimate effective-behavioral category. Play is accompanied by species-specific signals restricted to the play context; it has a definite place in the need hierarchy of the organism, and it shows a
consistent developmental relationship to other categories of behavior (see
Bekoff, 1972; Reynolds, *in press*; Welker, 1961, for reviews). If play
has its own underlying neural organization, it may be possible to show that play
functions as a drive by testing whether play behavior increases in frequency as a
function of play deprivation. Muller -Schwarze (1969) was unable to demonstrate any increase in play behavior after social play deprivation in black-tailed
deer, but Chepko (1970) obtained an increase in play behavior after play deprivation in goats, which she termed a *play rebound effect*. Our own experiments with rhesus monkeys (*Macaca mulatta*) indicate that the play rebound is a
highly reliable and easily reproducible effect of social play deprivation in this
species. Other experiments with the crab-eating monkey. *Macaca fascicularis*,
(=*irus*) did not show a play rebound effect, but this discrepancy can be attributed to the different age compositions of the particular rhesus and crab-eating
groups used. Two experiments were done with each species, one using the *Hardwork procedure*, the other using the *Hunger-distraction procedure*. The differences between these two procedures, which gave similar results, are discussed below.

Method

Two groups of subjects were used. One group was a colony of rhesus monkeys housed in an indoor-outdoor pen (outside dimensions 3.6 m. long by 6.0 m.
wide by 2.5 m. high) in a secluded part of the Stanford University campus. The
colony consisted of 2 adult males, 7 adult females, 5 juveniles about 2 years of
age, 6 juveniles about 1 year of age, and 3 infants born just prior to or during the
experiments. The immature group contained both sexes in about equal numbers.
The colony was formed three years prior to the beginning of the reported experiments. All infants and juveniles were born and reared in the colony. Behavior in
the group corresponds to behavior typical of the species, as described in the literature (Altmann, 1962; Hinde and Spencer -Booth, 1967).

The second group of subjects was a colony of crab-eating monkeys. Their
cage had the same location and physical dimensions as the rhesus colony, but the
group had a different social composition. The group was composed of 2 adult
males, 4 adult females, 2 two-year old juveniles (male and female), and 1 one-

190

year old juvenile (male), and 2 infants (both male). The colony was formed one year prior to the reported experiments by combining 2 one-male groups, but all of the immatures were born and reared in captivity.

A stopwatch and/or interval timer was used to time scoring periods. Behavior was narrated by the observer into a cassette tape recorder and transcribed to paper after the observation period. Manipulation of play involved the manipulation of feeding (see below) but required no special apparatus.

Social play was scored by one or two observers according to the method described in detail by Reynolds (1972). The basic technique is to record episodes of play in terms of what we call "play encounters."[2] *Play encounters* are considered to be encounters that exhibit one or more of the qualities of play: (1) the presence of play signals, such as the play face or other play initiating gestures; (2) the absence of nonplay signals, such as fear grimaces or threats; and (3) a bouncing, jerky quality to locomotor behavior.

Social play was measured by counting the number of dyadic play encounters per 5 minute scoring period. The two colonies were observed in alternating five minute periods. Each five minute period for the rhesus was preceded and followed by a five minute score period for the crab-eating monkeys, and *vice versa*. Hence, both hardwork studies took place on the same days, as did both hunger-distraction studies.

In the hardwork procedure, each species was observed between 0730 and 1930 hours for alternating five minute periods for 5 consecutive days. This technique allowed assessment of the total amount of social play of the groups, and of the diurnal distribution of play. In the distraction procedure the groups were observed twice a day between 0730 and 0900 hours, and between 1630 and 1830 hours. The procedures were identical to those already described. The *distraction* study ran for 12 days.

Both studies were done in May and early June of 1973. Animals were always observed in the outside portion of their pen and were not allowed access to the inside portion during the observation hours. Weather was warm (c. 75 to 80° F) and clear during the day. The observers sat outside the cage in full view of the animals. The fact that young infants were often off from their mothers and within several feet of the observers indicates that the animals' habituation was complete. Each day the cage was cleaned and the animals fed at 0900 hours.

In each experiment the animals were deprived of social play on one or two days, termed *deprivation* days, and were not interfered with on the remaining days. In the hardwork method, the amount of social play was reduced (on deprivation day, Day 3) by feeding the animals a mixture of unshelled sunflower seeds and birdseed, instead of their regular ration of Purina Monkey Chow. Qualitative observation indicated that the animals spent almost all day foraging for the seeds, with grooming, sleeping, and undirected locomotion reduced to well below normal levels. Quantitative data on play showed that play was greatly reduced. Rosenblum   et al (1969) have provided a systematic account of the

191

effects of food deprivation on behavior in two other species of Macaques, and their results indicate a reduction in play also. This finding is consistent with that of Loy (1970), who found that long-term deprivation in free-ranging rhesus monkeys reduced play behavior, although his graphs give no evidence of a play rebound.

With the hunger-distraction method, which was similar to the method used by Chepko (1971) and Muller - Schwarze (1968), play encounters were terminated by throwing food into the cage, which distracted the animals. Peanuts, grapes, orange slices, and banana slices were used to interrupt play whenever it occurred. Other activities were not directly interfered with. However, as the animals became satiated with food, its effect as a play depriver disappeared. The technique was completely ineffective by 1800 hours on deprivation day (Day 5) even though the animals were fed only half their normal ration of Monkey Chow at 0900 hours that morning. In the distraction experiment, the deprivation day was preceded on the previous day by a postponement of feeding until 1830 hours in the evening, which also had the effect of play deprivation. Since the animals were not normally fed until 0900 hours, the morning (0730-0900 hours) of Day 4 was equivalent to baseline scores, while the evening showed a significant drop in social play when compared to baseline evening scores. On the deprivation day (Day 5), both morning and evening scores showed significantly lower levels of social play than baseline scores.

Two groups of colony-housed monkeys, one *Macaca mulatta*, and the other *M. fascicularis*, were each subjected to social play deprivation by two different procedures: a hardwork procedure in which the monkeys were forced to spend most of their day foraging and a hunger-distraction procedure in which the animals were fed less than their normal rations and then had their play bouts interrupted by food thrown into the cage. Play was scored by the number of play encounters per 5-minute period over a number of 5-minute periods per observation day. Each procedure utilized a deprivation day and 2 or more non-deprivation days preceding and following it. With both procedures, the rhesus monkeys showed significant social play deprivation on the deprivation day and a significant increase or rebound effect above baseline levels on post-deprivation day 1. The *M. fascicularis* showed neither deprivation nor rebound by either method. The discrepancy is explained in terms of differing group composition in the two species. Other factors influencing the social play rebound effect are also discussed.

Results

The data for the rhesus reveal that both the hardwork method and the hunger-distraction method (a) significantly reduce social play on deprivation days to below baseline levels, and (b) that this is followed on post-deprivation day 1 by a significant increase in social play above baseline levels. The crab-eating monkeys show neither a reduction in social play nor a rebound effect with either method (Tables I and II and Figures 1 and 2).

The fact that the experiments with each species took place right next to each other, subject to the same extraneous factors, and at the same time, is a striking demonstration of the problems encountered in comparison across species in the study of play.

The differences between the crab-eating monkeys and the rhesus may reflect species-specific differences in response to hunger rather than in play. Rosenblum   *et al* (1969) found that food deprivation in pigtail macaques decreased play but increased it slightly in bonnet macaques on the deprivation day, suggesting that hunger is not an effective play depriver in all species. It is our contention that play rebound effects could be demonstrated in *Macaca fascicularis* if an effective play deprivation technique were available.

In this case, the discrepancy in the effectiveness of food manipulation techniques may be due to the different age compositions of the rhesus and crab-eating groups. In the rhesus, 98% of the total number of social play encounters contained one or more juveniles while only 45% of the crab-eating monkeys' play dyads contained juveniles. The nursing infants were not significantly affected by the food manipulation techniques, and the play between adults was probably already close to its floor level. The fact that rhesus play was primarily performed by juveniles with low rank in food competition made the food manipulation technique successful with that group. Tempermental and/or population density factors may play a role in the different results between the rhesus and the crab-eating groups. The crab-eating monkeys give the impression of being more resistant to manipulations of any kind, and the high population density of the rhesus cage may result in proportionately more encounters, which in juveniles are likely to be playful.

Discussion

The data indicate that social play behaves like a drive in that deprivation results in an increase in frequency above baseline levels when deprivation is ended. This replicates previous work by Chepko (1971) and extends her findings to primates. More importantly, the data demonstrate that social play is a variable that can be manipulated under the appropriate circumstances and with the appropriate techniques. The results also give some indication of the best way to achieve a positive effect to use in future investigations.

The baseline level of play is quite important. If the level is too low, no deprivation can result; and if too high, the rebound will be lost in a ceiling effect. Care should be taken to maintain the subjects at a constant level and at a constant degree of satiation of the drives prepotent over play. The morning observations proved to give good results in these and subsequent experiments, even though only a very small percentage of total play is represented in them. This is probably due to the fact that this play period is delimited so precisely by sleep on one side and feeding on the other, a situation we term *drive bracketing* of play.

TABLE I

Social play rebound effect, hardwork method, spring, 1973

SPECIES	N 5-minute periods per day (0730-1930 hrs)	Total number of play encounters per day				
		5/8	5/9	5/10	5/11	5/15
M. mulatta*	65	384	382	157^d	579	294
M. fascicularis	65	150	152	185^d	194	167

d = deprivation day, seeds given, no monkey chow

*Friedman's two-way analysis of variance:
Days 4 > 1,2,5 > 3
$P < 0.001$

TABLE II

Social play rebound effect, hunger-distraction method, spring, 1973

SPECIES	N 5-minute periods per window	Window	Total number of play encounters per window per day										
			5/22	5/23	6/4	6/5	6/6	6/7	6/8	6/9	6/10	6/13	6/15
Macaca mulatta	6*	0730-0900 hours	2	46	47	71	9^{d2}	127	59	39	75	42	74
	10	1600-1800 hours	40	X	81	14^{d1}	12^{d2}	33	9	0	X	X	X
Macaca fascicularis	6	0730-0900 hours	4	0	11	2	2^{d2}	3	11	10	2	1	3
	10	1600-1800	30	X	16	9^{d1}	8	33	33	6	X	X	X

d1 = deprivation day, feeding of monkey chow delayed until late afternoon
d2 = deprivation day, ½ ration of monkey chow and food thrown to interrupt play
X = no observation
*Friedman two-way analysis of variance: Days > 2, 3, 4, 7, 8, 9, 11, 12, > 1,5.
$P < 0.001$

FIGURE 1

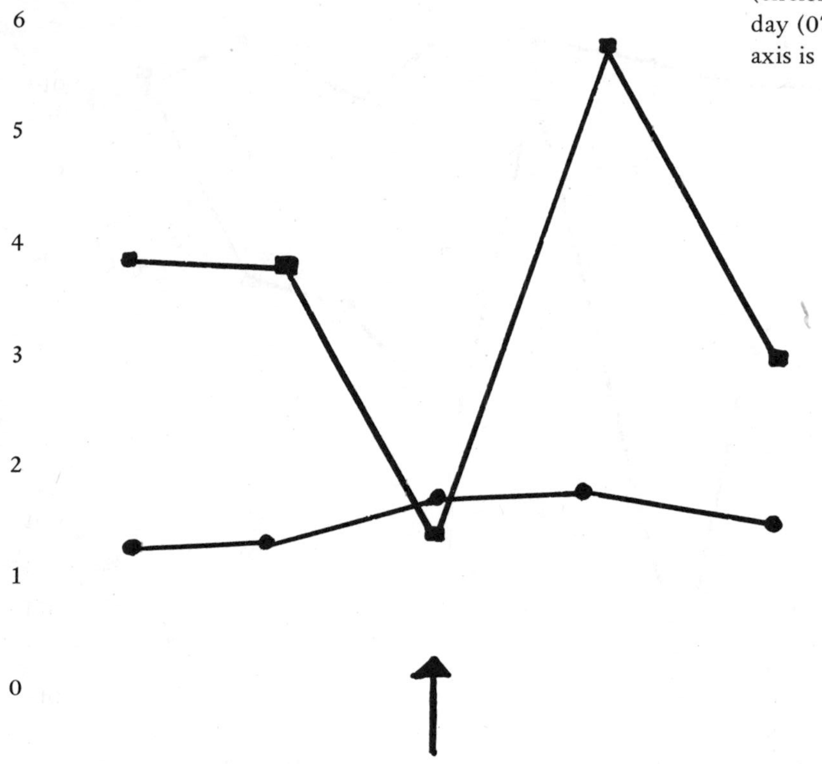

Hardwork study. *M. Mulatta* (squares) & *M. fascicularis* (circles). Y-azis is total numberof play encounters per day (0730-1930 hours) in hundreds of encounters. X-axis is days. Arrow indicates deprivation day.

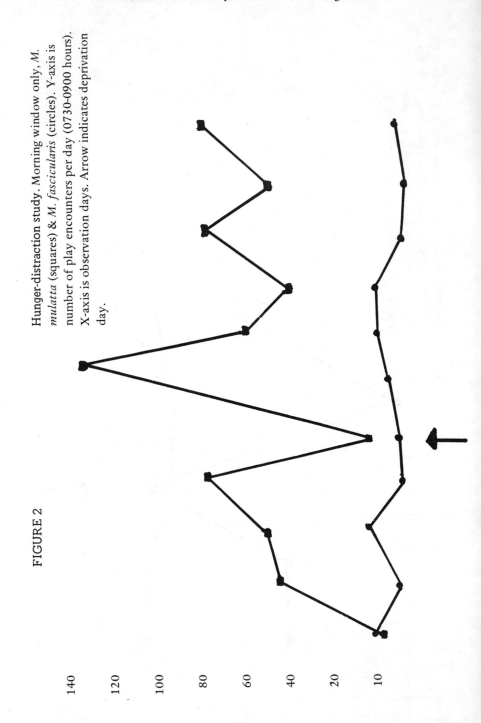

FIGURE 2

Hunger-distraction study. Morning window only, *M. mulatta* (squares) & *M. fascicularis* (circles). Y-axis is number of play encounters per day (0730-0900 hours). X-axis is observation days. Arrow indicates deprivation day.

Baseline records spanning many continuous days should be kept to delineate periodicities and fluctuations independent of experimental manipulation. We found that the weekday scores were quite stable and at a high level but that weekend scores sometimes plummeted to levels equal to deprivation day levels, presumably due to a lower level of environmental stimulation and more feeding irregularities on weekends. For this reason, weekend days were excluded from baseline scores, and experimental manipulations were confined to the middle of the week. On rare occasions, weekday scores also dropped as low as deprivation day levels (cf. day 1 in Figure 2), but such "natural" drops were followed by rebounds.

Age composition of the group is probably important. Infants are relatively impervious to food manipulation, while adults may vary little in their maximal or minimal levels of play. Changing age compositions in the experimental group is also a factor. We observed a change in social play baseline between May/early June of 1973 and July of 1973 for the rhesus group. The drop is probably due to the observed emergence of mothering of infants by juveniles, which Lancaster (1971) suggests is "play mothering."

In terms of actual technique, there is at present no known method for depriving animals of social play without depriving or increasing some other behavioral category. Our results can be thought of as increasing work (at foraging) as well as reducing play. Conceivably, hardwork itself might facilitate play in the absence of any play reduction. To control for this, the hunger-distraction method was used in addition, since there is very little work involved in picking up an occasional piece of fruit. The results indicate that the play rebound is not due merely to the addition of hardwork, since it is induced by either technique. The hardwork method gives results comparable to the hunger-distraction method with less hardwork by the experimenter. The distraction method is ideal for those with good pitching arms and a need for observer participation.

Lastly, play is subject to reductions by naturally occurring exogenous events. Hot weather reduced play in our monkeys, as did rain. Some unscheduled events, such as workmen repairing a clogged drain may, in fact, increase play by raising the level of arousal in a context of curiosity rather than of fear.

It is our contention that the play rebound effect is easily demonstrated if large numbers of juveniles are used, satiation of nonplay drives is maintained at constant levels, an appropriate observational period is employed, extraneous variations in weather and environmental stimulation are controlled for, and the species response to food deprivation is known. Social play, far from being chaotic and unpredictable, is in fact a highly regular and quantifiable phenomenon, which can be manipulated by techniques similar to those used for other affective-behavioral categories and endogenous rhythms. We hope to show in subsequent experiments (forthcoming) that the social play rebound effect can be used to investigate the nature of play with more precision than is available with any other technique.

NOTES

[1] We wish to thank Karl H. Pribram for allowing us access to his monkey colonies for this study and James H. Dewson, III, for his helpful suggestions and encouragement.

[2] The basic unit of social play is considered to be the *play encounter* between two individuals. Encounters between more than two individuals are considered to be combinations of *dyadic* or two-individual encounters. Encounters are demarcated by the behavior of the participants. An encounter is said to begin when an action by one individual is responded to be another. By this definition, behavior by one individual that is not responded to by another is not part of an encounter, even if it is socially directed. An encounter is said to end whenever either (a) there is an increase in physical distance between the two participants or (b) one or both participants cease responding for more than two seconds.

REFERENCES

Altmann, Stuart A.
    1962 *A field study of the sociobiology of rhesus monkeys, Macaca mulatta.* Ann. N.Y. Acad. Sci. 102:338-435.

Bekoff, Marc
    1972 *The development of social interaction, play, and metacommunication in mammals: an ethological perspective.* Quart. Rev. Biol. 47:412-434.

Chepko, Bonita Diane
    1971 *A preliminary study of the effects of play deprivation on young goats.* Zeitschrift fur Tierpsych. 28:517-526.

Hinde, Robert A. and Y. Spencer-Booth
    1967 The behavior of socially living rhesus monkeys in their first two and a half years. Anim. Behav. 15:169-196.

Lancaster, Jane B.
    1971 *Play mothering: the relations between juvenile females and young infants among free-ranging vervet monkeys (Cercopithecus aethiops),* Folia Primat. 15:161-182.

Loy, James
    1970 *Behavioral response of free-ranging rhesus monkeys to food shortage.* Amer. J. Phys. Anthrop. 33:263-272.

Muller-Schwarze, Dietland
    1968 *Play deprivation in deer.* Behaviour 31:144-162.
    1971 Ludic behaviour in young mammals. In *Brain development and behavior,* M. B. Sterman, D. J. McGinty and A. M. Adinolfi, eds. New York, Academic Press.

Reynolds, Peter C.
    1972 *Play and the evolution of language.* Ph.D. dissertation, Yale University, New Haven, Ct.
    In press *Play, language and human evolution.*

Rosenblum, L. A., I. C. Kaufman and A. J. Stynes
    1969 *Interspecific variation in the effects of hunger on diurnally varying behavior elements in macaques.* Brain, behav. and evol. 2:119-131.
    1961 An Analysis of exploratory and play behavior in animals. In *Functions of varied experience,* D. Fiske and S. Maddi, eds. Homewood, Ill.: Dorsey Press.

THE DIFFERENTIAL EFFECTS OF MULTIPLE AND SINGLE NICHE PLAY ACTIVITIES ON INTERPERSONAL RELATIONS AMONG PRESCHOOLERS[1]

Patrick H. Doyle
Wayne State University

Introduction

The purpose of this paper is to provide a higher order dimension by which to understand the influence of preschoolers' play activities on their behavior. The study of the effects of the varieties of preschool play on behavior has had a long history probably beginning with the classic study of Parten (1932). She found that such play activities as house and dolls and sandbox resulted in different behavioral outcomes; the same children tended to engage in cooperative play in the former activity but were more likely to exhibit parallel play in the latter one. Subsequent studies (Green 1933; Shure 1963; Rosenthal 1973) confirmed that the activity was an important extraindividual influence on behavior. Though the same children participate in different activities such as tricycles or jungle gym or puzzles, they systematically exhibit what is often strikingly different behaviors in each activity. It appears that the adage of "when in Rome do as the Romans do" applies to children's behavior in each play activity. In addition to cooperativeness such variables as quarreling, constructiveness and even attention span have been shown to vary with the play activity.

Despite the evidence that the type of play is an important determinant of behavior and therefore indispensable to understanding it, there has been little attempt to delineate the broader principles which govern play activities' various behavioral outcomes. Typically the activity has simply been related to a certain behavior. For example, Lincoln logs play leads to more quarreling that jump rope or piano play.

Since no higher order dimensionalization is given, each activity stands alone as simply constituting an empirical relationship with some behavioral outcome. This does not provide the type of understanding usually sought in the sciences. It does not permit prediction of outcomes of other activities, nor does it suggest modifications in them which would result in more desirable behavior. Moreover it demands that each bit of information be remembered in its own right instead of being organized and comprehensible as special cases of a broader principle. Thus, though activities have been shown to influence behavior, as explanations, at this point, they would have to be considered low grade ones. The level of understanding they offer, while important, is far below what could be achieved.

The fact that this state of affairs exists in the case of preschool play does not mean that this area has been specifically excluded from dimensionalization in higher order terms. Rather this is a reflection of a long-standing general emphasis on the study of the personality rather than the person's context. Historically most research has been guided by an appreciation of the motivational dispositions in the person instead of the context such as the type of play. Thus, though important higher order relationships presumably exist between the type of play and the child's behavior, their investigation has largely been overlooked in favor of focusing on the individual. We know about oral and anal personalities, open and closed minds and inner and outer directed persons, but only that the sandbox causes quarrels. This is not to say that individual differences are not important, but it is to say they are not the whole story.

Investigators invariably recognize that the equation defining behavior has a situation as well as a person component; they simply have not examined the setting variables to the same extent as the person ones. As early as 1936 Murray had indicated that a dual emphasis, including both behavior and its context, was important. He even coined a term to be analogous to the concept of *need* in the person. Whereas the person's motivation was to be classified in terms of needs, the context's influence on motivation would be considered *press*. It would have seemed natural under the circumstances to develop further parallel constructs particularly of the higher order type which would account for the extraindividual influence of such contexts as play activities. This did not materialize, though. Instead there is a recent tendency to simply apply the voluminous personality terminology to the situation (Insell and Moos, 1974). Thus a play activity such as house and dolls which engenders abundant sociality might be considered an *extrovertive* activity. One investigator (Doyle, 1975) has even utilized an activity profile which is analogous to personality profiles but which indicates the relative strengths of the various motivational dispositions inherent in the activity rather than the person. Thus an activity is high in extroversion, low in achievement, etc. However, this tendency must be considered only a halfway measure. As it stems from personality theory it cannot be assumed adequate to dimensionalize the environment. What is needed is a point of view especially rooted in the environment and including principles for higher order dimensionalization.

The systematic study of the forms of environments is most apparent in ecology which as an area in biology is concerned with the natural habitats of animals. Thus, rather than adopt personality terms to dimensionalize play, it would seem far better to borrow the conceptualizations from ecology which are grounded in the environment. In this manner the context of behavior would be developed in its own right from its own point of view which is particularly environmental as opposed to personality related.

The particular concept which is to be considered in this regard is that of the *niche*. In ecology a niche is that part of the environment which is necessary for the species' or organism's survival. Thus if two species occupy a single niche there will be competition until one or the other is eliminated. The principle is that too many occupants for a niche is likely to result in antagonistic relations often to the point that one of the competitors becomes extinct. As an example

200

the red-shouldered hawk requires larger trees for its nest and must also have a fair-sized segment of surrounding woodlands for prey. If there are few trees in the area or the woodlands are moderate in size the ecosystem may only support one pair of the species. The intrusion of any more red-shouldered hawks results in competition for the modest resources so a fight generally ensues with the loser being expelled. The limited niches available did not permit entry of another of the species.

In the preschool, play activities can also be conceptualized as containing props with varying numbers of niches. For example, the teeter-totter is a multiple niche activity because it has provisions for two persons to participate concurrently, whereas sweeping with a child-sized broom or riding a tricycle are single niche with the prop in each case only providing for the use of one person. This means in teeter-tottering one child may invite another to join him, but in the latter activities, similar to the red-shouldered hawk example, if another child begins intruding competition and disagreement are likely. Such competition is exemplified by two children struggling over a tricycle until one is forced off and the other takes over. Thus the characterization of play activities in terms of the number of niches which their props provide may at least be an initial step toward the sought-after dimension explaining the different behavioral outcomes in the various play contexts. If so, diverse activities' fundamental nature can be understood in terms of the niche's size.

The following higher order dimensionalization is thus offered of the activities in a preschool. The activities each have their props which can be seen as the resources of the activities. The props can be categorized into providing for more than one or only one person at a time. Thus we are distinguishing the preschool activities into multiple and single niche categories. The multiple niche activity settings are ones containing a prop which provides for concurrent participation by two or more children. Single niche activity props only provide for use by one child at a time.

The following variables are those hypothesized to be dependent on this niche dimension and hence serve as a basis for determining whether it is a useful construct. They were largely selected in terms of their importance to the major goal of the preschool which according to Rowe (1972) is "children learning to get along with each other." The variables could have been selected for any particular goal though. The basic test of the niche explanation will be whether it can correctly predict whether multiple or single activities will be greater in each one.

The Dependent Variables[2]

For children to become more socialized it is necessary they engage in *sociality*. If the children typically engage in solitary play it is not likely that the goal of the preschool can be achieved. Sociality is defined as reciprocative behavior verbal or nonverbal. Children racing on go-karts or discussing what they are building from legos are examples. According to our niche understanding, children in multiple niche activities would tend to be more social since their use of the same prop would tend to induce or even require it, while those in single niche play would tend to be more solitary.

The second variable is *social arousal*. According to many psychological points of view, besides a person engaging in the desirable behavior, the individual must be properly aroused; thus a social interaction in which the children are only half interested is not as propitious as one in which the sociality has their full attention. Others emphasize that it is important for the child to be more aroused than just fully attentive. They contend that high degrees of it are important to learning, so social interactions which are excited are the more important ones in determining the learning which occurs. If this latter case is true then occasions when the child is enraged or ecstatic with someone else would be the most important situations for the child to learn desirable behaviors. The child who is involved in a fight with another child would exemplify the highest level of arousal. Based on the ecological analogy, single niche activities should result in higher arousal.

While arousal only relates to the intensity of the child's social response, *positive emotional tone* refers to the extent to which it is pleasurable. This was measured on a seven point scale with the maximum of seven corresponding to extreme pleasure in sociality and the minimum of one to extreme pain. The social goal of the preschool would seem likely to be achieved if children persistently engage in positive emotional tone social interactions. As an example, children are happily engaged in puppet play with one another. As opposed to sheer arousal, positive emotional tone is predicted higher in the multiple niche play where less competition for niches is likely.

The next dependent variable refers to forms of social interaction which would specifically indicate the children are getting along with each other. This type of behavior we will call *prosocial behavior*. (The opposite which includes quarreling, etc., would thus be antisocial behavior.) It is defined as including the following ten types of behavior: affection, altruism, comforting, cooperation, defending, friendliness, helping, pleasure giving, sharing, and valuing. In other words, if one child engages in any of the above behaviors toward another child then this would be prosocial behavior. For example, two children in operating the teeter-totter are sharing it so they would both be engaged in prosocial behavior. The preponderance of prosocial behavior would be predicted to occur in the multiple niche activities. Sharing, for example, would not tend to happen in the single niche activities since the prop is conducive to use by only one person.

Besides the occurrence of prosocial behavior it might also be important that they not be perfunctory acts. They should probably be warm ones. Thus we are concerned here with whether the prosocial behavior is (a) perfunctory, (b) warm, or (c) very warm. A child who shares with another with a smile on his face is more desirable than one who does so in a mechanical manner. This

202

quality should be greater in multiple niche play; *warmth* is basically incompatible with the competition likely in single niche activities.

Why is a child behaving prosocially by cooperating, sharing, etc.? It could be a matter of coercion; the teacher or another child is forcing the person to be prosocial. This would not be altogether desirable. Thus it is important to determine the child's motives rather than simply presume that prosocial behavior is sufficient. Kohlberg (1963), a developmental theorist, has indicated the lowest stage of *morality* corresponds to engaging in desirable behavior on account of coercion. Thus this dependent variable is measured as prosocial behavior forced or not forced. An example of the forced measure is the teacher restraining a child from pushing ahead so he must wait his turn for the slide. The coercion would tend to occur more in single niche activities where again sharing, etc., would be at a personal loss. Consequently if it occurred it would be more likely to be coerced.

If we characterize *antisocial behavior* as involving malicious teasing, name-calling, quarreling, fighting, or threatening, this is precisely the behavior to avoid in the preschool. The presumed rivalry for single niche props would indicate this category to be higher in this type of behavior.

Thus we have seven dependent variables some of which would be considered sine qua non to the goals of the preschool. The outcome in each was predicted on the basis of the niche concept. The method used to test whether the multiple and single niche quality of a type of play produces the expected differential effects on the above variables is presented in the next section.

Method

The location of the research was the Wayne State University preschool. The data were collected in the form of videotape chronicles of a preschool day for each of the 20 children attending the morning session. The videotape was then viewed and children's behavior in 66 play activities was transcribed on all the previously listed dependent variables. The technical advantages of the videotape record as opposed to direct observation made it possible to not only determine the presence or absence in each activity of the dependent variables but, where appropriate, their duration as well. The inter-rater agreement percentages ranged from 94 to 75 percent on the variables requiring reliability checks.

When each child's entire day was transcribed, the next step was to classify the 66 activities into multiple and single niche. It was pointed out that this might be confounding due to the preponderance of single niche activities also being fine muscle activities. Thus, if the multiple niche play activities were higher in emotional tone or arousal, for example, this would be due to the difference in muscle behavior since the large type involved in running, jumping, etc., is likely to be more joyful. To provide for this criticism only the large muscle activities were classified multiple or single niche. This left 24 activities of which 16 were identified as multiple niche and 8 single niche. Of the original 20 children this left 19 in multiple niche and 16 in single niche activities.

Such activities as teeter-totter, jungle gym, ball playing, and ring-around-the-rosy to recorded music were categorized as multiple niche; while such ones as tricycle, rocking horse and slide were considered single niche. It is important to note that there were many tricycles so that up to 15 children could ride the tricycles at one time, but this was still a single niche activity since the props were single niche ones. Each tricycle could only accommodate one child.

Some activities seemed to no longer be unitary using this system. Jump rope is an example. It was divided into two activities: long and short jump rope, because the physical length of the jump rope determines the number of children who can play with it at one time. If it is long, then three children are accommodated, one on each end twirling and one in the middle jumping. So it is a large muscle multiple niche. Short jump ropes, on the other hand, have to be used individually with the jumper holding each end and consequently are large muscle single niche.

More rigorous statistical inference was achieved in testing whether the two types of activities tended to engender different rates of a particular variable by only including the 16 children common to both. In this manner a within-subjects design was possible for Wilcoxon tests of the sociality, prosocial and antisocial behavior hypotheses. However, in the instances of ordinal data which includes the rest of the hypotheses there were not enough cases retained in this procedure for such tests. Thus they remain descriptive.

Results

The results are presented in Table 1. The differences between the two activity types are as predicted. This can be seen in the continuous succession of "yes" indications in the fourth column. For each of the seven dependent variables it was possible beforehand to indicate the outcome in terms of whether the multiple or single niche activity would be higher. The fifth and sixth columns indicate the magnitude of the scores which are involved in each comparison. The four digit decimal numbers of social interaction and prosocial behavior refer to the mean portion of the total time in the activity that the variable was occurring. Each child's time in an activity was divided into the time he exhibited the dependent variable. These rates were then averaged. So, in the case of social interaction in large muscle multiple niche activities, 19 children averaged .4818 of their time in social interaction while in the single niche counterpart 16 averaged only .2297 of their time in the activities this way. Thus the multiple niche activities engendered sociality at more than twice the rate of their single niche counterparts.

To obtain the activity rate of antisocial behavior, the other four digit decimal, the number of social interactions in the activity containing one or more antisocial behaviors was divided by the child's total number of social interactions in the activity. The mean of all the children's rates in each of the activities was

TABLE 1

Predictions and Results for 7 Dependent Variables Based
on the Multiple and Single Niche Distinctions in Large Muscle Activities

Dependent Variable	Predicted Higher Activity	Resulting Higher Activity	Prediction Confirmed	Higher Activity Score	Lower Activity Score	Wilcoxon Significance Tests	n (Untied Pairs)
Social Interaction	LMMN	LMMN	Yes	.4818	.2297	.0149	16
Social Arousal	LMSN	LMSN	Yes	+24%	+18%	—	—
Positive Emotional Tone	LMMN	LMMN	Yes	+18%	+ 9%	—	—
Prosocial Behavior	LMMN	LMMN	Yes	.2551	.0300	.0011	15
Prosocial Warmth	LMMN	LMMN	Yes	+87%	+40%	—	—
Prosocial Morality	LMMN	LMMN	Yes	−13%	−40%	—	—
Antisocial Behavior	LMSN	LMSN	Yes	.2823	.1478	N.S.	10

LMMN and LMSN respectively designate large muscle multiple niche and large muscle single niche.

then calculated to obtain the activity rate. This measure broadly considers the question of antisocial behavior. It simply indicates whether social interactions in multiple and single niche are more likely to contain antisocial behavior, rather than exactly what fraction of the time this would be occurring as in the previous two scores. Referring to the table, approximately 28 percent of the social interactions in single niche activities contain antisocial behaviors while less than 15 percent do so in the multiple niche ones.

In the case of the arousal and emotional tone of social interaction and the warmth and morality of prosocial behavior, it was necessary to provide a different measure. Since these scores are ordinal each child's median score on each measure was determined in the two types of activities. Due to the data presented here being a subset of that obtained for all 66 activities which were identified and coded, the results were then summarized in terms of the net percent of children's medians above the modal score for all the 66 activities on the dependent variable in question. These scores are calculated as the number of children's medians above the mode minus those below it and divided by the total number. In prosocial warmth, for example, 87 percent of the children in multiple niche activities obtained medians above the mode for all 66 activities as opposed to only 40 percent for the single niche ones.

In comparing the scores in the two types of activities there is a tendency for the differences to be quite substantial. In the case of prosocial behavior, the children obtained a mean of .2551 of the time in prosociality in the multiple niche activities and only .0300 in the single niche ones.

Conclusions and Discussion

The greater understanding afforded by higher order dimensions appears achieved in distinguishing multiple and single niche activities. The use of this dimension has organized a total of 24 different activities into only two types which appear fundamentally understandable in this light. The multiple niche activities are consistently characterizable as more apt to result in desirable behavior, while the single niche ones lead to undesirable behavior. Moreover, relative to the preschool's goal of teaching children to get along, this dimension appears absolutely vital. Not only are the results in the direction predicted, but the differences are often large as well. The niche distinction further provides a basis for predicting the behavioral effects of other activities. If an activity is multiple niche its effect will be positive, if single niche it will be negative. Regarding the changes in activities which would enhance their effects, these are also suggested by this activity dimension. Tricycles should have two seats and two sets of pedals; instead of a slide having one ramp it could have two, or one wide enough for more than one child. In general, the results indicate the importance of studying the context of behavior as well as personality in understanding social behavior.

NOTES

[1]This paper is part of a research project of which Dr. Jacob S. Kounin is principal investigator and which was supported by Grant No. MH-15472 from the National Institute of Mental Health.

[2]Copies of the precise criteria defining each variable are available in *The Efficacy of the Ecological Model: A Study of the Impact of Activity Settings on the Social Behavior of Preschool Children*, an unpublished dissertation, Wayne State University Libraries.

REFERENCES

Doyle, P.
 1975 *Efficacy of the Ecological Model: A Study of the Impact of Activity Settings on the Social Behavior of Preschool Children*. Unpublished Doctoral Dissertation, Wayne State University.

Green, L.
 1933 *Friendship and Quarrels Among Preschool Children*. In Child Development 4:327-352.

Insel, P. M., and R. H. Moos
 1974 *Psychological Environments: Expanding the Scope of Human Ecology*. In American Psychologist 29 3:179-188.

Kohlberg, L.
 1963 *The Development of Children's Orientations Toward a Moral Order: 1. Sequence in the Development of Moral Thought*. In Vita Humana 6:11-33.

Parten, M.
 1932 *Social Participation Among Pre-school Children*. In Journal of Abnormal and Social Psychology 27:243-269.

Rosenthal, B.
 1973 *An Ecological Study of Free Play in the Nursery School*. Unpublished Doctoral Dissertation, Wayne State University.

Rowe, R.
 1972 *Child Care in Massachusetts: The Public Responsibility*. A study for the Massachusetts Advisory Council on Education. Boston: Harvard University.

Shure, M.
 1963 *Psychological Ecology of a Nursery School*. In Child Development 34:979-992.

Van Alstyne, D.
 1932 *Play Behavior and Choice of Play Materials of Pre-school Children*. Chicago: The University of Chicago Press.

CHILDREN'S PLAY:
A SIDEWAYS GLANCE AT MAKE-BELIEVE[1]

Helen B. Schwartzman
Institute for Juvenile Research
Chicago, Illinois

". . . with my anti-experimental bias I don't save myself from trouble, but it does have a lot of sideways-opening effects."

"Say more about sideways: "Well classically, grass on the side of the road is more interesting than where the road's going. I find I make mistakes if I start worrying too much where the road's going . . ."

> Gregory Bateson in "Both Sides of the Necessary Paradox: Meditations on Gregory Bateson and the Death of the Bread and Butterfly" by Steward Brand, *Harpers*, 1973.

In this paper four major perspectives for the study of children's make-believe (symbolic, sociodramatic) play are illustrated. It is suggested here that each of these perspectives involves the use of a particular metaphor for play which may be seen to influence the researcher's description and interpretation of this activity. The three most commonly utilized approaches for the study of play may be characterized as: 1) the "upward" perspective (make-believe play is viewed as imitation of, or preparation for, adult activity); 2) the "inward-outward" view (play is interpreted as a psychological projection or as expressive behavior); and 3) the "turn-about" or "backwards" angle (this view involves the use of two metaphors, first play is described as a game activity, and then games are viewed as reversals or inversions of cultural systems). All of these approaches neglect to account for, what is proposed here as the very significant effect of the "sideways" perspective of the child in play. For, to the side of, or across from, one child there very often exist other children—his or her peers.

Adopting this fourth, or sideways, perspective it is proposed that make-believe play be considered as a text or 'a story the players tell themselves about themselves' (Geertz, 1972). In this sense, as Ehrmann (1968) has suggested, players become not only the subjects but also the objects, or the "stakes", of their "game". That is, in the creation of specific make-believe play events the players, as *subjects* of these events, are able to *interpret* and comment on their relationships to each other (as these are developed in specific social contexts) as the *object* of their play.

A Study of Make-Believe Play

In order to illustrate how these four perspectives may be used to interpret information on children's make-believe play an example of one play event will first be offered. This event was recorded during a one year participant observation research study of the make-believe play of 23 pre-school age children attending a Chicago day care center.[2] The goals, methodology and results of this project are described elsewhere (Beale, 1973; Schwartzman, 1974). However, it is necessary to mention here that a variety of research techniques were employed to gather information for this study (e.g., daily diary record of each child's activities, relationships, etc.; field notes written in the classroom during play activities; tape-recording, still-photography and film (Super 8) records of play events; informal interviews with children and staff; sociometric study).

The most useful approach for gathering information on make-believe play for this project was the written notes on play groups recorded during 'free play' time in the classroom. On these occasions I would situate myself in a place (e.g., block corner, doll house corner) where a play activity was already in progress or was about to be initiated. At this location notes were taken as carefully as possible on the play situation as it was in the process of being created and constructed by the children. Often the children would ask what I was doing and I would inform them that I was writing down 'what they did and said'. Occasionally I would ask them to clarify what a particular object stood for in the play situation, or what role such and such a person had in the play event, or why they were doing such and such. As I was, in fact, doing exactly what I claimed to be doing this explanation of my activity seemed to be satisfactory to both the children and the staff.

A Make-Believe Play Event

Of the many make-believe play incidents that were recorded in this manner during the research year only one brief example is offered here.

Date: 3/17/72   Time: 3:30 P.M.—4:00 P.M.   Place: Block Corner

Thomas, Paul, and Karen are playing in the block corner. Sonia enters the area and asks if she can play with Thomas and Paul. They emphatically say: "No!" Karen says: "Yes! She can. I know, you marry me (pointing to Thomas) and Sonia can marry Paul". Thomas and Paul respond again: "No!" Karen replys: "O.K. I'll marry her and you can marry each other". Thomas and Paul respond reluctantly: "O.K. She can play". Karen says to Sonia: "We'll be nurses and you sleep in the tent" . . . Karen explains to Sonia where the boat, tent, water and alligators are. Linda comes in from playing in the outside yard. She immediately comes over to the block corner and falls in the designated "water" area and screams: "Help! something is biting my legs!" The group responds to Linda's action and then Karen announces that "Captain Paul is dead!" At this point Thomas acts very upset and says forcefully (directing his statement to Paul and Karen) "You guys never know what to do!" Karen leaves the group here and goes over to the drawing tables. (During this period Sonia is busying herself in the 'water' area saying: "oh, I've found a small snail, look a baby alligator, a baby racoon, a baby parakeet, a baby bird.") Thomas, Paul and Linda shift their discussion to talk of 'angels, wings and heaven'. At this point Thomas, with very agitated body movements, falls to the ground saying "I'm dead". Linda responds to this by declaring that "Thomas is an angel." Paul now begins to figit and act restless and states his desire to return to the original boat play theme. Linda responds by saying: "Well, I guess it was just a dream". The boat play theme is resumed.[3]

Interpretations of Make-Believe Play

There are obviously many things to be noted in this event (and this is actually only one part of a much longer incident). First of all this presentation is itself, in fact, an interpretation of the actual play event. However, I would argue that rather than attempting to deny, disguise, or avoid the interpretive process involved in such a presentation one should accept this as an intrinsic and basic part of the research process.[4]

Once information such as this has been constructed, there are several ways for it to be analyzed, (and, of course, interpreted again). This paper is an illustration of four ways in which make-believe play either has been, or can be, interpreted.

The Upward View

Following a view of play as imitation of, and hence preparation for, adult activities, one would surely note the adult roles assumed by the children in this play event, and the opportunity for adult role practice afforded by this play experience. It would be specifically noted that appropriate and inappropriate marital roles are discussed and responded to. Also it would be seen that Karen and Sonia obviously assume appropriate female occupational roles (nurses) and Paul plays an appropriate male occupational role (boat captain). In other make-believe incidents, collected for this project, the familial roles of mother, father, sister, and brother were commonly employed for 'playing house' events.

The Inward/Outward View

The use of a 'play as projection' metaphor for the interpretation of this event would surely lead to comments about Karen's 'pushiness' and 'strange' marriage formulation. Thomas, Paul and Linda's anxieties about death would also be particularly noted (e.g., Thomas' response to Karen's statement that

210

'Paul is dead'; and Paul's response to Thomas' statement that he is dead and Linda's response to Thomas' declaration). Possibly, it would be suggested, all of these children had recently experienced a death or traumatic separation in their families and this play activity was an "expression" of their anxiety and confusion about separation and death. (And, in fact, each of these children's parents were divorced.) Adopting this projection perspective play would specifically be interpreted as a place for children to 'work out', or 'act-out' intra-psychic frustrations, anxieties, and hostilities.

The Backward View

The inversion or backward interpretation of play behavior is generally used to interpret children's games. However, in Sutton-Smith's (1974) recent discussion of this approach it appears (although his statements here are confusing particularly in regard to his use of the words play and game interchangeably), that he would chose to view this as a general approach to the study of all play activity. Adopting this perspective for interpreting this play event one would surely note the inversion of 'marrying rules' employed by Karen. Also it would be seen that the play theme itself inverts our lineal conceptions of reality and narrative (e.g., beginning-middle-end) as the play theme quickly shifts and weaves back and forth between boat play, talk of angels, the death scene, dream sequence and again boat play. Players here would be seen to adopt roles which obviously they do not hold in non-play situations. And the whimsicality by which they move in and out of these roles, and thereby shift the play theme, would be seen not as a reflection or imitation of adult life but rather as a challenge to, or mocking and inversion of, appropriate adult role behavior.

The Sideways View

In order to use a sideways or *play as text* perspective one must first learn something about the *social context* of the children at the day care center (i.e., the history of their relationships with one another in this location). For example, one would have to know the variety of play techniques used by these children to create make-believe play situations (e.g., entrance techniques, connection-integration techniques; rejection techniques; the trick; the counter-game; dominance-definition strategies; acceptance-submission, or counter-definition techniques, and disconnection-disintegration techniques).[5]

Following this one would next have to know the particular play styles (i.e., how individual children typically employ these techniques in play) of these particular players, and also the history of these players' relationships with one another (i.e., the social or dominance hierarchy existent in the day care center context). Here, one would want to know, for example, that Thomas and Paul almost always play together as a dyad—with Thomas generally dominating Paul. However, one would also have to know that Linda was *the* dominant child in the day care center.[6] (This was expressed in play by her ability to enter almost any play group without the formality of a request and then to establish control and leadership by assuming the defining and directing responsibility of the play group). It would also be important to know that Linda, Thomas, and Paul often played together, with Linda generally operating in the leader role. Karen also was a participant in this play group, but often she was reluctant to accept Linda's dominance, and to establish her control of play groups she would frequently bring in notoriously "submissive" (i.e., non-leader, non-directing individuals) players such as Sonia. Karen was also very adept at employing 'tricks' to get what she wanted in play groups.

With this brief social history it is now possible to begin to interpret this event from a sideways perspective. Initially Sonia enters the play area, but she does not move into the defined play space. Before she is able to move into this area she uses a *request-entrance* technique: "Can I play with you?", and she is immediately *rejected* by Thomas and Paul. However, Karen, who wishes to bring (or connect) Sonia into the play group, responds to this by defining a possible activity (marriage) whereby Sonia could be included in the play group. This suggestion is again rejected by Thomas and Paul. Karen then employs what is referred to here as a *trick* whereby she reformulates her original proposition, which (it is suggested here) she most likely knew to be an unfavorable marriage alternative, "I'll marry her and you marry each other" to Thomas and Paul. This trick or reformulation was attempted by Karen expecting a rejection of her proposal but an acceptance of Sonia into the play group. Thomas and Paul do, in fact, respond by rejecting the proposal but admitting Sonia into the group. Karen then assumes definition/leader responsibilities in her relationship with Sonia as she defines (a *dominance strategy*) their role as nurses and then explains what the play space and objects stand for in the play event.

When Linda enters the classroom she immediately goes over to this particular play group as it is composed of individuals with whom she often plays. Linda also almost always assumes a dominant leader role in reference to this group and so she does not have to employ a request, but rather she immediately employs a *dominance strategy* by defining an activity (keeping to the boat play theme) for the group to respond to as she falls in the water saying, "Help! something is biting my legs!" The group responds to this action immediately and then Karen (who occassionally has difficulty accepting Linda's dominant leader role) responds with a *counter-definition*: "Captain Paul is dead!"

At this point it should be noted that Thomas and Paul (particularly Thomas), Karen and Linda all have attempted to define activities for the group to engage in. Thomas appropriately responds to this potentially chaotic situation by saying, "You guys never know what to do!" implying that the group will not be able to continue if everyone is defining activities for the group and a permanent leader is not established. Shortly after this Karen leaves the group eliminating herself as a possible contender for the leader role.

The play group discussion now shifts to talks of 'angels, wings and heaven', a different theme from the original boat play theme. At this point, Thomas falls down saying, "I'm dead!" It is suggested here that Thomas is, in fact, dead as the play group leader and Linda now begins to exhibit control of the group by defining Thomas as an angel. Also, in response to Paul's restlessness about returning to the boat play, Linda defines this whole sequence (whereby leadership shifts clearly to Linda) as a dream. Shortly after this the group returns to the boat play theme and Linda exhibits her now clearly established leader role by defining various activities for the group.

Adopting this perspective for interpretation the textual and interpretative dimension of play for the players themselves (i.e., the process whereby players 'tell themselves stories about themselves' and their relationships with one another as these are developed in contexts like a day care center) can be described. And, if make-believe play is viewed as a text then it can be seen to be subject to various levels and types of interpretation (four of which have been described here).

'More About Sideways'

This view of play also suggests a number of other useful metaphors (or interpretive models) for play. For example, play can be viewed as communication, and this communication can be characterized in terms of its production of paradoxical statements about persons, objects, activities and situations in play (see Bateson 1955). The player's style in play, as he/she acts as both the subject and object of this activity, can also be viewed as a dialectic in terms of the player's assumption of a play-role. For here the player must be able to communicate information that simultaneously defines him/her as a player (e.g., a witch, a mother, a brother) and as an actual person in the social context (e.g., Linda, Thomas, Paul). That is, Linda must be able to communicate to other players that she is both *Linda* (i.e., a person who leads, dominants and directs activities as she is known for this in the general classroom situation) and *not-Linda* (i.e., a witch, or a mother in the play situation) (see Schwartzman, 1974).

In conclusion it is proposed that this sideways view reveals a new and potentially valuable approach for the study and interpretation of children's make-believe. This research is also significant in its attempt to combine studies of play *texts* with studies of play *contexts* (the importance of which has recently been discussed by Sutton-Smith 1974). Finally, it is suggested that this approach is particularly useful for the study of play activity because it serves to punctuate the "metaphorizing", as opposed to "mesmerizing", quality of research studies of all behavior.

NOTES

[1] I would like to thank John Schwartzman, Gary Schwartz and Merton Krause for their comments and criticism in regard to this paper.

[2] This research was conducted from 1971-1972 and it was supported by a grant from the National Research Council (Committee on Support of Dissertation Research in Recreation and Leisure) and by a Ford Foundation Dissertation Fellowship in Ethnic Studies (Grant #710-0252).

[3] Along with this record of social situation and dialogue a spatial diagram noting significant objects, boundaries, and player's definition of play area was also constructed.

[4] This focus on the interpretive process of social research studies grounds its claim for "historical" (as opposed to "scientific") objectivity (Palmer 1969) in terms of the nature of inter-subjective communication between one's informants (Hymes 1964) and between researcher and informant (Fabian 1971). For further elaboration of this approach in reference to social research in general see Geertz (1973) and Ricoeur (1971); and in reference to research on children's play see Schwartzman (1974).

[5] Sutton-Smith (1971:16) refers to the use of these sorts of techniques as "playmanship". These strategies make it possible to initiate and continue a play event so that all players are able to appropriately relate to the play space, objects, and other players in the situation. Goffman (1961) also discusses the importance of these techniques.

[6] Linda's "popularity" is inferred from the sociometric study (children's answer to question "Who are your favorite friends in the classroom?) in which Linda was chosen 11 times and no other child was chosen more than 4 times; and teacher and researcher observations.

REFERENCES

Bateson, Gregory
    1955 "A Theory of Play and Fantasy" in *Psychiatric Research Reports*, II, December.
Beale (Schwartzman), Helen
    1973 *"Real Pretending": An Ethnography of Symbolic Play Communication*. Ph.D. Dissertation, Northwestern University.
Ehrmann, Jacques
    1968 "Homo Ludens Revisited" in *Yale French Studies*, No. 41 (December) (Issue on Game, Play and Literature).
Fabian, Johannes
    1971 "Language, History and Anthropology" in *Philosophy of the Social Sciences*, 1: 19-47.
Geertz, Clifford
    1972 "Deep Play: Notes on the Balinese Cockfight" in *Daedalus* 101: 1-37, Winter.
    1973 *The Interpretation of Cultures*, New York: Basic Books.
Goffman, Irving
    1961 *Encounters*, Indianapolis: Bobbs-Merrill.
Hymes, Dell
    1964 "Introduction: Toward Ethnographies of Communication" in *American Anthropologist*, Special Publication, J. Gumperz and D. Hymes (eds.), 66: 1-34.
Palmer, Richard
    1969 *Hermoneutics*, Evanston: Northwestern University Press.
Ricoeur, Paul
    1971 "The Model of the Text: Meaningful Action Considered as a Text" in *Social Research*, 529-562.
Schwartzman, Helen
    1974 "Re-Metaphorizing' the Study of Children's Symbolic Play Activity". Paper

presented at the 53rd Annual Meeting of the Central States Anthropological Society, Chicago, March 27-30.

Sutton-Smith, Brian

1971 "The Playful Modes of Knowing" in *Play: The Child Strives Toward Self-Realization*. Washington, D.C.: National Association for the Education of Young Children.

1974 "Towards an Anthropology of Play" in *The Association for the Anthropological Study of Play Newsletter*, Volume 1: Number 2, Fall (condensed version of paper presented for the Symposium on Recreation at the State University of New York, Brockport, August 1974).

CHAPTER VI

Socio-Psychological Aspects of Play and Humor

Introduction

Anthropology and sociology have shown there are ample payoffs to society for play, but what are the payoffs to the individual? One well-argued theory (as discussed in Duthie) is that play satisfies an individual's need for sensory ·stimulation. Why animals play and the consequences to their subsequent behavior of varying play experiences are issues which have been fruitfully addressed by psychologists, less so by other social scientists. There is evidence in this volume, however, of a blurring of disciplinary distinctions as these and other issues in the study of play make the Individual/Society dichotomy meaningless.

Duthie points out the need to add an action component to the generally static descriptions of play. The earlier papers by Storey, Boyd, Salamone, Manning, and Schwartzman show that this action component is important in showing the forces which motivate individuals in play. Guilmette demonstrates that the nature of the Little League experience whether as a league player or as an all-star produces a sharp increase in tolerance for hostile stimuli for the all-star players. All-star play is "framed" in a manner sufficiently different from ordinary little-league so that it is no longer play. Yet, like the Choctaw/Anglo basketball comparison (Blanchard, Chapter III) the game here is also *the same*. From the standpoint of motivation, it would be interesting to find out why children choose to play baseball and of these why do some choose (when given the opportunity) to play in the all-stars.

LaFave and Mannell play devil's advocate to the many critics of ethnic humor who claim that ethnic jokes serve as a means of social control. These jokes often stress the inferiority of one or another ethnic group and thereby reinforce stereotyping and discrimination. Their statement *that stimuli do not have absolute stimulating value* is exactly parallel to the concept of cultural relativism. Common sense would seem to imply that, Poles, for example, would find Polish jokes unamusing or fail to understand them altogether. Their research shows, however, that ethnic group membership alone is not sufficient to account for amused/not amused reactions to ethnic jokes. Ethnic group members are likely to be non-members of some reference group. If a person's reference group is favorably cast in a joke, it will be found amusing even if that person's ethnic group is negatively cast in the joke, and the converse is also true.

Mannell and LaFave reiterate a theme seen elsewhere in this volume, that the overriding concern with the functions of play (or; in this case humor) has cast a pall over research and theorizing. Humor is treated as completely superfluous and unworthy of study or as so serious (functionally) that earnest research has obscured its essential playfulness. They point to the importance of a person's mental set when encountering a potentially humorous situation. In a great deal of research on humor, subjects were primed with a "serious" mental set and for this reason may not have had an amused reaction. There is a need to provide the subject with a "playful" mental set before he encounters the humorous stimuli so that amused/not amused responses truly reflect either features of the stimuli or features of the subject's socio-cultural background.

PLAY/NON-PLAY DETERMINANTS

James H. Duthie
University of Windsor

Play as a recognized form of human behaviour is of comparatively recent origin just as childhood is a novel concept. Aries (1962) through a study of themes of childhood as depicted in sculpture and portraiture of the middle ages concluded "the discovery of childhood began in the 13th century ... but the evidence of its development became more plentiful and significant from the end of the 16th and throughout the 17th." Giotto, Durer, Breughel and other painters of the Middle Ages reveal that the conceptual category of 'child' was not invented until roughly the 14th century for prior to that even anatomists' drawing of the time tended to show homunculi in uterus; that is, the human male sperm was considered to contain hundreds of tiny,facsimiles of the adult which when implanted in the female grew into the typical little old men of medieval times and we note that medieval paintings typically depicted children as such. As Stone in *Social Psychology through Symbolic Interaction* (edited with Farberman in 1970) has shown, both the social entity "child" as well as "child's play" are artifacts of an historical process. Thus, it should not suprise us that attempts to categorize and explain play were first formulated in the 18th century and that by the mid 19th century socio-scientific speculation had evolved the primary five or six explanations of play we now regard as classical:

1. Surplus Energy
2. Instinct
3. Preparation
4. Recapitulation
5. Relaxation
6. Catharsis

These mixed physiological, psychological and sociological explanations presented faithfully to all first year courses in physical education and leisure studies have undoubted heuristic value if only to lead us rapidly to a realization that we await an explanation of the cognitive dynamics of the active, participating individual. What we need is a psychological theory of play which describes what happened in the "little black box" to cause certain behaviours to be emitted or at least become increasingly likely.

We have all observed that as children accumulate experience there are demonstrable changes in the way they perceive and respond to the enveloping and developing world. For Piaget the world is developmental in its effects on the increasingly complex responses of the child which we can regard as sequential:

a) Sensorimotor   c) Concrete operational
b) Pre-operational   d) Formal operational

As the cognitive style of the child changes, one stage merges with another—at first no symbols, then symbolic functioning. If they are absent in play (imitation, for example, occurs at the second stage), word play, jokes that depend on reversals and transformations do not appear until the concrete operational stage or later. Better ordering by the child of his experiences provides the basis on which Piaget rests his two broad categorizations:

1. Assimilation   2. Accommodation

The former involves children in imposing their own interpretation of reality upon objects encountered while accommodation requires them to alter their schema, both cognitive and sensorimotor, to reality's demands. These all-inclusive explanations not only depict how children adapt to environmental requirements but also the effect such adaptation is likely to have on the child is implied. Piaget regards these as indissociable:

> "Accommodation of mental structures to reality implies the existence of assimilatory schemata apart from which any structure would be impossible. Inversely, the formation of such schemata through assimilation entails the utilization of external realities to which the former must accommodate however crudely ... However, in play there is a primacy of assimilation over accommodation." (Flavell, 1963, p. 65)

Play for Piaget is thus essentially assimilative as the primary process of psychologically ingesting new experience and situations and has for him six readily applied criteria. Play is:

a) an end in itself   d) unorganized
b) spontaneous   e) conflict-free
c) pleasurable   f) overmotivated behaviour

Reviewing rapidly socio-historical interpretations of play, these have focused on the relationship between play and culture as seen in George Herbert Mead (1934), Huizinga (1949), Caillois (1961) and Hoebel (1966). As succinctly summarized by Miller and Robinson "sociology and anthropology have contributed to play theory the findings that play is a cultural universal having a social function that produces institutional forms and social forces." (1963, p. 138). However, there is clearly a need to distinguish between the social or cultural contributions of play and the dynamics of play. Although both provide opportunities to categorize play, it is the latter task that the social psychologist accepts as a challenge. What we seek are common ways of thinking about behavioural phe-

218

nomena, in the last analysis causal explanations of that behaviour. Using the conceptual analytic approach, picture out there an Animal (A), human or otherwise, moving in certain ways, watched by a human Observer (O) who reports to WE (the conceptualizing commentator) on the behaviour of A. WE, the commentators, have available bits of theory, essentially an historical and situational framework with the task of bringing under review and revising common ways of thinking about play behaviour. Here our methods are those of testing out and classifying the implications of supposedly true reports of behavioural episodes in an attempt to explain one of the most important of human behaviours, play itself.

Classification of Play by Means of
Conceptual Epiphenomenalism

To classify behaviours is the task of WE—the thinking and thus theorizing commentators who have available: (1) stored information relating to the physical and social context, (2) the report of O who is to be regarded as an effective observer. Thus, we deal with an epiphenomenon, the verbal or other reports of an observer (O) rather than the phenomenon itself. What does O, the conceptualizing observer, report? The answer is: the sequence of movements observed, what the Animal (A) did rather than suffered. In simple English usage an answer to the question, "What did it do?" Answer—"It *something*ed." Coughed, stumbled, dived, galumphed—remember Piaget's over-motivated behaviour and the lines of the Jabberwocky by Lewis Carroll who gives us a brief description of someone galumphing. These reports must feature acts or actions, movements of a particular animal observed over time, something done or performed. Acts differ in several ways from activity—activity is the label given by WE; it is not what is observed. Acts are observed, episodic, technical and if galumphing is any key, in play, the play act may serve to elevate or heighten the psychic level by supplying the Animal (A) with sensory inputs which change its state. Animals enter into an activity (which the WE commentators interpret) by doing an act: the field of the activity supplies the setting against which the thinking theoorizer (WE) evaluates the unit of action, the act. Through this process, enigmatic behaviour reports of animal responses—rats who cross electrified grids, monkeys who learn discrimination problems for no apparent reward (reviewed by Butler, 1958 and more recently, Berlyne, 1960 and 1963)—have been shown to arise from an animal's desire to activate the reticulate arousal system. Schultz (1965) coined the word "sensoristasis" (analogous to homeostasis in physiology) to describe the process by which an animal responds in order to maintain an optimal information throughout once primary drives are satisfied. This behaviour which is closely related to behaviours which our conceptualizing theorizers (WE) can regard as play are acts which are seen to increase stimulation: the rate in the laboratory like the chicken crossing the road, is rewarded for traversing a painfully electrified grid by having the opportunity to explore the other side of the lab; monkeys indeed seem to solve discrimination problems merely to look out on the everyday tasks of a psychological laboratory. Some of us would theorize that this supplies the drive mechanism missing in Piaget's functional but essentially static model—an animal of given complexity, a child in any of the stages depicted, responds adequately to those environments which load its processing capacity to levels found stimulating. We have a limited capacity for overload—given too much uncertainty, too much information, too many inputs, then we won't play anymore and withdraw to a state of rest.

Describing and Identifying Play Behaviours

Actions are usually of many kinds. Not all that we say about an act contributes towards saying what kind of an act it is.

The Aristotelian doctrine of predication enables us to distinguish between what is predictable about an object (typal characteristic) and what is present in an object (non-typal characteristic). The observer (O) reports what he sees. "It is brown, it is hairy, it has a tail, a mane, large teeth." "It is a lion" is the typal decision of WE. Note that "It is brown and hairy" does not lead us to lion recognition very rapidly. To simplify and speed up the process WE can supply a check list of criteria; of subsidiary, non-typal aspects which enable rapid identification:

Lions have tails, teeth, size, shape, smell.
Tables have tops, legs, size, shape but lions remain lions without tails and teeth.

Play, like other objects, is thus made up of an incompletely specifiable collection of salient features. Here is a checklist to employ in its identification (Neumann, 1971). In applying, note where it fails to enable you to identify the activity which these frozen acts portray. What is lacking may be the contextual framework. You may not have enough information. The Observer tells you all he saw; it is frequently not enough.

Action Checklist

1. Does A act to obtain other than enjoyment payoffs?
2. Does A control the intensity and extent of action?
3. Do other than situational determinants impose external final consequences?
4. Are choices limited by constraints not self imposed?
5. Is there a relaxation of reality connections?
6. Is there a stream of behaviour with choices at each point?

REFERENCES

Aries, Phillipe
1962 *Centuries of Childhood: A Social History of Family Life* (trans. R. Baldick). London: Jonathan Cope.

Berlyne, D. E.
    1963 Motivational problems raised by exploratory and epistemic behaviour. In S. Kock (ed.), *Psychology as a Science*. New York: McGraw-Hill, Vol. 5. Pp. 284-364.
    1968 Laughter, humour and play. In G. L. Lindsey and E. Aronson (eds.) *Handbook of Social Psychology*. New York: Addison-Wesley.
Butler, R. A.
    1958 The differential effect of visual and auditory incentives on the performance of monkeys. *American Journal of Psychology*, 71, 591-593.
Caillois, Roger
    1961 *Man, Play and Games*. New York: The Free Press.
Flavell, J. H.
    1963 *The Developmental Psychology of Jean Piaget*. Princeton, N.J.: Van Nostrand-Reinhold.
Hoebel, E. Admanson
    1966 *Anthropology: The Study of Man*. 3rd ed. New York: McGraw-Hill Book Co.
Huizinga, Johan
    1949 *Homo Ludens: A Study of the Play Element in Culture*. London: Routledge and Kegan Paul.
Mead, G. H.
    1934 *Mind, Self and Society*. University of Chicago Press.
Miller, Norman P. and Diane M. Robinson
    1963 *The Leisure Age*. Belmont, California: Wadsworth Publishing Co. Inc.
Neumann, E. A.
    1971 *The Elements of Play*. Unpublished doctoral dissertation. University of Illinois.
Schultz, D. D.
    1965 *Sensory Restriction: Effects on Behaviour*. New York: Academic Press.
Stone, G.
    1970 Social Psychology through Symbolic Interaction. (Stone & Faberman, eds.). Lexington, Massachusetts: Xerox College Publishing.

BINOCULAR RESOLUTION AS A FUNCTION OF THE PLAY IDENTIFICATION CLASS

Ann Marie Guilmette
University of Windsor

This paper deals with the findings from a previously conducted study of Little League Baseball identification classes (Guilmette, 1975). The main concern here will be with the binocular resolution of hostile athletic stimuli as a function of the play or non-play identification class.

Binocular rivalry as described by Engel (1961) is a stimulus-ambiguity situation. It is induced by means of a stereoscope which allows for the simultaneous presentation of two different images to the monocular field of the observer. In this study the unstructured stimulus situation consisted of one non-hostile athletic picture being tachistoscopically presented to Little League participants. In situations of stimulus-ambiguity as in binocular rivalry, perceptual response relies upon the functional value of the stimulus to the perceiver. From Kilpatrick's (1951) transactional theory of perception, the dominant image emerging from the rivalry field will be that stimulus which has the greatest meaning or value to the observer. Lacking relevant meaning, the other image will be suppressed either completely or partially (Engel, 1956). Due to differing demands made upon Little League participants, allstar players become more ego-involved with hostility than do league players. The selective process of visual perception then relies upon allstar players being more receptive to hostile stimuli and league players being less receptive to such stimuli. Response differences in the binocular rivalry situation are thus seen as a function of an individual's identification class.

It has been shown that in Little League there exist two divergent socio-psychological models, one for which league players represent a play identification class and one for which allstar players represent a non-play identification class. An individual possesses a given identification class if and only if that individual has some symbol by which he represents this identification class to himself (La Fave, Haddad and Marshall, 1970). The cultural influences associated with hostility in sports and athletics become the symbol by which Little League play and non-play identification classes manifest themselves.

Within Moriarty's (1972) Management by Objectives model, the differences between the Amateur-Sport-Play dimension and the Professional-Athletic-Non-Play dimension can be seen. For the play dimension: participation and overall development of the child are emphasized; fun, relaxation and the game experience are considered as rewards in themselves; all players are granted equal playing time with the major emphasis placed on sportsmanship; and competition is held only at the local league level. For the non-play dimension; specialized skill development and winning are emphasized; trophies and banquets are the rewards provided for those who excel, are aggressive and work hard at winning; the best players are allotted more playing time with the major emphasis placed on gamemanship; and competition is held mainly at the state or regional level (Moriarty, 1972). The University of Windsor, CAR for CSM study (1974) employed the Management by Objectives model. By concentrating on Little League involvement, they were able to confirm the postulate that the allstar experience is dissimilar to the league experience. While the avowed goals for Little League are goodwill, cooperation and better interpersonal relations (Little League Handbook and Manual, 1972), or those of the play dimension, the allstar situation reflected the professional athletic non-play dimension. This conflict between goals, identified by audio interviews and written opinionnaires, is ineffective and inefficient for organizational functioning and subsequently dysfunctional for the participants.

In North American society research into the area of the role or function of hostility in sports or athletics is just beginning to surface. The present study was designed to determine if hostility in sports would be a significant percept for the allstar subculture but not for the league subculture. The main research hypothesis was formulated to show that a subject's identification class would determine the perception and resolution of certain hostile athletic stimuli in a binocular rivalry situation. Thus allstar and league perceptual selectivity was tested, with hostile athletic slides serving as stimulus cues. Each league and allstar identification class was represented by thirteen volunteer subjects. These subjects were divided into the control group and the experimental group. They were tested before and after the treatment condition allstar.

Six hostile athletic stimuli (surfing, baseball, rodeo, football, hockey and tennis) were paired with six non-hostile athletic stimuli representing equivalent activities. Hostile or non-hostile athletic stimuli were previously determined by judges. Each stimulus pair was viewed through a modified stereoscope inducing a binocular rivalry situation. A modified "View-Master" served as the stereoscope. Eye dominance was tested and an eye dominance effect was controlled for by repeated trials presentation and order of stimuli presentation to the right and left monocular fields. Verbal responses by subjects were recorded for each stimulus pair indicating binocular resolution and stimulus dominance.

Perceptual selectivity functioned in determining hostile or non-hostile athletic stimulus dominance. Results were interpreted from principles of transactional functionalism. Significant past experiences which direct the perception of objects, events and situations is the basic propositional fundamental of this theoretical model. Socialization and structural-functionalism were assessed in light of the results and identification class differences that were detected. The research hypothesis was confirmed by the results. The allstar non-play identification class perceived hostile athletic stimuli in an either/or choice situation significantly more times than did the league play identification class. Variance in results due to an eye dominance effect was shown to be absent, enabling the hypothesis of independence between eye dominance and response to be accepted. That is, the tendency for one of the subject's two monocular fields to exert visual dominance did not contribute significantly to perceptual resolution and dominance of images. Other variables such as ego-involvement, familiarity and relevant meaning contributed to the selections of image dominance. The significant chi square (p.=.01) confirmed that a respondent's identification class and his perception and resolution of dominant images were associated. Hostility in a dominant athletic image is associated with the allstar non-play identification class while non-hostility in a dominant athletic image is associated with the league play identification class.

At test time one the control group and the experimental group were made up of boys in the league situation. Campbell and Stanley (1963) state that the more similar the experimental and control groups are in their recruitment and the more that similarity is revealed in scores in the pretest, the more effective this control becomes. These subjects were chosen from a homogeneous population considering such variables as similar physical abilities, maturational level and achievement orientation. Their comparative scores in the pretest (time one) were very similar. The identification class differences reflected at retest (time two) can only be attributed to the treatment effect of the allstar non-play situation.

The boys who played allstar become more ego-involved with their situation. Losing a game was no longer an acceptable social norm in that loss of a game would disqualify the team from any further play (Little League Handbook and Manual, 1972). As Sherif and Sherif (1969) state for persons highly involved in an issue the threshold of acceptance for relevant stimuli is heightened while the threshold of rejection is lowered. The allstar situation provided relevant cues that influenced the threshold of acceptance for hostile athletic stimuli. Familiarity, with the intrinsic and extrinsic rewards associated with success, and the punishments and negative sanctions associated with failure, added to this perceptual framework of recognition. The hostile athletic stimuli transmitted relevant meaning to the allstar non-play identification class.

What an individual is and what he feels himself to be are largely conditioned by the particular constellation of values he learns and that become a part of him (Sherif and Cantril, 1974). Conflict within the Little League organization arises from incongruity between individual ideas and structures (University of Windsor, CAR for CSM, 1974). The Little League structure creates conflict when it permits two separate and different systems to operate; one, the league, reflects the amateur sport play dimension and the other, the allstar, reflects the professional athletic non-play dimension. These two divergent approaches cause stress. Goals are not achieved and tasks remain unfulfilled (University of Windsor, CAR for CSM, 1974). Not only is this diverse policy dysfunctional and ineffective for the organization but it places undue strain upon its participants. This combined goal blocking and threat component provides individuals with specific internalized values and significates. In this case it provided the allstar non-play identification class the necessary cues to perceive significantly more hostile athletic stimuli than non-hostile athletic stimuli. The league play identification class, only associated with league play, did not perceive significantly more hostile athletic stimuli than non-hostile athletic stimuli.

Transactional functionalism interprets perception according to the familiarity, significance and meaning of cues (Kilpatrick, 1961). Significant stimuli are readily perceived in stimulus-ambiguity situations. Both Engel (1956) and Bagby (1957) established how such meaningful cues determined the dominant stimulus response during binocular rivalry. Pettigrew, Allport and Barnett (1958) explained that responses represented a heightened concern and deep involvement in relevant issues. They were content to establish the fact that cultural memberships, certain particular expectancies and subjective attitudes play a part in the resolution of binocular rivalry. In 1959 Hastorf and Myro concluded that when two monocular stimuli had definite meaningful content, what was observed was no longer a function merely of the formal stimulus properties. An individual resolves binocular rivalry in such a way as to perceive that content which is most meaningful to him.

All of these studies support the notion that in this case hostile athletic content served as meaningful, familiar cues for members of the allstar non-play identification class. Allstar subjects selected hostile athletic pictures as dominant over non-hostile athletic pictures. League subjects did not discriminate between the two types (H,NH) of pictures in this way.

Many studies have recognized that sports involvement is an agency for socialization (Helanko, 1957, Luschen, 1967, Dunlap, 1971). The societal-functionalism model whereby an occurrence does not become an event until some significance is given to it clearly exemplifies this. A societal event is the sharing of significances (Hastorf and Cantril, 1967) and social situations are learned societal events within sports participation. In this study social learning at the league and allstar levels are shown to be important aspects of this process.

The allstar experience is different from the league experience. The organization's approach to the allstar situation shifts to the professional athletic non-play dimension. More monies are appropriated for the allstar situation and successful participation is expected (University of Windsor, CAR for CSM, 1974). Role modelling becomes a fundamental manifestation of performance (Bandura, 1969). If the allstar situation is to be treated like that of professional athletics, it is posited that allstar players will role model professional athletes. The most successful professional athletes are given much recognition, prestige and material gains. Allstar players recognise that if they are successful, social and material gains will be awarded them. Failure then is to be avoided at all costs and winning or success becomes the major desirable goal.

The emphasis, at the allstar level, shifts from the players to the primary ways of the coaches and managers and to the ambitions of the parents and spectators (University of Windsor, CAR for CSM, 1974). Winning becomes an important and necessary condition. Social reinforcers such as increased attention and recognition, social approval and material rewards are made available to successful allstar players. The goals for the allstar become less attainable and more easily blocked. The community as a whole is now a threat to any failure at this level. Perceptions about hostility are easily created from the dimensions of this new experience.

At the league level, excluding the playoff situation, winning is less emphasized and participation of players is required by league rules (Little League Handbook and Manual, 1972). The goals for league players are more attainable and disappointments are created mainly by the players themselves. There is much less to gain for community satisfaction and much more to gain for personal satisfaction. Relevant cues concerning hostility are less likely to be available to league players. The league play identification class did in fact perceive no significant differences between the hostile athletic stimuli and the non-hostile athletic stimuli.

Within the theoretical model, socialization builds up "assumptions" associated with past experiences from participation at the allstar level. The significance of allstar participation within the allstar non-play identification class was demonstrated by this classes' perception of the hostile athletic stimuli.

Binocular rivalry presents a disguised situation and thus eliminates responses felt to be desirable by the subject for the experimenter. This indirect method is valuable in attitude assessment. Response to the stimulus-ambiguity situation is both spontaneous and undistorted. Internal factors, significant in psychological patterning, are best revealed through such techniques (Sherif and Sherif, 1969).

Overall, results verified the hypothesis that allstar non-play identification class resolves binocular rivalry by perceiving hostile athletic stimuli as dominant. In this stimulus-ambiguity situation league players perceived no difference between hostile athletic stimuli and non-hostile athletic stimuli. In an exactly similar stimulus situation, children who were exposed to league for the same period of time as children who were exposed to allstar play, perceived no differences in hostile or non-hostile athletic stimuli. Such children have clearly not been sensitized or habituated to hostility in their sport situation. The transactional functionalism model of perceptual response is capable of explaining these findings in terms of sports activity and consequent identification class differences. In essence this paper points to the differences between athletics and sports within Little League. The league situation usually functions at the sport or play level while the allstar situation functions at the athletic or non-play level.

REFERENCES

Bagby, J. W.
  1957 "A Cross-Cultural Study of Perceptual Predominance in Binocular Rivalry", *Journal of Abnormal and Social Psychology*, 54, 331-334.
Bandura, A.
  1969 *Principles of Behaviour Modification*, New York: Rinehart and Winston.
Campbell; D. T. and Stanley, J. C.
  1963 "Experimental and Quasi-Experimental Designs for Research or Teaching", in N. L. Gage (ed.), *A Handbook for Research in Education*, Chicago: Rand McNally and Co., 1963.
Dunlap, H. L.
  1969 "Games, Sports, Dancing and Other Vigorous Recreational Activities and their Function in Samoan Culture," in J. W. Loy and G. S. Kenyon (eds.), *Sport, Culture and Society*. The MacMillan Company.
Engel, E.
  1961 "Binocular Methods in Psychological Research", in F. P. Kilpatrick (ed.), *Explorations in Transactional Psychology*. New York University Press, 1961.
  1956 "The Role of Content in Binocular Resolution," *American Journal of Psychology*, 69, 87-91.

Guilmette, A. M.
    1975 Identification Class Differences as Determinants of the Perception of Hostile or Non-Hostile Athletic Stimuli, Unpublished Thesis, University of Windsor.
Hastorf, A. H. and Cantril, H.
    1967 *Case Reports: They Saw A Game*, A Case Study.
Hastorf, A. H. and Myro, G.
    1959 "The Effect of Meaning on Binocular Rivalry," *American Journal of Psychology*, 72, 393-400 (1959).
Helanko, R.
    1957 "Sports and Socialization," Acta Sociologica, 2, 229-240.
Kilpatrick, F. P. (ed.)
    1961 *Explorations in Transactional Psychology*. New York University Press.
    1951 *Human Behaviour from the Transactional Point of View*. Princeton: Institute for Associated Research, 1951.
La Fave, L., Haddad, J. and N. Marshall
    1970 "Humour Judgements as a Function of Identification Classes," Paper read at the Canadian Psychological Associationg Meetings, Winnipeg, Manitoba.
Little League Baseball Handbook and Manual, Little League Baseball Incorporated, Copyright 1972.
Luschen, G.
    1967 "Interdependence of Sport and Culture," *International Review of Sports Sociology*, 2 127-141.
Moriarty, R. J.
    1972 "Canadian Intercollegiate Sports Organization: Challenge, Conflict and Change," An Address to the International Symposium on Sport and Physical Education, State University of New York, Plattsburg.
Pettigrew, T. F., Allport, G. W. and E. D. Barnett
    1958 "Binocular Resolution and Perception of Race in South Africa," British Journal of Psychology, 49, 265-278.
Sherif, M. and Sherif, C. W.
    1969 *Social Psychology*. New York: Harper and Row.
Sherif, M. and Cantril, H.
    1947 *The Psychology of Ego-Involvements, Social Attitudes and Identifications*. John Wiley and Sons Inc.
University of Windsor
    1974 *Sports Institute for Research, (SIR)*, "Change Agent Research for Citizenship, Sportsmanship and Manhood, (CAR for CSM)," Faculty of Physical and Health Education, 1974 Canada Council Grant #S72-1768.

ETHNIC HUMOUR AS A FUNCTION OF REFERENCE GROUPS AND IDENTIFICATION CLASSES

Lawrence LaFave and Roger Mannell
University of Windsor

The present paper is related to others in this symposium in the following way: the construct *Identification Classes* serves in our research as an independent variable in disguised attitude measurement as it does in the paper by Guilmette. Since the amount of ego-involvement generated by the activated Identification Classes is hypothesized to help determine whether the situation is defined as sport (i.e., playful) or athletic (i.e., serious), so her paper also ties to Duthie's on this play-serious dimension. Such a dimension is also focal to the remaining paper by Mannell and La Fave.

Ethnic Humour in the Vertical Mosaic

Counter to the assumption of many well-intended social scientists and lay-men, it is not invariably the case that humour directed at an ethnic group necessarily damages that group. Ample evidence (experimental and otherwise) exists to the contrary.

Nevertheless, there *is* also evidence that humour intended to ridicule ethnic groups *can* be harmful to the targets; the effects of such humour on ethnic group members is substantially more complex than commonly acknowledged. Experimentally controlled research is needed to determine the relative influences of the various factors involved in such ethnic humour.

Porter's (1965) sociological classic "The Vertical Mosaic" judges Canada as a pluralistic society whose ethnic cultures are vertically stratified. It seems abundantly clear that ethnic groups on the lower levels of this socio-economic pyramid have not infrequently proven the targets of ethnic jokes—'Newfie' jokes, French Canadian, Indian, Eskimo jokes, et al.

From such obvious facts many well-intended persons have concluded that all such ethnic humour is instrinsically anti-humane. This argument is sometimes even extended to suggest that supposedly satirical dramas (such as the TV series "All in the Family") have primarily aversive consequences (e.g., Vidmar and Rokeach, 1974). Those authors report the satire may be misused by most of the viewers and such bigots as Archie Bunker judged as heroes. Indeed the New York state commissioner of human rights (UPI, 1972) is reported to have said recently that anyone caught telling ethnic jokes in New York state will be charged with violating anti-discrimination laws. The Detroit, Michigan Common Council (Ravitz, 1973) recently passed a resolution decrying such humour.

While these well-intended critics appear at least partially correct, the facts render premature the conclusion that ethnic humour invariably discriminates against the ethnic group. It is too early to conclude that ethnic humour invariably discriminates against disadvantaged minority groups and serves the social control function of helping perpetuate the *vertical* mosaic.

Counter to the assumptions usually implicit in such a conclusion are the following possibilities: 1) Not all ethnic, racial, and/or minority group humour is at the expense of the target group; some may literally compliment that group. 2) 'Insults' directed at ethnic group representatives may be "left-handed insults" or compliments in disguise. 3) Perhaps even jokes which disparage the ethnic group are appreciated most *not* by the dominant, external group but by the ethnic group itself. 4) Ridicule humour at the expense of the minority group (often by other representatives of that very group) may provide heat for the melting pot—serving as negative social sanctions or punishment of minority group members who nonconform to the dominant culture, thus helping insure upward social mobility of that ethnic group.

Perhaps ethnic humour performs a multiplicity of functions—some of which actually increase ethnic group cohesiveness (Martineau, 1972) and even facilitate upward social mobility by the ethnic group in question. It would indeed be ironic and unfortunate if a totalitarian approach resulted in blanket legislation against such ethnic group humour so as to encroach upon the civil liberties of all Canadians and reduce the quality of Canadian life—even for the ethnic group 'victims' themselves.

Yet there already exist experimentally controlled social psychological studies which begin to suggest such a possibility. (For reviews of such experiments see La Fave, 1972; La Fave, et al., in preparation, b; Martineau, 1972; and Zillman and Cantor, in preparation).

The most relevant social psychological counterpart of the sociological construct *Vertical Mosaic* is, for purposes here, the *Marginal Man*. Yet it seems that such phrases as *Marginal Man*, Sense of Humour and *Self Hatred* (which allegedly provides the Marginal Man with an above average sense of humour) are ambiguous. Indeed the construct *joke* itself appears ambiguous in ways which impede understanding.

However, the most common concept of *joke* in the humour literature is as a *humourous stimulus*. Evidence is accumulating which challenges the very existence of jokes thus defined.

For instance, experimental evidence on *vicarious superiority* humour (La Fave, 1972; La Fave, et al., in preparation, b) suggests that so-called jokes may lose their ability to amuse when one's own proverbial ox begins to get gored. It seems also conceivable that under such circumstances the butt of the 'joke' may become sufficiently threatened that his "ego defenses" prevent him from perceiving its point. In such an instance of cognitive 'repression' he would not judge it a nonfunny joke, as in the former instance, but a nonfunny *non*joke.

However, not only may one man's joke be another's insult, nonjoke stimuli may also be judged amusing under appropriate background conditions. Nerhardt (1970) found, and Deckers and Kizer (1974) replicated, that highly discrepant weights from an established expectancy generate laughter (which in this context apparently 'operationally' defines amusement). It appears then that so-called jokes represent neither a necessary nor sufficient condition of amusement.

Is amusement at the expense of an ethnic group's culture *relative* to one's own culture Weltanschauung? For instance, a joke at the expense of an ethnic group raises the question as to what a joke is. A necessary condition of being a joke would seem to be to have a point. And many humour theorists and common sense would seem to agree that the point of a joke is based upon an *incongruity*.

The question then presents itself as to whether this incongruity is *objective* or *subjective*. That is, must the situation really contain an incongruity or is the necessary condition for amusement rather an apparent (i.e., *epistemic*) incongruity? If the latter, then perhaps the perceived incongruity is culturally relative and, consequently, 'jokes' themselves do not objectively exist in an absolute sense but are culturally relative.

To question the existence of jokes defined as humourous stimuli is important because if 'jokes' are culturally relative then no correct answer exists as to what is amusing. If no correct answer exists to what amuses then amused laughter at an ethnic group's expense may merely indicate the ethnocentrism of the amused, rather than anything intrinsically absurd about the ethnic group's behaviour. If so, an immediate consequence is that an educational campaign to alert people to the relativity of cultures could reduce their ethnocentric bigotry and reduce their feelings of superiority and ridicule at the expense of harmless ethnic groups.

Theoretical Significance and Practical Importance

It seems clear then an adequate theory of humour remains to be formulated, and doubtful that such an achievement will transpire in the near future. Two concepts do seem stubbornly to resist 'extinction', however, whenever one gropes for the quintessence of that which amuses: 1) some notion of happiness increment (e.g., superiority, heightened self-esteem, joke resolution, tension reduction) and 2) some concept of incongruity (whether object or subjective, culturally absolute or relative).

These two apparently essential ingredients of an adequate recipe for humour will be treated in terms of *superiority* and *incongruity*—as the research traditions under these two titles are those to which we are most indebted. In short, we need advance our understanding of both superiority and incongruity humour theory and find new connecting links between these two seemingly necessary ingredients.

Although humour formulations involving the concept of superiority are traced back at least to the ancient Greeks, it appears to be in the several hundred words on this subject by British philosopher Thomas Hobbes (1651, pp. 101-103; and 1968, p. 125) that superiority humour theory began to take on coloration useful for social psychological research. At least the first controlled experiment in this area appears to have been in the Hobbesian tradition (Wolff, et al., 1934).

The central concern of this research tradition quickly transformed (unconsciously at first, and later consciously) from superiority humour to *vicarious* superiority humour theory (i.e., from individual psychology to social psychology). One's 'sense of humour' appeared to depend upon one's group loyalties and hostilities rather than an "every man for himself" Hobbesian jungle of loyalty only to oneself. The way now opened for a set of 'jokes' to serve as a *projective*

230

test or *disguised-structured* measure of socialized components of his personality or of his *social attitudes* and *beliefs* as internalized from the social or *group norms* (La Fave, 1972; La Fave, et al., in preparation, b; Martineau, 1972; Zillmann and Cantor, 1972).

However, just as the step from Hobbesian superiority humour theory to *vicarious* superiority humour represents an important advance, another important step forward would seem to be the recognition that, in comparing groups, one need not always positively identify with one's membership group. Thus, when one is more ego-involved (whether positively or negatively) in a nonmembership group than a membership group, the vicarious superiority revision suggested here (and hinted at by Wolff et al., op cit.; and Middleton, 1959) is that the groups in the message communicated towards which one holds the strongest attitudes (not the membership grops per se) best predict humour judgements. This revision of vicarious superiority humour theory could solve an important paradox in ethnic group humour which well-intended proselytizers against ethnic jokes often overlook.

For instance, Anthropologist Sally Snyder of the University of Windsor has followed the recent history of anti-Polish 'jokes' in the Detroit area. A decade ago the Mayor of Hamtramack(a Polish suburb of Detroit) vehemently demanded the removal of an anti-Polish 'joke' book from local newsstands. And in which area of greater Detroit did Snyder find (personal communication) that anti—Polish book selling best? Hamtramack!

The Haddad and La Fave experiment, to be discussed later, provides support for such 'masochistic' ironies.

It is with such ironic facts as the above that serious students of humour must cope. Yet under our revision of vicarious superiority humour theory, the paradox resolves and we can distinguish several experimentally testable reasons that so-called jokes at an ethnic group's expense may be funnier to members of that ethnic group than to outgroupers.

There exist at least eight reasons a 'joke' at an ethnic group member's expense may apparently amuse that ethnic group member. (These are the same eight reasons discussed elsewhere—La Fave, 1971; La Fave et al., in preparation —that a sense of humour, defined as amusement at one's own expense, is an illusion.) One of these eight involves pseudo amusement. The ethnic group butt of the 'joke' *laughs* though unamused (to attempt to appear as a "good sport," to avoid being fired by his boss or deported by the immigration official who told the 'joke' and so on). For instance, the southern United States Negro was stereotyped by the bigot as "happy-go-lucky"; as a means of survival the Uncle Tom needed to pretend to be amused whenever the bigot attempted to be amusing.

Second, the ethnic group victim of the 'joke' may be amused because language or cultural barriers cause him to misinterpret the message in the decoding process—mistaking it as portraying him in a complimentary light. Third, the 'joke' may have more than one amusing aspect (as the best 'jokes' often do) and

231

amuse its butt not because he is victim per se but because of the 'joke's' other alleged amusing properties.

Fourth, the communicator may misunderstand the level of generality at which the ethnic group member is decoding the 'joke.' Thus a Chinese may be amused at an anti-Confucian 'joke,' because (counter to the communicator's expectation) he did not judge the 'joke' to be directed against all Chinese (and therefore not against marxist Chinese such as himself) but only against reactionary Chinese still committed to decadent feudalism.

Fifth, the latter-day immigrant may tell with obvious amusement a story of an embarrassing event (unfunny at the time) which happened to him when he first arrived in this country. However, further analysis should indicate that he is only capable of being amused because he has made a *temporal differentiation* between *past me* and *present me*. (Both the fourth and fifth reasons an ethnic group member may appear amused at his own expense, even though he is not, are instances of what we have called *attitude switching*—La Fave et al., 1974, pp. 189-190—to be sharply distinguished from *attitude change*.)

A sixth reason an ethnic group member may seem to hold a sense of humour is that he may be amused at the expense of his *membership ethnic group* because it is *no longer his positive reference group*. For instance, it is common knowledge among sociologists that the first generation of immigrants to the United States may have a lower crime rate than the national average but their children a higher than average crime rate. Their children apparently get trapped between conflicting cultures—the home, immigrant culture and the school or *peer-group culture. This conflict seems often to* get resolved by denouncing one's ethnic culture and assimilating to the new world. In fact colorful names are given to such "Uncle Toms" by their own ethnic groups when they assimilate to the dominant Caucasian culture. (Such Chinese are often called bananas, Indians apples, Negroes Oreo cookies, and so on.) These "Uncle Toms" often suffer so many frustrations with respect to their ethnic group that they learn to develop a more negative attitude towards it (social psychologist Kurt Lewin's concept of "self-hatred") than do representative members of the dominant culture. Hardly surprising then that anti-Polish 'joke' books sell best in Hamtramack.

Closely related, but striking perhaps a more positive note, is a seventh reason an ethnic group member may find 'jokes' at the expense of his own group funny; he may hold *conflicting positive reference groups*. In such instance, this marginal man may hold more than one Weltanschauung—one for each positive reference group or internalized culture. He appears to hold a sense of humour because one part of himself (i.e., one positive reference group) is always capable of being amused at the expense of another, conflicting part. Yet unlike the sixth, he does *not* permanently renounce either part. The resultant vacillation may be sometimes painful, but the ability to maintain such "ambiguity tolerance" can also result in a highly cosmopolitan, creative, sensitive marginal man with a very apparent sense of humour. (Perhaps in this type of marginal man inheres a very beautiful aspect of the *mosaic* part of the vertical mosaic and a strong argument for maintenance of the cultural pluralism of Canada.)

An eighth and last reason an ethnic group member may find 'jokes' at the expense of his own group amusing provides an *irony of irony*. Often ethnic group members may be observed (especially when engaged in repetitious, menial work) insulting each other's ethnic group ("You stupid polack!" "Dumb dago!" etc.). Closer analysis seems to suggest, however, that these are "left-handed insults" or compliments in disguise. That is, the message is neither encoded nor decoded literally, and represents a pseudo hostile communication between friends. Under such circumstance, the irony of irony is that an extreme insult is less insulting than a mild insult (since the former is less likely to be taken literally and more probably cognitively restructured as "He's only joking").

Such a pseudo insult is then transformed into a disguised compliment— since the 'butt' believes his friend thinks him a good sport capable of taking a joke. The judgment that one has been complimented by a friend results in a happiness increment which, conjoined with the incongruity between the literal and the contrary intended meaning of the communication, results in the mental experience of amusement.

Some of the above eight reasons help explain why ethnic groups are often butts of 'jokes.' There exist two important theoretical reasons why such should be the case. First, there seems great wisdom in the Gestalt psychologist's assault on the philosophical doctrine of naive realism with the adage *stimuli do not have absolute stimulating value*. Recall the psychophysical experiments begun by Nerhardt in which a 'nonjoke' (weight) may be experienced as amusing if lifted in a contextual background of previously lifted weights which form a range from which the amusing weight is highly discrepant. Had that same weight been lifted against a background of earlier weights of which it were a geometric mean, it would hardly be perceived as amusing. Yet that weight hasn't changed—though judgment of it has, due to variance in the contextual background.

Much slapstick comedy is apparently based on such manipulation of background to render the stimulus highly discrepant from a range of expectancy or social norm and consequently incongruously amusing. It is hardly far fetched to extrapolate from such data to the assumption that the 'outlandish' costumes and customs of newly arrived immigrants will often appear ridiculously amusing to the provincial ethnocentrics, who will consequently feel smugly *superior* because of such perceived *incongruities*. In fact, two different types of social norms seem in need of distinction here—*belief* and value (or *attitude*) social norms; belief norms refer to what the society expects one *is* likely to do and value norms to what one *should* do. The social psychological counterpart to these two types of norms is La Fave's construct of *identification classes* (La Fave et al., in preparation b)—a replacement for the construct of reference group (La Fave et al., 1974, pp. 185-187).

A second important theoretical reason why ethnic groups are often butts of 'jokes' relates to the earlier discussion concerning the *cultural relativity of perceived incongruity*. A custom which is perceived as amusingly incongruous from the perspective of one cultural Weltanschauung may not be from the perspective of another.

It would be misleading, however, to overlook some obvious ways in which 'jokes' at the expense of ethnic groups are anti-humane. What truth inheres in the Hobbesian version of superiority humour theory would seem to argue for such inhumaneness. So might the findings of anthropologist Radcliffe-Brown (1940) regarding the joking relationship.

The issues regarding the social psychological functions of ethnic group humour are quite complex, and the evidence appears neither completely on one side nor the other. A surprising number of arguments exist for humanitarian functions of ethnic humour. Further, it is possible to formulate a fair number of these arguments quite clearly, and in experimentally testable ways which hold significant theoretical implications not only for the social psychology of humour but for general social psychology as well.

Does ethnic humour increase prejudice and discrimination against ethnic groups? Can ethnic humour be employed as a dramatic means of furnishing positive information about the ethnic group which suffers from victimization by negative stereotyping (as perhaps United States Negro comedian Dick Gregory often has used Negro humour)?

Would governmental legislation or formal censure of humour directed at ethnic groups serve latent functions counter to the benevolent intentions of the sponsors?

Relationship to Existing Research and Literature

The superiority humour tradition most influential on the present proposal traces to the several hundred words on this subject by the British philosopher Thomas Hobbes (1651, pp. 101-103; 1968, p. 125). The first attempted experimental test of Hobbesian theory was by Wolff et al., (1934).

However, it proved technically inconvenient for Wolff et al. to test Hobbesian superiority humour theory directly by presenting subjects with 'jokes' at their own expense. Rather 'jokes' were employed that tested 'superiority' theory *vicariously* by making the butts of these 'jokes' *not* the personal name of each subject, but rather his *ethnic group* membership.

In offering such a substitution the authors inadvertently social psychologized Hobbes' individualistic superiority theory. In other words they did not test (nor has anyone since) his theory at all but, inadvertently, their own *vicarious* superiority humour theory.

They found, consistent with prediction, that anti-Jewish 'jokes' were unfunnier to Jews than to gentiles. However, counter to prediction they also reported anti-Scottish 'jokes' less funny to Jews than to gentiles.

With serendipitous hindsight they blamed the mistaken prediction on

234

faulty experimental control, rather than their vicarious superiority theory—reasoning that the Jews had sympathized with the Scots attacked as stingy in the anti-Scottish 'jokes' and consequently found such 'jokes' unfunny—having been negatively stereotyped as stingy themselves.

The next experiment in this tradition was by Middleton (1959). Half of his similar vicarious superiority predictions also failed of substantiation and he too, in hindsight, blamed the experimental design, rather than the theory. He did, however, introduce Hyman's (1942) *reference group* construct to this area for the first time (albeit ad hoc). Middleton reasoned that anti-Negro 'jokes' had proven as amusing to Florida Negro college students as white, counter to prediction, because he had failed to consider that their membership group (Negro) may not be their reference group (i.e., that these Negro college students were "Uncle Toms" and "Aunt Jemimas").

The third experiment in this vicarious superiority tradition was by La Fave (1961). Here such predictions, based on four religious reference groups, were substantiated. In addition mathematically interrelated subhypotheses were substantiated which contradicted humour theories by G. H. Mead, Freud, and Eastman and previous related inconsistencies in the literature were reconciled (La Fave, 1967; 1972). That experimental design systematically varied not only the butt of the 'joke' but also the *victor*. In addition, La Fave's construct of *attitude switching* with respect to levels of generality (as distinct from attitude change) was substantiated (La Fave, 1972; La Fave et al., 1974).

Three more experiments have since been performed by the La Fave group. These involve the social issues of Canadian-American relations (La Fave, et al., 1973), a student sit-in (La Fave, et al., 1974), and Women's Liberation (La Fave, Billinghurst and Haddad, in preparation). These three experiments were semi-replications of La Fave (1961)—breaking no essentially new ground but being necessary to show that substantiation of the vicarious superiority humour hypothesis was not just a consequence of artifactual contamination of the social issue employed in La Fave (1961).

The basic theoretical proposition from which the more specific hypotheses utilized in our four vicarious superiority humour experiments discussed above are derived is as follows:

> Let S believe J is a joke in which A seems to S victorious and/or B appears the butt. Then the more positive S's attitude towards A and/or towards the 'behaviour' of A, and/or the more negative S's attitude towards B and/or towards the 'behaviour' of B, the greater the magnitude of amusement S experiences with respect to J.

A fifth vicarious superiority humour experiment, by Haddad and La Fave (La Fave, et al., in preparation, b) tested (for the first time) the 'masochistic' irony referred to earlier. In this experiment the following six hypotheses were tested, the last five for the first time.

1: Ss will judge more amusing those 'jokes' which esteem their positive reference group (i.e., positive identification class) and membership group and disparage their negative-reference-nonmembership group than 'jokes' of the other permutation (i.e., which esteem their negative-reference-nonmembership group and disparage their positive-reference-membership group).

2 and 3: Ss will judge more amusing those 'jokes' which esteem their primary-reference-membership group and disparage their negative-reference-nonmembership group than will Ss whose secondary-reference-membership group is esteemed and primary-reference-nonmenbership group is disparaged. (Primary and secondary reference groups are both positive but primary is preferred to secondary. Also, since there are four experimental groups, listed below, so two hypotheses are deduced—one hypothesis compares two groups and the other the remaining two.)

4: Ss will judge more amusing those 'jokes' which esteem their primary-reference-nonmembership group and disparage their secondary-reference-membership group than 'jokes' of the other permutation. (Although hypotheses 2 and 3 above provide a hint of the marginal man's alleged 'masochistic sense of humour,' it is only hypothesis 4 which predicts completely along this line).

5 and 6: Ss will judge more amusing those 'jokes' which esteem their positive-reference-membership group and disparage their negative-reference-nonmembership group than 'jokes' which esteem their primary-reference-nonmembership group and disparage their secondary-reference-membership group.

A total of 111 Ss were partitioned into four groups—27, 28, 28, and 28 respectively, as follows: 1) Pro-Professor Professors. For this group professors are the positive-reference-membership group and students the negative-reference-nonmembership group. 2) Pro-Student Students. This group is the converse of 1). 3) Pro-Professor Students. For this group professors are the primary-reference-nonmembership group and students are the secondary-reference-membership group. 4) Pro-Student Professors. This group is the converse of 3).

All hypotheses were substantiated at the .05 level or better. Thus results are unambiguous; whenever the membership and reference groups conflict, the reference group is the more important determinant of humour judgements.

This experiment tests a marginal man who feels positively both about his ethnic group and the dominant group. Therefore, he becomes socialized to both cultures and, instead of denying his original ethnic culture, may resolve his conflicts by a creative synthesis of the relevant aspects of both cultures. Creative genius throughout human history seems to have been produced by such cosmopolitan marginal men in amounts disproportionate to their numbers.

A common technical criticism of our vicarious superiority research concerns so-called demand characteristics. More specifically, these critics maintain that since our experimenters were deliberately chosen to have good rapport with their subjects, each experimenter holds the same relevant positive reference group as his subjects. Thus subjects try to please the experimenter by providing answers which spuriously support our hypotheses.

If this criticism is valid, then the Haddad and La Fave experiment discussed above had "the cards stacked against" its hypothesis 4. That is, the pro-student professors should have preferred the pro-professor-anti-student permutation of 'jokes' to the pro-student-anti-professor permutation relative to the pro-professor students. Yet, consistent with our vicarious superiority humour hypothesis, the opposite occurred.

Five experiments relevant to vicarious superiority humour theory have also been performed by the Priest group. Four of these experiments (reviewed in La Fave, 1972; and La Fave, et al., in preparation, b) seem to provide no essentially new developments and appear to suffer in varying degrees from experimental design problems. However, the remaining experiment by Gutman and Priest (1969) offers two important contributions: 1) It provides a connecting link between the superiority humour and hostility-and-humour traditions. 2) Even more important, that experiment considers (for the first time) attitudes towards the *messages* in the 'joke'—unlike all prior superiority humour research which had focussed upon attitudes towards the communicators of such messages.

The remaining several experiments relevant to vicarious superiority humour theory have been performed by the Zillman group (Cantor and Zillmann, 1973; Zillmann and Cantor, 1972; Zillmann et al., 1974; and Zillmann and Bryant, 1974). The major relevant theoretical innovation of this group is to introduce to the humour area the construct of *retaliatory equity* as a model which Zillmann and Bryant believe is half-contradictory to that employed by Gutman and Priest (op. cit.). However, the value of retaliatory equity theory for qualifying vicarious superiority humour theory remains an open question at this writing as the Zillmann and Bryant experiment (op. cit.) fails to exclude plausible alternative interpretations (La Fave et al., in preparation, b).

REFERENCES

Bergson, H.
    1911 *Laughter: An Essay on the Meaning of the Comic.* New York: Macmillan.
Cantor, J. R. and Zillmann, D.
    1973 Resentment toward victimized protagonists and severity of misfortunes they suffer as factors in humor appreciation. *Journal of Experimental Research in Personality*, 6, 321-329.
Deckers, L. and Kizer, P.
    1974 A note on weight discrepancy and humor. *The Journal of Psychology*, 86, 309-312.
Gutman, J. and Priest, R. F.
    1969 When is aggression funny? *Journal of Personality and Social Psychology*, 12, 60-65.
Hobbes, T.
    1651 *Humane Nature.* London: Anchor.
    1651 *Leviathan.* Marmondsworth, Middlesex, England: Penguin Books Ltd., 1968.

Hyman. H.
1942 The psychology of status. *Archives of Psychology*. No. 269.

Jones, J. M.
1970 *Cognitive factors in the appreciation of humor: a theoretical and experimental analysis.* Unpublished doctoral dissertation, Yale University.

La Fave, L.
1961 *Humor judgments as a function of reference groups: an experimental study.* Unpublished doctoral dissertation, University of Oklahoma.

1965 *Some supplemental variables to assimilation-contrast principles in psycho-social 'scales.'.* Paper read at a symposium on "Social Judgment" at the annual convention of the American Psychological Association, Chicago, Illinois, September.

1967 Comment on Priest's article: "Election jokes: the effects of reference group membership." *Psychological Reports*, 20, 305-306.

1969 Humor as a supplemental variable to assimilation–contrast principles in psycho-social 'scales.' *Symposium proceedings 1969 Western Psychological Association Meetings*, Vancouver, British Columbia.

1971 *Sense of humor: a myopical illusion?* Paper presented at the annual convention of the American Psychological Association, Washington, D.C., September, in symposium on the Cultural Relativity of Humor.

1972 Humor judgments as a function of reference groups and identification classes. In J. H. Goldstein and P. E. McGhee (Eds.), *The Psychology of Humor*. New York: Academic Press, pp. 195-210.

La Fave, L., and Sherif, M.·
1968 Reference scale and placement of items with their own categories technique. *Journal of Social Psychology,* 76, 75-82.

La Fave, L.; Billinghurst, K.; and Haddad, J.
Humor judgments as a function of identification classes: Women's Liberation. In preparation (a).

La Fave, L.; Haddad, J.; and Maesen, W. A.
Superiority, enhanced self esteem, and perceived incongruity humour theory. In A. J. Chapman and H. C. Foot (Eds.), *Humour and Laughter: Theory, Research, and Applications.* Sussex, England: John Wiley & Sons, Ltd., in preparation (b).

La Fave, L.; Haddad, J.; and Marshall, N.
1974 Humor judgments as a function of identification classes. *Sociology & Social Research,* 58 (2), 184-194.

La Fave, L.; McCarthy, K.; and Haddad, J.
1973 Humor judgments as a function of identification classes: Canadian vs. American. *The Journal of Psychology*, 85, 53-59.

Martineau, W. H.
1972 A model of the social functions of humor. In J. H. Goldstein and P. E. McGhee (Eds.), *The Psychology of Humor*. New York: Academic Press, 81, 721-730.

Middleton, R.
1959 Negro and white reactions to racial humor. *Sociometry*, 22, 175-183.

Nerhardt, G.
1970 Humor and inclination to laugh: emotional reactions to stimuli of different divergence from a range of expectancy. *Scandinavian Journal of Psychology*, 11, 185-195.

Osgood, C. E. and Tannenbaum, P. H.
1955 The principle of congruity in the prediction of attitude change. *Psychological*

Review, 62, 42-55.

Piaget, J.
1932   *The moral judgment of the child*. London: Kegan Paul.

Porter, J.
1965   *The Vertical Mosaic*. Toronto: University of Toronto Press.

Radcliffe-Brown, A. R.
1940   On joking relationships. *Africa*, 13, 195-210.

Ravitz, M.
1973   Resolution—Detroit Common Council. December 4.

Sherif, C. W.; Sherif, M.; and Nebergall, R. E.
1965   *Attitude and attitude change: the social judgment-involvement approach*. Philadelphia: Saunders, 1965.

Sherif, M. and Hovland, C. I.
1961   *Social judgment: assimilation and contrast effects in communication and attitude change*. New Haven, Connecticut: Yale University Press.

Sherif, M.; Harvey, O. J.; White, B. J.; Hood, W. R.; and Sherif, C. W.
1961   *Intergroup conflict and cooperation: the Robbers Cave Experiment*. Norman, Oklahoma: Institute of Group Relations, University of Oklahoma.

Shultz, T.
1972   The role of incongruity and resolution in children's appreciation of cartoon humor. *Journal of Experimental Child Psychology*, 13, 456-477.

Suls, J. M.
1972   A two-stage model for the appreciation of jokes and cartoons: an information-processing analysis. In J. H. Goldstein and P. E. McGhee (Eds.), *The Psychology of Humor*. New York: Academic Press, pp. 81-100.

UPI
1972   New York to charge tellers of ethnic jokes. *Toronto Daily Star*, January 27, p. 3.

Vidmar, N. and Rokeach, M.
1974   Archie Bunker's bigotry: a study in selective perception and exposure. *Journal of Communication*, Winter, 36-47.

Wolff, H. A.; Smith, C. E.; and Murray, H. A.
1934   The psychology of humor. 1. A study of responses to race-disparagement jokes. *Journal of Abnormal and Social Psychology*, 38, 345-365.

Zillmann, D. and Bryant, J.
1974   Retaliatory equity as a factor in humor appreciation. *Journal of Experimental Social Psychology*, 10, 480-488.

Zillmann, D. and Cantor, J.
1972   Directionality of transitory dominance as a communication variable affecting humor appreciation. *Journal of Personality and Social Psychology*, 24, 191-198.
       The dependence of mirth upon affect toward protagonists. In A. J. Chapman and H. C. Foot (Eds.), *Humour and Laughter: Theory, Research, and Applications*. Sussex, England: John Wiley & Sons, Ltd., in preparation.

Zillman, D.; Bryant, J.; and Cantor, J.
1974   Brutality of assault in political cartoons affecting humor appreciation. *Journal of Research in Personality*, 7, 334-345.

HUMOR JUDGEMENTS AND THE "PLAYFUL ATTITUDE"

Roger Mannell and Lawrence La Fave
University of Windsor

Humor is serious business. At least, this is the impression one gains from a review of the social science literature concerned with humor. Humor and joking are described as playing a role in the maintenance of social structure (Radcliffe-Brown, 1940; Bradney, 1957), a social control mechanism (Martineau, 1972), a leadership technique (Goodchilds and Smith, 1964), a persuasive communication technique (Markiewicz, 1974), a psychotherapeutic procedure (Cassell, 1974), etc. The psychological experience of humor is also viewed to be a function of motive arousal (cf. Bryne, 1958; Singer, 1968; Levine, 1969), reference groups and identification classes (cf. La Fave, 1961, 1972, in press), intuitive notions of social justice (Gutman, 1967; Zillman and Bryant, 1974), and the perceived intentions of the source (La Fave, 1969, 1971; Gutman and Priest, 1969; McGhee, 1974). Underlying social motives assumed to influence the humor experience include: Mirth as a neutralizing mechanism to ward off sympathetic distress to the suffering of others (McDougall, 1903, 1922), repressed sexual and aggressive tendencies (Freud, 1960), and enjoyment of dominance over others (Hobbes, 1651) to mention only a few.

Some social scientists have not infrequently forgotten about humor as play, particularly those who argue that the "social" content of humor has important implications for an individual's experience of that humor. The first author (Mannell) has suggested that an adequate conceptualization of the way an observer experiences a so-called humorous situation or communication ("joke") needs not only to be based on whether he *believes* this communication "real" or "fantasy" but also on whether the observer *adopts* a "playful" or "serious" 'attitude' (Judgemental set) regarding the intention of the communication. Given these two dimensions, a typology in which they are orthogonal can be developed resulting in four categories (playful-real, serious-real, playful-fantasy, and serious-fantasy). From this model we argue that much of the research which stresses the mediating function for the observer of socially and culturally determined values, attitudes and norms should be re-examined, and the conditions under which these factors operate in humor should be specified.

Humor Appreciation: A Function of
Social and Cultural Realities

To summarize the more or less explicit assumptions of much of the humor research and theory—including much of our own work, it is assumed that through the socialization process, as a result of social learning, the individual comes to distinguish and form stereotypic attitudes with respect to various races, social roles, religious and political persuasions, and dominant personality traits. Also notions of social justice and norms regarding the endorsement and acceptability of certain "social behaviors" (particularly interpersonal aggression, harm, and hostility) are learned in this socialization process, and these internalized attitudes and values structure and influence the appreciation generated in an observer by a humorous communication or situation.

La Fave's (1961, 1972) vicarious superiority theory of humor predicts that an observer's reference groups or identification classes may influence or modify his reaction to a humorous communication or situation:

"Let S believe J is a joke in which identification class A is victorious over identification class B. The more positive S's attitude with respect to A and/or the more negative S's attitude toward B, the greater the magnitude of amusement S experiences with respect to J" (La Fave et al., in press).

Gutman (1967) argues that humor reactions to communications depicting the interaction of two protagonists in interpersonal hostile ways will be a function of the reader's intuitive notions of justice and definition of the protagonists' behavior as socially acceptable-unacceptable:

"If the joke victim stimulates anger by bad behavior, then the readers should feel that he got what he deserved in the punch line, and should rate the joke as more humorous. The outcome of such a joke is consistent with intuitive notions of justice (Heider, 1958), and justice is, of course, an important rationalization for the enjoyment of aggression. On the other hand if the joke victim had, prior to his victimization, behaved well, his fate is perceived by the reader as unjust, and should not be rated as humorous" (Gutman and Priest, 1969).

Zillmann and Bryant (1974) suggest a model which also introduces notions of social justice (equity) as a factor affecting humor appreciation. They dealt with the squelch format in which the communication depicts a protagonist who is provoked and who then retaliates against his provoker. Manipulations were made to effect a variation in the degree of retaliation achieved, from extreme underretaliation, through fair retaliation, to extreme overretaliation.

"It was proposed that retaliatory equity, i.e., a situation in which the negative consequences inflicted upon the provoker by the retaliator are of similar magnitude as the negative consequences initially inflicted upon the retaliator, constitutes an optimal condition for mirth, and that both types of retaliatory inequity, under- and overretaliation, impair humor appreciation in proportion to the magnitude of the resultant inequity" (Zillmann and Bryant, 1974).

Cantor and Zillmann (1973) and Zillmann, Bryant and Cantor (1974) suggest that the degree of interpersonal aggression and hostility expressed should effect or modify the observer's reaction to the humorous communication.

These models provide conflicting predictions in certain cases. This discussion will ignore these issues and merely point out that there are models and experimental support to suggest that the members of a cultural or social group who internalize the dominant values and norms of their group will tend to give humor judgements and react to certain situations and communications in highly consistent and predictable ways (when these communications contain socially significant content).

The above approaches suggest or assume that humorous communications are taken "seriously". In fact, the research done has typically attempted to ensure that Ss would take the "jokes" seriously. La Fave (1961) in setting up his experiment, which provided the first adequate test of the reference group construct in explaining humor judgements in socially relevant humor, indicated that:

> "An attempt was made to select jokes which would be taken seriously, otherwise S, thinking the speakers were only joking, might detach himself and become humored at his own expense—detachment which likely would hurt the present hypotheses" (La Fave, 1961, p. 28).

Gutman went to extra lengths to have S react to his stories as depictions of actual events and in a serious manner. Ss were told to think of the stories as situations and base their rankings on the entire story. This was done to avoid "the tendency of Ss to treat them as jokes" (Gutman, 1967).

The only study which may not have influenced the Ss to react to the materials as real situations and not approach the humor judgement task with a serious 'attitude' is Zillmann and Bryant's (1974). The results of this study are in question due to methodological problems discussed elsewhere (La Fave, et al., in press).

Where has All the Play in Humor gone?

Certain theorists have argued,though, that the humor experience is only possible when the element of the playful or unreal is present, and when social norms and values do not intrude into the judgement of humor. Levine (1967) maintains that both the "game illusion" and the "comic illusion" are expressions of voluntary withdrawal from the real world into a world where the rules and procedures are of one's own choosing and making. Both play and humor supposedly express freedom from realistic cares and problems of reality. Does this assumption of Levine's, mentioned above, suggest that the interpretation of an event or humorous communication as unreal or fantasy is sufficient to induce amusement, even when the content exhibits violations of social conventions?

Max Eastman (1936) stressed the importance of the playful-serious distinction (p. 15). He argued that any attempt to approach a joke in a serious manner negates its ability to amuse (since he viewed humor the result of holding a playful attitude toward a situation which would normally cause pain). If we assume that one person's victory over another causes pain in an observer, La Fave's (1961) results would appear to cast doubt on the absoluteness of Eastman's all-or none argument (since it was shown that when a positive reference-group member squelched a negative reference-group member, the humorous communication was judged more amusing than when the reverse occurred). Clearly, humorous communications can amuse, even when taken seriously.

Flugel (1954) equated *unrealism* and *playful*. "This playfulness or unrealism serves as a constant background upon which the special characteristics of different forms of humor . . . are, as it were, superimposed" (p. 723).

Do the concepts of reality-fantasy and playful-serious hold any value in explaining the role of an observer's attitudes (with respect to social justice, and norms regarding the appropriateness of aggression, hostility and damage) in his humor experience? Does humor allow the participant to transcend (at least momentarily) social and cultural realities?

Imaginary 'Play' and Reality-Fantasy in Humor

Singer (1973) in focusing on the study of imaginary 'play' and McGhee (1972, 1974) on reality-fantasy assimilation in humor have stressed some psychological processes which affect fantasy production and the factors affecting the adoption of a "pretend" or "make-believe" orientation. The same processes may underlie both 'play' and humor. Piaget (1932), while he did not address the phenomenon of humor, classified children's play into games of mastery, games with rules, and games of make-believe. This latter classification is of particular interest and has been described by Singer (1973) as:

> "Those aspects of play which involve "make-belicve" or "as-if" elements, the creation from thin air of additional companions in adventure, the attribution of events to different times and places, and the shifting of roles and voices within the same child (p. xi) . . . In a sense one can see that much of one's capacity to produce and appreciate humor also takes its beginning in some aspect of make-believe play or in general in the accommodation-assimilation sequence" (p. 257).

For Piaget (1962) play derives from the child working out two fundamental characteristics of his mode of experience and development. These are *accommodation*, which represents an attempt to imitate and interact physically with the environment, and *assimilation*, which represents the attempt to integrate externally derived percepts or motor actions into a relatively limited number of categories or schemata. Imaginary play as visualized by Singer seems more associated with the assimilation process. The similarity of this concept to that

243

hypothesized by McGhee for humor appreciation is striking. McGhee (1972) stresses the need for the child to "fantasy assimilate" rather than "reality assimilate", if the individual is to be amused by a violation of expectancy (a stimulus event discrepant from a cognitive schema—Piaget, 1952) and the novel object or event can not be assimilated into the appropriate schema or cognitive category or with previous knowledge, the child attempts to accommodate or change the concept so as to incorporate the new object or event. Failing this the child may continue to modify his schema until the new stimulus is fully assimilated. McGhee suggests that this process does not always occur upon encountering stimulus situations that are inconsistent with already established knowledge, for example, when the inconsistency does not in fact occur in the "real world". If a child were to see a cartoon showing a mother elephant sitting on a nest of eggs in a tree, the child would probably not reality assimilate or accommodate his concept of elephants to this depiction. That is, he does not change those relevant conceptual categories to incorporate this new information about elephants.

McGhee (1975) found that when violations of weight conservation were presented to conserving children under "reality" conditions (in which violations of conservation were demonstrated using a balance) or "fantasy" conditions (in which the violation occurred in the form of a story), surprise at the violation was most amusing when fantasy cues were present. Many incongruities are encountered in which external cues (e.g., seeing the incongruity in a drawing or cartoon form, or seeing a smile on the face of the source of the incongruity) are present which suggest that the stimulus events could not really occur as depicted. McGhee also points out that internal cues, that is, a high level of knowledge or conceptual mastery over the content area depicted, is essential.

How do humorous communications or events in which socially unacceptable behavior is depicted, that is, humor with hostile and aggressive themes or communications where injustices are depicted, fit into the above scheme. As previously discussed, high hostility, injustice (Gutman and Priest, 1969) and inequities (Zillmann and Bryant, 1974) have been shown to decrease the amusement generated by a communication when the punchline is held constant. It has been argued that the Ss in most of these experiments were under conditions which forced them to react seriously. Would it then be expected that if these depicted events were viewed as not real, fantasy or make-believe, that the amusement generated would no longer be inhibited? If a cartoon character is shown having his head cut off, do we tend to find this less amusing than the same character being slapped in the face or simply verbally rebuked? Do an observer's notions of social justice and his internalized norms with respect to interpersonal aggression function under reality rather than fantasy conditions?

The Symbol-Minded Man's Reaction to Humor in Fantasy: Playful versus Serious Attitudes.

Levine (1967) has argued that in the world of play the child is freed from the restraints and prohibitions of the real world and he can enjoy the licence of aggression with immunity. Poole (1966) found that "aggressive play" and "real aggression" are clearly distinguishable in polecats. Axline (1971) argues that in play therapy the child is free to "act" out aggressive and hostile themes since no sanctions or adult values with respect to the social acceptability of these make-believe behaviors are allowed to intrude into the play activity. Is a humorous communication or event which depicts socially unacceptable behavior also free of intrusion by an individual's social norms and values, when it is fantasy assimilated rather than reality assimilated?

It will be argued here that the interpretation of a communication as fantasy is not a sufficient condition to guarantee that an observer's internalized attitudes and values will not modify his humor judgement. The observer may approach something he defines as fantasy (not real) with a serious 'attitude'. By playful attitude is meant a temporary suspension of the observer's social values concerning depicted behaviors normally defined as socially unacceptable or unjust. Man is symbol-minded. He has the capacity to create symbols, react to symbols as he would their referent and to react to various stimuli as symbols in ways which the original creator did not intend. Therefore, it would seem that an observer can process or approach a situation he defines as fantasy with one of two mental sets: (1) a serious 'attitude' (judgement set) which leads the observer to call into operation his internalized values, norms, and notions of social justice in evaluating and subsequently reacting to humor which contains socially relevant content; or (2) a playful 'attitude' (judgemental set) in which these social values are not salient and therefore do not operate in modifying humor judgements.

We interpret a theatre play as fantasy yet we can react to the injustice, damage and interpersonal aggression exhibited by the characters either as extremely amusing (playful attitude) or extremely sad (serious attitide). A typical reaction to a Picasso painting depicting the mutilation of quasi-human figures, while defined as not real, is not one of amusement but horror, sadness, etc. Why do we then find amusing certain cartoons showing equally exaggerated depictions of human figures undergoing disfigurement.

Some of the conditions which tend to determine which mental set is adopted by an observer when judging a humorous communication can be specified. It is suggested that a serious attitude will be adopted when: (1) the observer's attention is focused specifically on the socially unacceptable behavior depicted, (2) the observer sees the communication as symbolic of the human condition, man's plight or man's inhumanity to other men, and/or (3) the observer is aware that not only are unacceptable behaviors being depicted but that his humor judgement of the communication is public knowledge and can be taken as an indicator of his endorsement of socially unacceptable behavior. The observer's awareness of these conditons may result from : 1. certain characteristics of the communication itself (e.g., cartoons which depict highly realistic

245

human characters versus distortions of human characters versus animal characters), 2. a task or experience the observer has performed or had prior to the humor judgement task (e.g., having viewed, read about, participated in a situation which evoked a serious mental set as a result of the actual or described injustice, interpersonal aggression; or experimental instructions to take the 'jokes' seriously), or from 3. the observer's awareness that his humor response is being monitored or is under surveillance by a relevant reference group or person (e.g., fear of experimenter evaluation and interpretation of a humor judgement task as indirect assessment of endorsement of interpersonal aggression, etc.). Gollob and Levine (1967) and Singer, Gollob and Levine (1967) believe they have shown that focusing an observer's attention on the hostility depicted in cartoons tends to decrease enjoyment of the more hostile items.

The present model has a number of interesting implications for the social psychology of humor. If, as previously discussed, researchers have typically forced or encouraged the observer into a serious judgemental set prior to judging humor stimuli which have been systematically varied to determine the effects on humor judgements of the observer's attitudes towards interpersonal aggression and violence, and the effects of the observer's notions of social justice, then the question arises as to how these manipulations affect humor judgements when the observer adopts a playful mental set. Gutman and Priest (1969) argue that the greater the social acceptability of the behavior of a retaliator in a humorous communication the greater the amusement generated in an observer. Zillmann and Bryant (1974) suggest that amusement is rather a function of the degree of equity of a retaliator's behavior, while earlier versions of superiority theory (La Fave, 1972) may appear to predict that the greater the damage done by the retaliator the greater the amusement. The present model suggests that the generalizability of these theories may be restricted to accounting for humor judgements under certain conditions only. By taking into consideration the judgemental set (playful-serious) of the observer, it is hoped that the inconsistencies found in the research and the disagreements between theories can be accounted for.

REFERENCES

Axline, V. M.
    1969 *Play Therapy*. New York: Ballantine Books.
Bradney, P.
    1957 The joking relationship in industry. *Human Relations*, 10, 179-187.
Bryne, D.
    1958 Drive level, response to humor and the cartoon sequence effect. *Psychological Reports*, 4, 439-432.
Cantor, J. R., and Zillman, D.
    1973 Resentment toward protagonists and severity of misfortunes they suffer as factors in humor appreciation. *Journal of Experimental Research in Personality*, 6, 321-329.

Cassell, J.
  1974 The function of humor in the counseling process. *Rehabilitation Counseling Bulletin*, 17, 240-245.
Eastman, M.
  1936 *Enjoyment of laughter*. New York: Simon and Schuster.
Flugel, J. C.
  1954 Humor and laughter. In G. Lindzey (Ed.), *Handbook of social psychology*. Special fields and applications. Reading, Mass.: Addison-Wesley.
Freud, S.
  1960 *Jokes and their relation to the unconscious*. New York: Norton.
Gollob, H. J., and Levine, J.
  1967 Distraction as a factor in the enjoyment of aggressive humor. *Journal of Personality and Social Psychology*, 1967, 368-372.
Goodchilds, J. D., and Smith, E. E.
  1964 The sit and his group. *Human Relations*, 17, 23-31.
Gutman, J.
  1968 The effects of justice, balance, and hostility on mirth. (Doctoral dissertation, University of Southern California), Ann Arbor, Mich.: University Microfilms, No. 28 (7-A), 2774.
Gutman, J., and Priest, R. F.
  1969 When is aggression funny? *Journal of Personality and Social Psychology*, 12, 60-65.
Hobbes, T.
  1651 *Humane Nature*. Anchor, London.
La Fave, L.
  1961 Humor judgements as a function of reference groups: on experimental study. Unpublished doctoral dissertation, University of Oklahoma.
  1969 Humor as a supplemental variable to assimilation-contrast principles in psychosocial "scales". *Symposium Proceedings 1969 Western Psychological Association Meeting*, Vancouver, British Columbia.
  1971 Sense of humor: a myopical illusion. Paper presented at the annual meeting of the American Psychological Association, Washington, D.C., September.
  1972 Humor judgements as a function of reference groups and identification classes. In J. H. Goldstine and P. E. McGhee (Eds.), *The Psychology of Humor*. New York: Academic Press, 1972.
La Fave, L., Haddad, J., and Maesen, W. A.
  In press Superiority, enhanced self-esteem, perceived incongruity humor theory. In A. J. Chapman and H. T. Foot (Eds.), *Humor and Laughter: Theory, Research and Applications*.
Levine, J.
  1967 Humor and play in sports. In R. Slovenko and J. A. Knight (Eds.), *Motivation and Play, Games and Sports*. Springfield, Ill.: Charles C. Thomas.
  1969 (Ed.). *Motivation in humor*. New York: Atherton Press.
Markiewicz, D.
  1974 Effects of humor on persuasion. *Sociometry*, 37, 407-422.
Martineau, W. H.
  1972 A model of the Social functions of humor. In H. J. Goldstein and P. E. McGhee (Eds.) *The Psychology of Humor*, New York: Academic Press.
McDougall, W.
  1903 The theory of laughter. *Nature*, 67, 318-319.
  1922 A new theory of laughter. *Psyche*, 2, 292-303.

McGhee, P. E.
   1972   On the origins of incongruity humor: fantasy assimilation versus reality as-
          similation. In J. H. Goldstein and P. E. McGhee (Eds.), *The Psychology of
          Humor*. New York and London: Academic Press.
   1974   Cognitive mastery and children's humor. *Psychological Bulletin*, 81, 721-731.
McGhee, P. E., and Johnson, S. F.
   1975   The role of fantasy and reality cues in children's appreciation of incongruity
          humor. *Merril-Palmer Quarterly*, 21.
Piaget, J.
   1932   *The moral judgement of the child*, London: Kegan Paul.
   1952   *The child's conception of number*. London: Routledge and K. Paul.
   1962   *Play, dreams and imitation in childhood*. New York: Norton.
Poole, T. B.
   1966   Aggressive play polecats. In P. A. Jewell and C. Loizos (Eds.), Play exploration
          and territory in mammals. *Symposia of the Royal Zoological Society of Lon-
          don, #18*. London: Academic Press, pp. 23-28.
Radcliffe-Brown, A. R.
   1940   On joking relationships. *Africa*, 13, 195-210.
Singer, D. L.
   1968   Aggression arousal, hostile humor, catharsis. *Journal of Personality and Social
          Psychology*, Monograph Supplement, 8, No. 1, Part 2, 1-14.
Singer, D. L., Gollop, H. J., and Levine, J.
   1967   Mobilization of inhibition and the enjoyment of aggressive humor. *Journal of
          Personality*, 35, 562-569.
Singer, J.
   1973   *The child's world of make-believe*. New York: Academic Press.
Zillman, D., and Bryant, J.
   1974   Retaliatory equity as a factor in humor appreciation. *Journal of Experimental
          Social Psychology*, 10, 480-488.
Zillman, D., Bryant, J., and Cantor, J.
   1974   Brutality of assault in political cartoons affecting humor appreciation. *Journal
          of Research in Personality*, 7, 334-345.

APPENDIX A: CONSTITUTION OF THE ASSOCIATION FOR THE ANTHROPOLOGICAL STUDY OF PLAY

ARTICLE I: Name

Section 1: The name of this association shall be The Association for the Anthropological Study of Play.

ARTICLE II: Purpose

Section 1: The purposes of the Association shall be to promote, stimulate and encourage the anthropological study of play: to support and cooperate with local, national, and international organizations having the same purposes; to organize and arrange meetings and issue publications concerning the purpose of the association.

Section 2: The Association shall conduct its activities solely for scholarly purposes.

ARTICLE III: Membership

Section 1: There shall be three classes of members. Members, Fellows, and Constituent Members.

Section 2: Members are those individuals who maintain professional interest in and support of, the anthropological study of play. Members may be designated as Contributing or Sustaining Members by the payment of additional dues, as established in accordance with Article VII.

Section 3: Fellows of the Association are those Members who are actively engaged in furthering the body of knowledge in the anthropology of play as evidenced by their current scholarly research.

Section 4: New members of the Association will be enrolled as Members. Members who wish to become Fellows must apply in writing to the Council. Election to a Fellowship will be the result of a majority vote of the Council at each annual meeting. The application submitted should include evidence of the Member's qualification for a Fellowship, as stipulated in Article III, Section 3.

Section 5: Any organization, such as a society, club, institute, or library, which encourages or supports the purposes of the Association, shall be eligible for membership as a Constituent Member upon application to the Membership

Committee. Each Constituent Member may choose one delegate to attend the annual meeting of the Members, who, on that occasion, shall have the same voting privileges as Members.

Section 6: Membership shall not become effective until the Treasurer has received the first year's dues, such dues establishing membership for each fiscal year.

ARTICLE IV: Officers

Section 1: The officers of the Association shall be a President, President-Elect, Immediate Past President, Secretary-treasurer, and Publications Editor, all of whom shall be Fellows of the Association. All officers shall be elected by the Members of the Association by mail ballot prior to an annual meeting (see ARTICLE X) for two year terms, by a plurality of members voting. Their terms of office shall begin at the close of the meeting immediately prior to their election, and shall terminate at the close of the meeting at which their successors assume office.

Section 2: The officers shall have the powers and duties customarily incident to their respective offices in similar organizations, such as shall be specifically delegated to them by the Council, and must include:

Section 2A: President: The president shall preside over the business of the Association and chair the meetings of the Council.

Section 2B: President-Elect: The President-Elect shall plan the program for the meetings of the Association, such as symposia, workshops, and annual meetings, for the furtherance of communication, enlightenment and exchange of information. The President-Elect shall assume the duties of the President when the President is unable to continue said responsibilities or at the request of the President.

Section 2C: Immediate Past-President: The Immediate Past President shall assist the President and the Council in the conduct of the Association, insuring that there is continuity in the progress of the Association.

Section 2D: Secretary-Treasurer: The Secretary-Treasurer shall keep and distribute to the Association Members the minutes of the Association meetings, including the meetings of the Council; shall inform the membership of the annual business meeting at least one hundred and twenty (120) days prior to the meeting; shall mail a list of nominations for the Association's officers and Council Members-at-large according to ARTICLE X; and shall be responsible for conducting the voting on any proposed amendments to the constitution or by-laws of the

250

Association in accordance with ARTICLE XI.

The Secretary-Treasurer shall promote membership, collect and disperse the Association's monies, and make available the Association's books for audit by an individual or firm appointed by the President in accordance with ARTICLE VI. The Secretary-Treasurer shall report the financial status of the Association to the Members at the annual meeting, and shall make that report available for inclusion in the Association's *Newsletter* or *Proceedings*.

Section 2E: Publications Editor: The Publications Editor shall be responsible for the publications of the Association; e.g. the *Newsletter*, the *Proceedings*, and other publications determined to be appropriate by the Council.

ARTICLE V: Council

Section 1: Except as otherwise provided by these By-Laws, the management of the affairs of the Association shall be vested in a Board of Directors which shall be known as the Council.

Section 2: The Council shall consist of the Officers of the Association and three Members-at-Large, all of whom shall be Fellows of the Association. The President shall act as Chairman of the Council. Five members shall constitute a quorum of the Council.

Section 3: Council Members-at-Large shall be elected to a two year term of office, except for the first set of Members-at-Large, who shall serve a one year term.

Section 4: The Council shall hold an annual meeting not more than one week preceding the annual meeting of the Association at a time and place designated by the President. Special meetings may be called at any time by the President or by any five members of the Council upon at least two weeks written notice to each member of the Council.

Section 5: In the event that Members of the Council cannot attend the annual meeting or special meetings which may be called, they may appoint a proxy to cast votes in their name. A proxy must be in writing and must be delivered to the President of the Association.

Section 6: The Council may decide to submit specific questions by mail ballot, to insure that each member, present at the annual meeting or not present, can cast his vote. Such ballots shall be distributed by the Secretary-Treasurer to members of the Council, and shall include a clear statement of the questions and a summary of the arguments presented for and against the question.

Section 7: In the event that an elected member of the Council cannot fill his term of office, he shall present his resignation to the President in writing. Upon the acceptance of such a resignation the President shall appoint a Fellow to fill the vacant position on the Council.

Section 8: Except as otherwise provided by law and these By-Laws, decisions of the Council shall be by majority vote of those members of the Council present and voting.

ARTICLE VI: Meetings

Section 1: There shall be an annual meeting of the members of the Association after which time officers and Council members-at-Large shall assume the offices to which they were elected. Prior to, or during the annual meeting of the members the Council shall hold its annual business meeting as required under ARTICLE V. The President, in conjunction with the appropriate officers of the Association shall designate the time and place of both meetings. The President shall arrange the order of business at these meetings.

Section 2: The Secretary-Treasurer shall mail notices of the annual meeting of the members and the annual business meeting to the Members of the Association not less than one hundred twenty (120) days prior to those meetings. Such notification shall state the time, place and general purposes of the meetings. The notification of meetings may be included in the ballot containing nominations for elected officials or Council Members-at-Large, as stipulated in ARTICLE X.

Section 3: The Council of the Association shall present at the annual meeting of the members a report dated as of the close of the last complete fiscal year, verified by the President and Secretary-Treasurer, or by a majority of the members of the Council. This report shall also show the names and addresses of the persons and organizations who have been admitted to membership during such year. This report shall be filed with the records of the Association and an abstract thereof entered in the minutes of the annual meeting of the members at which the report is presented. The President shall appoint an individual or a firm, who shall not be a member of the Council, to act as an auditor, who shall examine the annual report referred to in this section prior to the annual meeting of the members, and shall express his opinion thereon in writing at the annual meeting of the members.

Section 4: The Council may sponsor or sanction other meetings or symposia which contribute to the purposes of the Association.

ARTICLE VII: Dues and Finances

Section 1: The amount of the annual dues for all classes of membership shall be determined by vote of the Council.

Section 2: The Council shall set a date for the annual payment of dues.

Section 3: The Council of the Association shall set the dates of the fiscal year.

ARTICLE VIII: Publications

Section 1: There shall be a Newsletter published on a regular basis; such basis to be determined by the Council.

Section 2: There shall be an annual Proceedings published.

Section 3: Other publications may ensue as determined to be desirable by the Council.

Section 4: All members shall receive regular subscriptions to the Newsletter and other official publications of the Association, subject to the current financial status of the Association.

ARTICLE IX: Committees

Section 1: Standing Committees: There shall be five (5) standing committees of the Association, as follows:

Section 1A: The President shall appoint annually a Membership Committee consisting of three members, the Chairman of which must be a member of the Council. The membership committee shall review all membership applications and refer qualified applicants for Fellow status to the Council at the annual business meeting.

Section 1B: The President shall appoint a Budget and Fiscal Committee of three members, the Chairman of which shall be the Secretary-Treasurer. An annual report shall be given at the annual meeting of the members of the Association. The Budget and Fiscal Committee is responsible for the collection and dispersement of Association funds.

Section 1C: The President shall appoint a Program Committee of three members, the Chairman of which shall be the President elect. The Program Committee is responsible for the organization and preparation of the program for any Association meeting.

Section 1D: The President shall appoint a Time and Site Committee of three members, the Chairman of which shall be a member of the Council, to make the necessary local arrangements for the annual meeting of the Association, exclusive of the program for the meetings.

Section 1E: At each annual meeting of the Association the President shall appoint, subject to the confirmation by the Council, a Nominating Committee consisting of three Fellows of the Association, none of whom shall be members of the Council, who shall continue in office for one year. The Nominating Committee is responsible for the preparation of a list of nominees for the elected offices of the Association, in accordance with ARTICLE IV, Section 1, ARTICLE V, Section 3, and ARTICLE X.

Section 2: Special Committees: Special Committees shall be appointed by the President and approved by the Council from time to time as the occasion demands. These committees shall be limited in activities to the purpose for which they are appointed and shall have no power to act unless such is specifically conferred by action of the Council.

ARTICLE X: Nominations and Elections

Section 1: The Nominating Committee shall present a list of nominations, for officers and Council Members-at-Large, in the appropriate years, to the Secretary-Treasurer for the elections to be held prior to any annual meeting, not less than six (6) months before such meetings. The secretary-treasurer shall mail a ballot to each eligible member, containing the list of nominees one hundred twenty (120) days prior to the annual meeting at which time newly elected officers would take office (i.e. the first, third, fifth, seventh, etc. annual meeting of the members). Additional nominations may be made in writing to the Secretary-Treasurer by any five members of the Association at any reasonable time prior to the distribution of the list of nominations, provided that the candidate's written permission is available.

Section 2: The voting in all elections for officers and Council Members-at-Large shall be accomplished by mail. The ballot distributed by the Secretary-Treasurer (see ARTICLE X, Section 1) shall be used for these elections. The ballot shall include, but not be limited to: (A) a list of candidates for each office or Council Member-at-Large position, and (B) a brief statement by each candidate expressing his qualifications for the office, a summary of his publications, and a report of his professional activities, and may include other pertinent information on candidates and offices, as long as the additions are the same for each candidate for each office.

ARTICLE XI: Amendments

Section 1: Amendments to the constitution or by-laws of the Association shall be accomplished by two-thirds majority of the Members of the Association voting on such changes.

Section 2: Voting must be accomplished by mail ballot to insure that each Member has an equal opportunity to voice his opinion.

Section 3: Amendments may be proposed by: (A) a majority of the Council, (B) a majority of members present at an annual meeting of the Members, or (C) by any 10 members of the Association, when presented in writing to the Secretary.

Section 4: Ballots shall be distributed to all Members of the Association who are in good standing by the Secretary-Treasurer. Ballots shall include a summary of the arguments in favor of or opposed to the changes in question.

ARTICLE XII: Parliamentary Authority

Section 1: The rules of procedure contained in Robert's Rules of Order, Revised, shall govern meetings of the members of the Association so far as they are applicable and when not inconsistent with these By-Laws.

ARTICLE XIII: Seal

Section 1: The seal of the Association shall be that adopted by the Council and shall be used on all official transactions and publications. The seal must include at least (A) identification of the Association, (B) the date of the origin of the Association, and (C) a symbol depicting the purpose of the Association.